Fort Concho

and the

Texas Frontier

By J. EVETTS HALEY

Illustrations by H. D. BUGBEE

SAN ANGELO STANDARD - TIMES
SAN ANGELO TEXAS 1952

DESIGNED AND PRODUCED BY
CARL HERTZOG AT EL PASO TEXAS

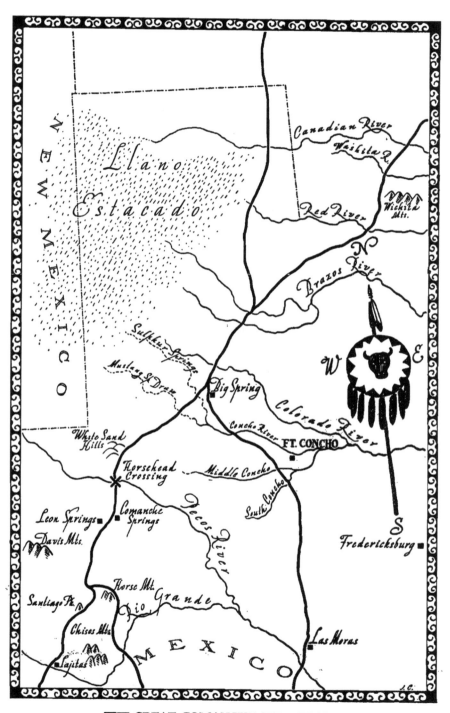

THE GREAT COMANCHE WAR TRAIL

Contents

Maps and Illustrations

DRAWINGS *by* H. D. BUGBEE

Preface

THIS book presents a picture of life on the frontier as it centered around an important Texas fort. Despite the isolation of the early border posts they did not stand completely alone. They were part of a vast pattern of policy, of movement and of action through which life sometimes ebbed but mainly flowed from east to west across the face of America. Thus this story is written broadly into the historical background of the time and place.

Both these elements combined to enhance the importance of some posts. Others in the same strategic design came to life and withered into oblivion on the vine of history. Fort Concho was born in that expansive period when free men—impelled by the lust for land and cattle and commerce, but impelled most by the vital force of simply being free—pushed zestfully west in spite of the limitations of distance and danger. It was conceived at the proper time and its camp was pitched in the right spot.

For hundreds of miles on either side wild and difficult land and stubborn and hostile men combined to funnel the westward flow of people past the fort, through the valleys of the Conchos. Thus in addition to being thrown up as a shield in partial defense of the settlements of Texas, Fort Concho became the jumping-off place for many important trails. From this advanced bastion eager men and apprehensive women pointed their herds and the tongues of their wagons into the arid and largely unknown world that separated them from the West Coast. It became the focus of concentration and maneuver for far-flung campaigns designed to break forever the resistance of the Comanche, the Kiowa and the Apache. And at last, somewhat living down its bucolic past, it became the nucleus of a gracious city and a distinctive culture.

This book is an effort to trace the sometimes faltering policy and the chain of dynamic circumstances by which this development came about. It owes its existence completely to the devotion and drive of Houston Harte, of the *San Angelo Standard-Times*, who through a period of many years, unstintingly spent his time, money and influence to bring it to completion. The volume itself is thoroughly provincial. It was conceived, written, illustrated, designed and printed by West Texans.

As usual the illustrations of H. D. Bugbee have their unusually authentic touch and appeal. The hand and the consummate taste of Carl Hertzog shows on every page. Of all the sources, the old army files in the National Archives at Washington were most revealing. Locally, Miss Susan Miles and her associates in the Tom Green County Historical Society were always helpfully at hand. The careful reading in script by Francis Fugate, of El Paso, levelled off some of the rough spots, while the conclusions and the errors are definitely mine.

J. EVETTS HALEY

Canyon, Texas, June 7, 1952

CHAPTER I

The Great Comanche War Trail

THE GREAT PLANE TABLE called the *Llano Estacado* tilts a little into the sun from the Canadian River, on the north, to break again in gentle undulations toward the Conchos on the south. When seen by the first white man it was devoid of growth except for a blanket of grass, and barren of shelter except for the short canyons that seemed to writhe in search of an outlet along its eastern edge. It was a formidable barrier to the first travelers through the Southwest. They approached it with respect bordering on awe.

The eastern rim of this broad plateau is little changed. For hundreds of miles it lifts its rugged and florid face to the morning sun. Its eroded lines of character are cut deep by the sudden dash of its rain, and by the eternal force of its restless winds. A sort of protective stubbly beard of twisted cedar and an occasional mesquite softens its visage from a distance, though the beetle-brow of the caprock frowns severely, as if in contempt, upon the gentler land below. Above and beyond this rocky ledge the Staked Plains stretch west for more than a hundred miles into the setting sun.

Their awesome effect is completely lost in the unnatural present. In the unsettled past a man from a region of landmarks turned into a derelict upon this ocean of grass. His squinting eyes sought the shimmering horizon in vain for an object of orientation, interest and rest. But the illimitable bounds of these Plains suggested nothing short of infinity, and in the sober reflection imposed by their ringing silences, they threw the isolated traveler back upon himself in contemplation of the spiritual end of man. Great religious philosophies were not born by chance in such arid and awesome lands.

But the first Anglo-Saxons who pushed their way west were hunting action and adventure rather than sober philosophy and a short cut to heaven. They avoided the Staked Plains as a careful mother shuns the plague. The earliest reports contended that wood and water could not be had. Thus the first maps of the Southwest warned the wayfarer against this desert wilderness — against this "great Zahara of North America."

In the restless flow of human life that lapped at the edge of this wilderness, however, was the historic force that was taking the West. In the first quarter of the nineteenth century bold and imaginative men from the frontiers of Missouri were venturing by a long and hazardous trail toward Santa Fe and the Spanish Southwest. They took a central route across the Great Plains. In the seven hundred miles of uncertain land dedicated to God and the Indians between the settlements and the Rio Grande, not another blazed and beaten course pointed the way to the West Coast.

One great trail, however, crossed this region for more than a thousand miles from north to south. It was blazed in blood long before this land was settled. It began in the Comanche range where the upper tributaries of the Arkansas and the Red finger for their sources in the breaks of the Great Plains. It stretched across Texas to carry destruction to the Mexican settlements as far south as Durango. It was known a hundred years and more ago as the Great Comanche War Trail.

It was well named. It was blazed for savage rapine, based on a war of movement. The youngest and the best of the Comanche braves, astride mustangs that would lope the longest trails, "that would take them there and bring them back," periodically took this broad highway that skirted the Staked Plains. The clouds of dust raised by the hoofs of their mounts as they headed south across the Red, the Brazos and the Colorado were a fearful portent of the storm that would surely strike the frontiers of Mexico when the next moon grew full. September was the time. So regular were the raids that the Indians called the period the Mexican Moon, and the Mexicans knew it as the Comanche Moon.

Raiders from Indian Territory took a course that passed the western extremity of the Wichita Mountains. Others came down from the Arkansas across the upper reaches of Red River. The Staked Plains shunted their converging lines by way of game, water and grass along the base of the Plains to come together at Sulphur Springs, near the lower end of Sulphur Draw. From there the main trail pointed by Mustang Springs, east by north of the site of Midland, and by a hard and dry ride to permanent water in the Sands. It struck the Pecos at Horsehead Crossing, cut its broad course across the alkali flats, and gave name to that bluish flood pouring out of the bowels of the earth at the site of Fort Stockton — Comanche Springs.[1]

From the Leon Water Holes, about ten miles west, it cut across the long ridges to the head of San Francisco Creek, below present Marathon. Just north of the Camel Hump or Horse Mountain, the trail forked. The western prong led to water at Maravillas Creek, past Santiago Peak, west of Nine Point Mountain to Terlingua Creek, down it for a few miles, and then again bore off to the southwest to cross the Rio Grande at Lajitas. It swung around the mountains near the

[1] Randolph B. Marcy, *Exploration of the Red River of Louisiana*, Sen. Ex. Doc., 33rd Cong., 1st Sess., 1854, p. 95. The Springs dried up in the summer of 1951.

village of San Carlos, and then pointed like a lance toward the heart of Chihuahua.²

The eastern fork, or the main trail, kept to the left of Horse Mountain, south through Persimmon Gap by Bone Springs, and passed just east of the ghostly ridges of the Chisos Mountains. It bent back to the west, and crossed the Rio Grande south of that imposing range at what was called "The Grand Indian Crossing."

Captain John Love, in his pioneer navigation of the river from its mouth by flatboat in 1850, discovered that this was the first ford in four hundred miles of meandering stream above the mouth of Devils River, because, he reported, the river was then from twelve to eighteen feet deep the entire distance. Here, however, the Comanches could cross on good bottom with the water lapping just four feet up on their horses' sides. Love noted that the Indian traffic was heavy, and said that the trail "is very wide, well beaten, and resembles a much traveled thoroughfare." It could be seen for many miles back in the mountains.³

Nearby on the Mexican side, at the mouth of the Arroyo Altares, is a monument marking this trail. It indicates the point from where the Comanches set their dark faces into the southern sun for hundreds of miles. At first they bore a little to the west. When the boundary between Coahuila and Chihuahua was designated, it followed, in part, The Great Comanche War Trail.⁴ Off-shoots led toward Saltillo, but the

2 E. E. Townsend to J. E. H., July 10, 1947; John W. Pope, *Report of Exploration for a Route for the Pacific Railroad*, Sen. Ex. Doc. No. 78, 1885, pp. 14-16, 72, 78. Marcy found one of their trails through the Sands in 1849. See *Report of Captain R. B. Marcy's Route from Fort Smith to Santa Fe*, Sen. Ex. Doc., No. 64, 31st Cong., 1st Sess., 206-207.

3 M. L. Crimmins, "Two Thousand Miles by Boat in the Rio Grande in 1850," West Texas Historical and Scientific Society, *Publications*, No. 5, pp. 51-52.

4 This route through the Big Bend has been traced by that late eager student and old-time resident of the region, E. E. Townsend. The great and lasting work by Dr. R. N. Richardson, *The Comanche Barrier To South Plains Settlement*, Glendale, 1933, devotes a chapter to the Mexican war trails but does not trace them in detail. See pp. 192, ff.

[4]

main trail drove south toward Zacatecas and Durango, five hundred miles into Mexico. .

Back in Texas another prominent branch of this same trail forked off adjacent to the South Plains and pointed to the Big Spring, which Captain R. B. Marcy, in his exploration of 1849, found to be a prominent camping place of the Comanches. Marcy explored the region, named the spring, and reported that "there are remains of lodges in every direction." His Comanche guide told him there was another good road from there to the Pecos. It kept off the Plains completely, south by way of the Conchos.

This trail likewise forked in the Concho Country.[5] The main branch bore west and crossed the Plains to the Pecos by way of Castle Gap to join the Great Trail at Horsehead. The left-hand fork kept south across the Edwards Plateau, touched at the head of Las Moras and the upper Nueces, and thence pointed its way to the ultimate pillage of Mexico.[6]

Just when these sweeping Comanche forays, reaching from the summer buffalo range on the plains of the Arkansas clear down to the cattle ranches of Durango, actually started is still to be dug from the records of Spanish Mexico. Dr. R. N. Richardson, historian of the Comanches, has noted that this trail was in existence in the eighteenth century. The Spaniards were trading with the Plains Indians as early as 1785. By 1831 the raids were serious enough to be taken up in treaty between the United States and Mexico. But savage nature designs while diplomats dicker across the tables, and by 1840 the incursions reached farther than ever into Mexico. In the late forties and early fifties they seemed to be at their worst.[7]

September's growing moon found the lithe Comanche warriors on the sunny side of the *Rio Bravo*, looking toward the haciendas. They struck in large and even punitive expeditions.

5 Marcy, *Report* etc., as cited, 208.

6 Joseph E. Johnston's report in *Reconnaissances of Routes from San Antonio to El Paso*, Sen. Ex. Doc., No. 64, 31st Cong., 1st Sess., p. 28. O. W. Williams, *Baja El Sol*, n.p., n.d., makes mention of the approach to the Pecos. See Richardson, map, p. 194.

7 Richardson, as cited, 70, 192, 200-201.

In 1847 the veteran chief, Buffalo Hump, gathered six to eight hundred warriors on the Rio Grande. He made no pretense of the fact that he planned to strike Chihuahua City and Parras on his march south, and maybe rattle his lances on the doors of San Fernando, which is now San Antonio, on his return. There was grim humor, as Dr. Richardson observed, in the reason he gave for this venture: during the Mexican War the Missouri Volunteers of the American Army had whipped him near Parras, in Mexican Territory, and now Mexico must pay the penalty.[8]

The Kiowas and Apaches likewise took this trail. Their methods were the same: terror, pillage and devastation based on a war of movement. They spread out in wide areas in Durango, Zacatecas, and Chihuahua to strike the towns and ranches. Then with dead men and destruction behind them, with terrified prisoners in their clutches, and with herds of horses and mules — sometimes as many as a thousand head — before them, they swept their savage way back toward the Rio Grande in the waning light of the bloody Comanche moon.

Rarely were they worried; rarer still were they caught. By long and dry drives they clattered through the Big Bend and headed for the Pecos. When they reached the salty Pecos water many of their famished horses drank their fill and died. Their bones so littered the range about, the ancient story goes, that early travelers gathered the skulls and marked this welcome ford across that once bold and treacherous stream. Thus Horsehead Crossing, the surviving landmark of this trail through Texas, got its name.[9]

From here the Comanches drove their herds back to their home ranges, and trailed their surplus stock to the outposts of Indian Territory and Missouri for traffic with Indian traders there. They were the Tartars, the Asiatics, of the Western World, scorching the earth and carrying hundreds of Mexican

[8] Richardson, as cited. 199.

[9] John S. Ford, MS., "Memoirs," University of Texas, III, 515-516; John R. Bartlett, *Personal Narrative*, New York, 1854, I, 96.

women and children into abject slavery.[10] On the frontiers of Mexico, there was no terror to compare with the Comanches and Apaches.

While Captain John Pope was crossing West Texas in 1854 making one of the preliminary railway surveys for the government, he met some Kiowas near Mustang Springs with horses stolen in Mexico. He was astonished by the heavy traffic that had beaten out this great trail, and observed that the Indians,

unsupported, penetrate into the densest settlements of the northern states of Mexico; and in broad daylight, and nearly unopposed, they carry into captivity hundreds of human beings, and thousands of horses and mules, and lay under contribution populous towns, and even large cities. They are objects of extremest terror to the Mexicans; and it is related that a single Comanche, even at mid-day, dashed at speed into the public square of the City of Durango, and by his mere presence caused the hasty closing of the stores and the retreat of a population of thirty thousand souls to their barred houses. He remained an hour roaming through the deserted streets, and was only captured by being lassoed from the window of a house as he was riding triumphantly but carelessly from the suburbs.[11]

Even as late as 1840 the heart of San Antonio was not secure against the Comanche lance, and the poor frontiers of Mexico were shorter still on defense. When that observant English adventurer, George F. Ruxton, passed through northern Mexico in 1846, he noted that the "haciendas in Durango and Chihuahua are all enclosed" by high walls, "flanked at the corners by circular bastions loopholed for musketry. The entrance is a large gate, which is closed at night; and on the flat roof of the building, a sentry is constantly posted day and night." At La Noria he found a warning had just been sounded and everybody was "in greatest alarm and dismay. . . . The women were weeping and flying about in every direction, hiding their children and valuables, barricading the houses,

[10] Richardson notes that one responsible party estimated about 300 captives, "principally Mexicans," living with the Comanches in 1853. The Mexicans estimated 652 people "killed, wounded, or captured in the state of Nuevo Leon from 1847 to 1857." As cited, 201, 206.

[11] Pope, as cited, 14; also 12, 16, 76, 78.

and putting what few arms they could collect into the hands of the reluctant men." [12]

Julius Froebel, a German traveler through the same sections in 1852 and 1853, noted similar devastation. Ranches and even towns were abandoned and entire regions were laid waste. One section between Durango and Chihuahua was known as the "Desert of the Frontier." [13] The Mexican War undoubtedly encouraged raids by the savages from north of the Rio Grande, and stimulated a market for their horses and mules—and sometimes captives—among the traders on the American frontier. [14]

The virtue of the Comanche brave came to be measured by his efficiency as a horse thief, and Captain Marcy, one of the most observant and literate of the early army explorers, noted that among these Indians "a young man who has not made one or more of these expeditions into Mexico is held in but little repute." To bear this out he said that old Is-sa-keep, a chief of the Northern Comanches, had confided that his "four sons, who he said were as fine young men as could be found; ... were a great source of comfort to him in his old age, and could steal more horses than any other young men in his band." [15] Thus paternal pride sped his declining years and spurred his fine boys along the Great Comanche War Trail, further to compound the miseries of northern Mexico.

From that land of mountain rock and mescal growth beyond the Pecos, the Mescalero Apaches took their toll of captives and lives, horses and cattle. When Captain W. H. C. Whiting scouted out of San Antonio for a course to El Paso del Norte in 1849, and reached the Davis Mountains, he ran into hundreds of these Indians, mainly under the great chief Gomez. Each lodge had its captive and each band its droves of

[12] George F. Ruxton, *Adventures in Mexico and the Rocky Mountains*, London, 1849, pp. 111-113.

[13] Ruxton, as cited, 112; Julius Froebel, *Seven Years Travel in Central America, Northern Mexico and the Far West of the United States*, London, 1859, pp. 346 ff.; Richardson, as cited, 196, 203; Bartlett, as cited, II, 447-448.

[14] Randolph B. Marcy, *Exploration of the Red River of Louisiana*, 105, 114-115; Richardson, as cited, 199, 210.

[15] Marcy, *Exploration*, as cited, 105-106.

[8]

Mexican horses, mules and cattle in its trailing commissary. Whiting's party replenished their own meat from wild stock the Apaches had lost in the Big Bend. And at last, as a further stimulus to their depredations, Santa Fe traders were even then venturing into the Big Bend to barter trifles for these horses and mules,[16] and take them back for sale to the Forty-Niners at prices ranging from fifty to seventy-five dollars a head.[17]

But the complexion of the Southwest was changing while this traffic in human lives and property was at its height. With the annexation of Texas the United States and Mexico had gone to war. In one of the greatest marches of history, Doniphan and his Missouri Volunteers had tramped down the Santa Fe Trail and through Paso del Norte to take Chihuahua. General John E. Wool had marched west from San Antonio to cross the Rio Grande, and both had meshed their efforts with General Taylor to take northern Mexico.

The conflict had come to an end with the Treaty of Guadalupe Hidalgo in 1848, and not only Texas, but New Mexico, Arizona and California were secured to the Union. By the

[16] Ralph P. Bieber, *Exploring Southwestern Trails, 1846-1854*, Glendale, 1938, pp. 273, 295-296, 323.

[17] Mabelle Eppard Martin, "From Texas to California in 1849; Diary of C. C. Cox." *Southwestern Historical Quarterly*, XXIX, 47.

same treaty the United States agreed to restrain the Indian raids. While this unfulfilled and immediately impossible obligation was lifted by the Gadsden Purchase Treaty of 1853, the Comanche Moon was regularly dimmed with a ring of blood above the unhappy borders of Mexico.

In 1849 Captain Whiting observed that nothing short of an offensive war on this side would stop the Indians, and made his recommendations accordingly. By 1854 the slow processes of government ground out the decision to place what became Fort Stockton squarely upon the trail at Comanche Springs. Later another was located on a favorite camp where Gomez's warriors had proudly carved their raiding exploits in Indian sign on the bark of trees at the head of the Limpia. Still these past masters of mobility swept around the forts and levied on Mexico.

In the 1840's desperate authorities there, however, had resorted to a bounty on the Apaches. With co-operative spirit adventurous Texans — mainly under the leadership of Major Mike Chevallie, a Jack Hays' ranger; the notorious James Kirker; and another Texan, John Glanton — brought their zestful missionaries into Chihuahua for the purpose of converting the Apaches into "good Indians" by strictly frontier standards. Thus the scalp-hunters were organized for the bloody business of killing Indians.

Their forces were augmented at El Paso del Norte by a company of American emigrants in July, 1849, where the Mexican authorities were offering "great inducement to those . . . fond of fighting." Here a Texan on the way to the gold fields recorded in his diary that "Apache scalps are worth two hundred dollars, prisoners two hundred and fifty. . . . A company is being made up among the Americans here for that purpose and no doubt at least a hundred will join it." [18]

Chevallie and Glanton were from Houston, while James Kirker was variously described as "an Irish adventurer" and a Scotsman. Froebel, while passing through Northern Mexico

[18] Martin, as cited, *Southwestern Historical Quarterly*, XXIV, 131.

in the early fifties, learned that the price was "200 dollars for every adult Indian, alive or dead . . . An Indian woman, alive, is valued at 150 dollars; a living boy at the same sum, while for one dead 100 dollars is given." He found that the Indian children were placed "in good families . . . the girls making commendable servants." But the boys usually ran away to rejoin the wild bunch.

Possibly Kirker was the most noted of the scalp-hunters. By report he had been a Rocky Mountain trapper and had been taken into the Apache tribe, but had deserted them for the refinements of civilization. Whatever the alleged disparities in the bounties, he was experienced enough to know that fortune smiled in the offers of the Mexican government. He went into Chihuahua, organized a company of Shawnee Indians, Mexicans, and Americans and took the field.

He tolled a party of Apaches into Galeana under the ruse of friendship and tanked them up on liquor. When the festival was at its height he fell upon them with his band, and with the effective aid of the Mexican populace ended the orgies. Bancroft reported that he killed 182 men, women and children, and took eighteen captives. Ruxton, claiming to get his report from an eye-witness a few months later, said that with 160 scalps fluttering from poles, "Kirker's party entered Chihuahua in procession, headed by the governor and the priests, with bands of music escorting them in triumph to the town." [19]

Anyway it was a valorous day. The venture had been a decided success. Only in settling up did a sour note intrude. Kirker's heavy raid placed such a strain upon the treasury that the government refused to pay but a portion of the bounty. This penurious policy and breach of honor discouraged his men and cooled their ardor for the chase.

Meanwhile, John Glanton, a veteran ranger and a gentleman whom Froebel could hardly have libeled as "a dangerous desperado from Texas," reached Chihuahua and joined the enterprise. But personal jealousies, the mounting strain on the

[19] H. H. Bancroft, *North Mexican States and Texas*, San Francisco, 1889, II, 397, 599-600; Ruxton, as cited, 154.

state treasury, and the fact that dried Mexican scalps and ears—difficult to distinguish from those of legitimate Indians—began bobbing up with disturbing frequency, all combined to upset this commercial venture designed to settle the Indian troubles.

In the resultant confusion Glanton was run out of Mexico by the authorities. In 1850 he made his way west on the California trail to the crossing of the Colorado, and was operating a ferry when the Yumas rose in commendable wrath and killed him.[20]

In 1852 one Colonel Langberg, long in the service of the Mexican government, also got into the scalp-hunting business. He managed to gather some Seminole Indians with their leaders—Wild Cat and the Negro, Gover Jones, expatriates from Florida—and brought them to Chihuahua to take up where the others had left off. But the initial experience with this buccaneering pursuit had put a damper on both the Indians and the Mexicans. The officials refused to ratify Langberg's "treaty" with the Seminoles, and those blood-thirsty worthies left in indignation, declaring there was not a "gentleman" within the government.[21]

Notwithstanding this temporary set-back, the Apaches, who had suffered most from this inhuman traffic, fell upon the settlements of Northern Mexico and the California trail with renewed vigor. But the raids did not last long. In the late fifties they diminished in intensity, and by 1860 they had become infrequent. In 1873 the Mexican Border Claims Commission urged that the losses to Indians from this side should be an offset to American borders claims against its own government. Yet the problem originally imposed on both countries

[20] H. H. Bancroft, *Arizona and Mexico*, 487-488. J. Frank Dobie, in *Apache Gold and Yaqui Silver*, Boston, 1939, pp 363-366, has given the best bibliography available on the scalp-hunters.

[21] Froebel, as cited, 350-351, 354; *Telegraph and Texas Register*, (Houston) reprint in *Southwestern Historical Quarterly*, XLVIII, January 3, 1950, p. 272; Bancroft, *North Mexican States and Texas*, II, 397, 599-600. Bancroft says that the bounty offered was $100 per scalp for adults, $25 for children. Bartlett, *Personal Narrative*, II, 322-323.

by the traffic of the Great Comanche War Trail did not come to an end until the early eighties.

Then with the settlement of West Texas and the eventual confinement of the Comanches, the Trail—"worn deep by the hoofs of countless travelers, man and beast, and whitened by the bones of animals"—passed into history. But deeper still than its traces through the scanty grass along the Rio Grande were its bitter memories of desolation clear down to Durango, and the awful anguish of hundreds of wailing women and terrified children carried into Indian slavery. For everyone except the Comanche it was a trail of tragedy.

$\mathcal{S}$eeking a $\mathcal{W}$estward $\mathcal{W}$ay

AFTER TEXAS was annexed, the Mexican War fought, and the Southwest acquired by the United States, new routes to the West were eagerly sought. With enterprising human nature, exploration and appraisal logically follow acquisition. When the powerful lure of gold in California was added to the natural challenge that the unconquered wilderness held for the vigorous Anglo-Saxon race, the trend to the West was strong.

These positive forces exerted themselves through Washington to influence federal policy, and policy prompted action through the ready organization of the regular army. Out of such historical movements came the first effectively organized efforts to find trails across the appallingly wide-open world called West Texas.

Already the traders of the Missouri frontier had pushed out to tap the profits and the exotic pleasures of Santa Fe. Nor did they stop there. Far down the Rio Grande, where it loops at last through a rough pass in a spur of the Rockies and veers southeastward on its long way toward the Gulf, was the drab but considerable settlement of Paso del Norte. Some two hundred and thirty miles more of arid trail connected it with the next sizable city in Mexico.

Chihuahua needed American goods. The vigorous breed to the north that loved adventure and fortunately never scorned to profit soon took its caravans through these hazards. It was a long trail that looped in a great and erratic arc from the settlements on the Big Missouri to the upper reaches of the Arkansas, down by Santa Fe, through the Pass of the North and at last to Chihuahua. As a burro intuitively takes the easy grades and makes a proper trail, bold and healthy men naturally seek the short cuts to their objective. The devious approach is a part of diplomacy; the direct is honest and natural. Thus with such a round-about test of endurance and distance between Independence and Chihuahua, some enterprising soul was bound to seek to cut across.

Dr. Henry Connelly left the practice of medicine in Missouri for the zestful life of the trail. He made his way to Santa Fe in 1824, and on to Chihuahua City in 1828, where he went into business. He knew at first hand the uncertainties of the old trail and eleven years later decided to travel straight to the American settlements.

He made his plans with five Mexicans. Special concessions in low import duties were arranged with the state authorities. Fifty dragoons were detailed as a guard, and on April 3, 1839, a party of about a hundred men set out with seven wagons and a herd of seven hundred mules. They took the old Spanish trail to the village called Presidio del Norte that clung to tenuous life on the lowest crook of the *Rio Bravo*. They worked their way northeast out of the Big Bend, and followed the deep-cut course of the Comanche Trail to the Leon Water Holes and Comanche Springs.[1]

From there this cavalcade of mule-men headed for the spring called Escondido, but for some reason left the main Indian Trail and kept east to the Pecos below Horsehead' Crossing. By a course north-of-east Connelly passed over the Staked Plains, close by the Flat Rock Ponds, to the head of

[1] William Elsey Connelly, *Doniphan's Expedition and the Conquest of New Mexico and California*, Topeka, 1907, pp. 276-280; Ralph P. Bieber, *James Josiah Webb, Adventures in Santa Fe Trade, 1844-1847*, Glendale, 1931, pp. 102, 108.

[15]

the Middle Concho, and then bore back toward the Colorado. Because of continued hostility between Mexico and Texas, the party turned to the north across the Brazos and the Red, keeping west of the Cross Timbers to be sure of missing the Texas settlements.

They mistook the Red for the Brazos and did not realize their mistake until they got to the Canadian. There a party of friendly Delaware Indians happened upon them and piloted them back to their destination of Fort Towson, in southeastern Indian Territory. They had intended to load their train—as the creeping caravans were then called—and back-track to Chihuahua that fall. But lost time and heavy rains caused them to lay over until spring. Then with sixty to seventy wagons, and recruits swelling their forces to 225 men, they left Fort Towson for Mexico.

To their great surprise they found the Texans friendly. They passed directly through the Red River settlements and headed southwest. Beyond the Cross Timbers they missed their earlier trace and were lost for several days on the Brazos, but eventually took off to the south and picked up their old trail on a prong of the Colorado. And so again they passed near the site of San Angelo, swam their stock across the Pecos, ferried their goods on a wagon-bed buoyed by kegs, and headed back down the Great Comanche Trail to Presidio del Norte.

When they got there they found that the political picture had changed. The Governor of Chihuahua had died, and in keeping with the gentle tradition of politics a new set of customs officials was in charge. To Connelly's dismay the promised reduction of duties had gone a-glimmering. But after forty-five long days of Latin negotiation they compromised the levies, crossed the river, and drove into Chihuahua City, August 27, 1840, almost seventeen months after their original embarkation. Their venture had soaked up so much time and expense that it proved unprofitable, and so "Connelly's Trail" fell on the debit side of the ledger and passed

[16]

into history. But those enterprising men who blazed it still figured prominently in this region.[2]

When the Mexican War broke out the veteran Santa Fe and Chihuahua traders—Connelly, Magoffin, Skillman and others—became the advance and trusted agents of the United States Army when it marched into Mexico by way of Paso del Norte.[3]

After Alexander Doniphan made his remarkable march from the settlements of Missouri to take Chihuahua, Connelly's Trail was followed by the merry-eyed, six-foot-two, blond, curley-haired Major John P. Campbell who was sent from Chihuahua with dispatches for Washington.

He, like Connelly, cut straight across. On March 14, 1847, he set out with a detail of thirty-two men. He made it to Presidio del Norte without serious mishap, though his interpreter died on the way. From there he too apparently came up the Comanche Trail, but instead of keeping on toward Fort Towson, as he must have originally planned to do, he turned east. After being hounded unmercifully by the Indians, he reached the settlements in a starving condition. He contracted scurvy and died from its effects four years later.[4]

The interest in a direct route from the American settlements to the Mexican outposts took fresh and tenacious hold with the discovery of gold in California. The Army was then released from war. Eager men from the East, having fallen to the strange but strong lust that took men West, were being mustered out of the services. Those and others turned, not in frustration at seemingly insuperable odds that a dangerous destiny entailed, but zestfully and courageously to the blazing of new and ample trails into the West.

2 Connelly, as cited; Reuben Gold Thwaites, *Early Western Travels*, (Gregg's *Commerce of the Prairies*), XX, 224-227; 250; C. G. Raht, *The Romance of the Davis Mountains and Big Bend Country*, El Paso, 1919, p. 230; Froebel, *Seven Years in Central America*, etc., 410; Bieber, *Exploring Southwestern Trails*, 267; *Southwestern Historical Quarterly*, XLVIII, 263. *Reconnaissances of Routes from San Antonio to El Paso*, Ex. Doc. No. 64, 31st Cong., 1st Sess., 19, 46.

3 Bieber, *Adventures in the Santa Fe Trade*, as cited, 102.

4 Connelley, as cited, 107, 451-453; Ralph P. Bieber, *Journal of a Soldier Under Kearney and Doniphan*, Glendale, 1935, p. 36.

In the summer of 1848 San Antonio merchants, anxious to take the Chihuahua trade away from Missouri, raised a little money and enlisted the interest of the noted Texas Ranger, John C. Hays, in exploring and laying out a route by way of El Paso. Hays took hold of the enterprise with characteristic courage. With a small party and Indian guides he left San Antonio, August 27, 1848, and struck north for a ranger camp on the Llano near Castell, where Colonel Peter Hansborough Bell had assured him an escort.

There he was joined by Captain Sam Highsmith and thirty-five Texas Rangers. Early in September they pulled out up the Llano and crossed the divide to the Nueces, and continued to Las Moras and the San Pedro. With them was a Mexican who had learned the country as an Indian captive, as well as the Delaware guide, John Conner, Major Mike Chevallie, ranger and scalp-hunter-to-be, and other valorous souls. They experienced so much trouble near the San Pedro that they renamed it the Devils River. From here west their trip grew tougher still. Samuel Maverick, one of the party, suggested their troubles in a diary he kept. He noted that on September 26, 1848, they reached the Pecos "in great thirst."

From there they plunged into the rocky wilderness to the west. None of the party knew the country and even the guide soon confessed that he was lost. Supplies ran out. Fortunately the party came upon four old buffalo bulls that had been whipped out of the herd and had drifted west of the Pecos, far out of their accustomed range. Eventually this meat was exhausted.

Maverick wrote that by the first of October they were "eating mustang meat." They turned south to the "banks of the Rio Grande," where, he said, "we killed and ate a panther." Then they left the river and pushed west until they struck the Great Comanche Trail, down which they turned again "to the Rio Grande at a great Indian crossing." They left the stream again and bore west-northwest, until, on the 7th day, they were so starved that they began "to eat bear grass." Next day the record grew terser still. "In worst hills. Find a trail. Meet three Mescalero Indians (Apaches) take their back trail and enter the canon of Mescal Creek."

"Oct. 9—Travel up Canon. Determined to kill a mule, having nothing but mezcal bear grass to eat. [October 10] Kill mule and eat our breakfast. Travel up same canon. Found abundance of fine tunas. Our mule meat very poor and tough. R. A. Howard's bear grass soup. Here we are at the highest mountains," which meant the Chisos. They then lost eight horses and mules to the Indians, but struggled on, as Maverick recorded: "Dr. Wham crazy."

They turned back south-southeast toward the Rio Grande, "breaking down ten or fifteen horses" and scattering the command in an attempt to reach water. On the night of the 12th they made another dry camp, pushed on next day fourteen miles to water, and Maverick said on the 14th "wait for our benighted men. Dr. Wham rode off in a fury last night. Suppose he is lost. Send back for lame and crazy." The searchers "Finally lost the unhappy crazy man in the black ravines," and the starving party pushed ahead, "S.S.W. on big Comanche road (of twenty trails) to Durango" and across the river into Mexico. On the 17th they quit the great trail, killed another pack mule, and next day camped near the Mexican village of San Carlos. On the 19th Maverick noted that they had at last gotten aid and were in camp, "recruiting on bread and milk."

They apologized to the authorities for being on Mexican soil, marched up the river to Presidio del Norte, crossed back into Texas, and turned down the river to camp at Ben Leaton's newly-established fort. There they ate and rested for sixteen days, during which time Leaton gave them a barbecue with tortillas and coffee, and the Bishop of Chihuahua blessed them with a consignment of supplies.[5]

Leaton had come from the Chihuahua country with other American soldiers after the Mexican War, apparently in 1848. About five miles down the river from where Presidio was built, he laid claim to the best land in that section, diverted the waters of the river to it, and built a 'dobe fort—the pioneer establishment of the Big Bend.[6]

Hays and Highsmith recruited their men and mounts and to their dismay found that they were still a long way from El Paso. As the season was far advanced, supplies gone, and men dressed only for summer, they wisely decided to turn back. With a supply of *pinole* or ground parched corn and thirty days' rations of meat, they took the Comanche Trail towards civilization — or as near thereto as the settlements of Texas lay.

Apparently they quit the trail before reaching Comanche Springs, as they suffered two and a half days without water, and came to it again at Escondido, east of Fort Stockton. From there they reached the Pecos at Horsehead, turned down to Live Oak Creek, passed near the site of Fort Lancaster, and then split into three parties. Twenty-eight men decided to march directly toward San Antonio while Hays took six men and headed southwest, by way of Las Moras Creek.

Captain Highsmith and his Texas Rangers determined to

[5] Bieber, *Exploring Southwestern Trails*, 32-33, gives a good summary of the expedition. Samuel Maverick, "Chihuahua Expedition," MS., U. of T., Austin; J. D. Affleck, "History of John C. Hays," MS., II, 739-749; John Salmon Ford, "John C. Hays in Texas," MS., 173-174, all U. of T., Austin; John Henry Brown, *Indian Wars and Pioneers of Texas*, Austin, n.d., 104-106.

[6] Bieber, *Exploring Southwestern Trails*, 284-285; Froebel in 1853, as cited, p. 409-410, vouched for this remarkable character, though he says that Leaton was then dead. As cited, 408-410.

Mrs. O. L. Shipman, in *Taming the Big Bend*, n.p., 1926, pp. 10-11, says his house, which comprised his fort, was of forty rooms, some of immense size. For other detail, see *Voice of the Mexican Border*, Marfa, December, 1933, pp. 85-86.

bear northeast to the Concho and thence to the settlements. Those who took the southern route got in after considerable suffering. Hays reached San Antonio, December 10, 1849, and though he had not succeeded in reaching El Paso, he had, after 107 days of marching and starving, gotten back alive, which was so remarkable that a ball was given in his honor. Little mention was made of the fact that he had hoped to reach El Paso and return in sixty days.[7]

Highsmith's men had even worse luck. They pushed east from Live Oak Creek toward the head of South Concho. When his stragglers, slowed on account of failing horseflesh, camped one night in a thicket, a party of Indians rode over them, stampeded their horses, and set them afoot. By a forced march they caught up with the main command. Yet while it was on the head of the South Concho a sentinel went to sleep and the Indians stole thirteen more of their horses.

Time wore on and Highsmith, knowing that their extended absence would have everybody worried, pushed ahead to report and send help back to his men on foot. Meanwhile the others made it as far as Brady Creek, where a snowstorm caught them, and where they shivered around an open fire in their tattered summer clothes for five days. After intense suffering both parties made their way to the ranger camp on the Llano, but Highsmith died from the effects about a month later.

Remarkably enough Dr. Wham, who had ridden off from the party in mad delirium, was picked up by Indians, who, following their practice of refusing to kill a crazy man, fed and cared for him. He showed up at San Antonio sound of mind and body about a year later, and Captain W. H. C. Whiting, on his exploration in the spring of 1849, found Wham's lost horse doing well on the grass beyond the Pecos.[8]

The Hays and Highsmith party had discovered that the country to avoid was the torn mass of land around the lower Pecos. They found that the Comanche Trail was the right

7 Bieber, as cited; Brown, as cited, 105-106; Affleck, as cited, 747.
8 Brown, as cited, 106; Bieber, as cited, 262.

approach to Chihuahua. When splitting up on their return from Live Oak Creek they had unconsciously but roughly pointed out the two routes of western travel which would come into general use.

Meanwhile the absorbing news had broken. Just before Hays had left San Antonio, an account of the discovery of gold in California was printed in the *New York Herald.* Apparently it was dismissed as "just another newspaper story," as it passed almost unnoticed. But while the exploring party was floundering around in the Trans-Pecos, the New Orleans *Daily Picayune* came out with a colorful account of the discovery and the diggin's, September 12, 1848. The temperature of the whole country mounted to the fever point while Hays and Highsmith stubbornly fought their way back to the settlements.

Meanwhile, men were congregating by way of boat upon the Texas coast, and elsewhere by pack and caravan, hell-bent for California and the land of gold. The movement was swelled by many who had been through Texas during the Mexican War and was spurred by the further obvious fact that a trail through the southern latitudes should be opened first. It was given additional impetus by the knowledge that Phillip St. George Cooke and his Mormon Battalion had pushed their way west during the war, by forced marches southwest through central New Mexico, and across the deserts to California.

These seekers of gold reasoned that they should cut straight across Texas and do the same thing. Further to add to the pressure upon the Texas frontier, the Corpus Christi, San Antonio, and Austin papers were advertising the superior virtues of the Texas routes — though obviously nobody knew just what they were.[9]

They could safely predict a shortage of snow, and they did

9 Ralph P. Bieber, in his tremendous work of editing Southwestern journals, gives a fine picture of this movement in the historical introduction to his book, *Southern Trails to California in 1849*, Glendale, 1937, pp. 28-23.

See map of region, p. 32.

contend that the army would offer protection. The basis for this claim seemed to have been the fact that the popular clamor had prompted orders from Washington, December 10, 1848, for General W. J. Worth, in charge of the district at San Antonio, to send details to find if there really was a practicable route west toward the land of glitter, glamour and gold. San Antonio, full of buccaneering spirits, was already a-bustle with their enterprise.

Furthermore, the American Army was distinguished with a group of young, capable, and ambitious officers. They had been grounded in the solid fundamentals at the Academy, had won their spurs with zest and courage in the Mexican War, and were now being seasoned in service on the frontier. They were to graduate into great generals on both sides of the conflict that came to a showdown in the Civil War. The frontier of Texas, with her tough and vital problems, drew a full and fortunate share.

General Worth issued orders looking towards the explorations. The winter of 1848-1849 at San Antonio was alive with preparations to delve into the unknown. Colonel Joseph E. Johnston, Captain Whiting, and Lieutenants W. F. Smith, Francis T. Bryan, N. Micheler and S. G. French organized their ventures to find the way to the West.

William Henry Chase Whiting got off first, February 12, 1849, a few weeks ahead of his twenty-fifth birthday. This remarkable young man, born at Biloxi, Mississippi, March 22, 1824, had come out of West Point at twenty-one years of age with the highest average in the Academy up to his time, and had been sent to San Antonio in 1848.[10] He was a cultivated man who deserves remembrance in West Texas. The record of his trip is still designed to challenge the healthy spirit that inclines to do and dare.

[10] George W. Cullum, *Biographical Register of the Officers and Graduates of the U. S. Military Academy*, etc., 3rd ed., Boston and New York, 1891, II, 208-209; Bieber, *Exploring Southwestern Trails*, 30-31; Whiting's Report, House Ex. Doc., No. 5, 31st Cong., 1st Sess., pp. 281 et. seq.; and Smith's Report, *Reconnaissances of Routes from San Antonio to El Paso*, as cited, 4 ff.

In December before, Hays had reported that the best route for a wagon road was from San Antonio north to the San Saba, and thence through the Concho country to the Pecos. The valiant Highsmith, in the short while spared between debilitation and death, also reported to Governor P. H. Bell, December 15, that "a first class road" with "wood, water and grass, over a fine and level country, unobstructed by mountains or any natural opposing difficulties," could be had by this course. It was a bravely optimistic conclusion upon the vicissitudes of a land that took his life![11]

Major General Worth had their reports before him when, on February 9, 1849, he ordered Whiting and Smith to scout out Hays' course into Presidio del Norte and find "if there be a practicable and convenient route for military and commercial purposes between El Paso and the Gulf, passing by or near Austin or San Antonio de Bexar in Texas." If such a quest along the Rio Grande west from Presidio proved unprofitable, they were to return from El Paso del Norte by a direct route to the Pecos, and into the settlements by way of the San Saba.

Whiting left San Antonio with an experienced escort of nine men, Lieutenant Smith, Dick Howard as guide, two Mexicans —one of whom was Jose Policarpo Rodriguez—and Whiting's body-servant, fifteen men in all. Howard had been with Hays. Policarpo had the native Mexican's intuitive bent for the out-of-doors and was to become a noted guide.[12]

On account of bad weather and incorrigible mules they were seven days in reaching Fredericksburg, about seventy miles away, which was then the extreme outpost in Texas. There they picked up a recruit and struck out through the hills north and a little west, "partly by the old Pinta trail to the headwaters of the south fork of the San Saba River." On the way they ran into a party of friendly Delaware Indians and enlisted Jack Hunter as an additional guide. They paused long enough on the San Saba to view and speculate upon the

[11] Quoted in Bieber's *Exploring Southwestern Trails*, 33.

[12] See Jose Policarpo Rodriguez, *The Old Guide*, Nashville, Dallas, n.d., 18-21.

[24]

old Spanish Mission and fort,[13] near present Menard. From there they kept west along a Comanche trail to the head-springs of the San Saba, March 1, 1849. That night they had their first Indian scare.

Even though the guards had been doubled on account of fresh sign seen during the day, the Indians attempted to steal their mules, and Whiting noted in his journal:

About one at night the mules stampeded with a great snorting. The strength of the new ropes with which they were fastened was all that saved them to us. The night was dark; and pulling back with all its force upon its lariat, every animal appeared with ears pricked, looking in one direction. . . . After some moments of anxious suspense the crack of the sentry's rifle showed he had discovered the cause. The Indians, for such they proved, disappeared incontinently, and the mules resumed their grazing. I was pleased with the conduct of my men at this alarm. Awakened at the least sound, when the startling tramp of the frightened herd came upon the still air, not a man arose from where he lay. Each one quietly turning on his rude bed with head slightly raised from the saddles which served as pillows, and every sense alert, remained with rifle cocked until the disturbance ceased, watching for the slightest motion before them.[14]

From here Whiting kept on the Indian trail up the head-draws of the river, bearing south of west, and fortunately finding abundant water in holes. When the trail turned off to the right, toward the Conchos, he continued up the draw, finally to turn out across the ridges to the west and "emerge upon the arid table prairie. Found it barren and thinly clad with scattering mesquite [he wrote]. Occasional groves or thickets of live oak were seen in the lowest parts." On the

[13] This establishment was set up in 1757 by the Spaniards in an optimistic attempt to Christianize the Apache Indians. On March 16, 1758, the Comanches and allies attacked the mission and prematurely ushered Father Terreros and nine others off to heaven. The presidio, remains of which may still be seen, was occupied for sometime thereafter without converting the Apaches. See Wm. Edward Dunn, "The Apache Mission on the San Saba River, Its Founding and Failure," *Southwestern Historical Quarterly*, XVII, 379 ff.; Herbert E. Bolton, *Athanase de Mezieres*, Cleveland, 1914, pp. 48-49; Carlos E. Castaneda, *Our Catholic Heritage in Texas*, Austin, 1938, III, 386-409.

[14] Bieber, as cited, 256-257.

night of March 3, they were thirty-four miles from the head of the river and forced to make a dry camp.

Next day they turned due west, crossing alternate ridges and draws until, near noon, they struck Highsmith's trail, made as he struggled back toward the settlements. Within two hours they cut the course taken by Hays. They were then west of the site of Eldorado, in present Schleicher County. Again on the night of the fourth, with men and mules beginning to suffer for water, they made another dry camp.

Next morning they started without breakfast, as famishing men have no hankering for food, and took up the march that had now "become painful and almost insupportable...." The guide, Howard, found each depression and water hole that had sustained Hays the fall before now dry as dust. Still they kept to the west, into Crockett County, and that day stopped in a deep draw to let their "train, now nearly broken down," graze for awhile on freshly green, wild rye.

Their road from the San Saba had been fine, but they had unknowingly kept to the dry divide with

the curse of thirst upon it.... Judging we could not be far from the Pecos or its tributaries [Whiting recorded] and knowing that another night without water would set us afoot, it was thought best to push on. How weary were the miles of that last march! Silent, unmurmuring, each man rode on, his weary mule unable to make more than a mile and a half an hour. We took an old trail; and traveling through a canyon, or ravine, about s. 60° w., at half past twelve the grateful sound of rippling water reached our ears, and we were soon encamped on the west bank of Live Oak creek, a little tributary of the Pecos.

They made forty-two miles that day in spite of the condition of their mules, and lost only one. Here with water, wood and shade they laid over to rest.[15]

Fortunately they dropped into a Comanche trail and followed it five miles to the Pecos, a river "generally so deep as to be unpassable—a pocket edition of the lower Rio Grande." They crossed and turned up the stream through a country that Whiting found "bleak and utterly desolate... in its monoto-

15 Bieber, as cited, 257-265.

nous and somber features its destitution of trees and foliage. ... Even game seem to shun it..." They picked up Dr. Wham's horse, met a party of Lipans, and on March 12 turned west. In the afternoon they struck the Great Comanche Trail, which, Whiting wrote, "filled us with astonishment. Close together, twenty-five deep worn and much used trails made a great road, which told us that this was a highway by which each year the Comanche of the North desolate Durango and Chihuahua." They turned down it and camped that night at what came to be called the Escondido, "a singular spring in the prairie."

They next came to what was then called Awache Spring, where the Comanches had a habit of stopping to rest their *caballados* stolen in Mexico — a place soon to be known as Comanche Springs. They passed the Leon Water holes, struck the mountains, and made ineffectual efforts to find a way through them. Upon starting to skirt them to the right, they met a small party of Apaches, who told them they were headed in the wrong direction to reach Presidio, and turned back.

From here on it was touch and go with the Apaches, who, principally under old Gomez, swarmed the region by the hundreds. Whiting's party was pocketed by his bands and would have been wiped out but for the cool and determined stand of their Texan escort. On March 30 they rode through and named the Wild Rose Pass and the Limpia. They intended to camp in the cottonwoods at the future site of Fort Davis, but signal smokes behind and before warned them that the Apaches were again gathering. They staked out their mules, ate supper, lit their fires that night, and then silently packed up and stole a march of eighteen miles to the west.

Next morning they took a southerly course toward Presidio, passing through a prairie dog town and killing an old panther, which they ate for breakfast late in the afternoon. On the early morning of the 24th they reached Leaton's Fort.

After a good rest and the replenishment of their supplies with high-priced *pinole* and jerky, and after paying their respects to the Mexican officials across the river at Presidio, they were joined by John Spencer, from there, and took off upstream for El Paso del Norte. Presidio, Texas, had not been started.[16]

Whiting's party continued by hard and rough marches up the river to the first settlements on "the island," as the valley below El Paso, which had become a part of Texas, was then called. This rich spot, with its irrigated Mexican farms, was set like an emerald oasis in the bleak world that sloped out and upward on either side. There at San Elizario, the first town, Whiting rode off to see the local priest. This accomplished young officer, being unfamiliar with Spanish, opened the conversation in Latin. But for that "obese, sensual-looking, heavy-eyed man with a dull, Father Gorenflot expression," Whiting "might as well" have spoken in Sanskrit. All that he learned was that the padre had his own woes and regretted that the island had passed to the Americans.[17]

From there the explorers rode through Socorro and Isleta, and on April 12, 1849, arrived at the first settlement at the site of El Paso, Texas — Ponce's Ranch, opposite El Paso del Norte. They had been exactly two months in making the trip from San Antonio and were lucky — extremely lucky in view of the Apaches — to get there alive. They had found that a wagon road to Presidio del Norte was practicable, but that one right up the Rio Grande would be a tough route. On their way back they would, in keeping with their orders, try for a better course. But first they had to recruit their stock and replenish their commissary.

16 Carl B. Raht, in his *Romance of the Davis Mountains and the Big Bend Country*, 84-85, said that Spencer, John Burgess and John Davis came up from Chihuahua to Presidio del Norte in 1848, and that Spencer crossed and founded Presidio a short time later, acquiring the land from "four or five Mexican families whom he found living there." Apparently no one was on this side in late March, 1849, except Leaton, as the observant Whiting would have noted them. See Bieber, as cited, 284-286. Henry Fletcher mentions that Presidio was settled in 1848, though this, too, is obviously in error. See *Southwestern Historical Quarterly*, XLVIII, 295-296. Whiting passed right over the site and observed that it would make a pleasant location for a post. Bieber, as cited, 290.

17 Bieber, as cited, 304.

Upon learning that Lieutenant Sackett, of the First Dragoons, was at Doña Ana, New Mexico, Whiting employed Captain Henry Skillman at El Paso del Norte to carry a dispatch asking for supplies. Whiting then crossed the river in a dugout to look over the Mexican town. Almost the first person he met was that vigorous Amazon known to history as the "Great Western" who had been dropped while sick "by Major Graham's command on its way from Saltillo to California," and "had since passed through much privation, suffering and hardship." Now she was planning to move to the American side to await the arrival of the army. Whiting observed that "Never was anyone more delighted at the sight of American officers than she appeared. Her masculine arms lifted us one after another off our feet."[18]

This noted, well-made woman, six-feet-one-inch in height, had done splendid service in several battles of the Mexican War. Old Rip Ford recorded that "she had the reputation of being something of the roughest fighter on the Rio Grande; and was approached in a polite if not humble manner...", while other "Forty-Niners" recalled her with gratitude because "she treated us with much kindness."[19] It was apparently something for the record to be treated kindly by a double-fisted woman in '49. By mid-July, after Whiting met her, she had moved to the site of El Paso, on the Texas side, and set up a hotel.

Whiting found the valley and the town of Paso del Norte short on stock and supplies. There was not enough in the place to eat, and the levies of the late war, plus the rush to California, had shot prices out of sight. Whiting enlisted Skillman for his return trip, recruited his stock, and was ready to march. Skillman, Spencer and another hardy soul named Gifford proposed to take Whiting's back-trail to Presidio to carry dispatches, to pick up some valuable papers that Whiting had left at Leaton's Fort, and to rejoin him on the Pecos.

[18] Bieber, as cited, 308-309. See also Brantz Mayer, *History of the War Between Mexico and the United States*, New York, 1848, vol. I, pp. 185-188.

[19] Martin, "From Texas to California in 1849," as cited, 132, 219.

Whiting's party left El Paso, April 19, 1849. They turned from their old trail and cut east through the Eagle Mountains to come out on what is now known as Lobo Flat. They worked their way with difficulty through the then unnamed Davis Mountains, again eluded the Apaches, picked up Connelly's Trail, and reached their crossing on the Pecos just above the mouth of Live Oak on the morning of May 8th. There they were to meet the Presidio party if it managed to get through the Indians. But Skillman had not arrived.

Whiting left a note, passed down the river to where the bluffs closed in, and prepared to cross. While thus engaged Skillman caught him to report that he, too, had met the vicious Gomez, who, fearful that the army would move against him after Whiting's escape, had gone back into the Big Bend and made a treaty with Leaton.

From here the combined parties crossed to the Devils River, finding water on the way. They turned downstream, feasting on fat does and bear. Whiting sent Smith, Skillman, and the guide, Dick Howard in advance with dispatches, but the Indians set them afoot on the Nueces. Whiting came in more leisurely with the main force by way of the Zoquete, Las Moras, and newly-founded Camp Leona. Here he found that the entire party had long since been given up for lost. But their joy upon reaching the outpost was tempered by the news that cholera was "raging in San Antonio," and that Major-General Worth had just died with the plague.[20]

They reached San Antonio over the Wool Road after an absence of 104 days. They had accomplished their mission and determined two suitable routes across the wilderness of West Texas.

The course by which they returned, with some refinements of route, came to be called the Lower Road. The other through the German settlements, north to the San Saba and out through the Concho country, obviously became the Upper Road, and the best. Still both were hard going. Whiting made

20 Bieber, as cited, 310 ff.

[30]

his report. The conclusion of this competent soldier and outstanding graduate of West Point who could one day meet the
Apache on roughest ground in a test of life and death, and
next converse with a man of God in the eternal Latin, is
interesting to observe:

> This meager outline of our labors is now closed, but I cannot part
> from my brave companions without expressing here my gratitude for
> the resolute and unmurmuring courage with which they invariably
> followed and supported me, and which was equally conspicuous as well
> in the presence of a numerous and treacherous enemy as in enduring
> the privations of hunger and thirst. Skillful in the use of their arms,
> careful of their animals and their provisions, watchful, cautious and
> daring, these hardy frontiersmen of Texas combine all the qualities
> which make the successful border soldier.[21]

Thus after all was said and done, there was no substitute
for seasoned, self-disciplined men of tough fiber and courage.
The trail they opened west would tolerate no other kind.
The times found them in Texas.

[21] Bieber, as cited, 350.

WESTWARD TRAILS

Marcy's Trail
Connelly's Trail
Upper Road
Ford & Neighbors
Lower Road

Canadian River
Washita River
Fort Towson
Preston
Cross Timbers
Wichita Mts.
Red River
Fort Belknap
Brazos River
Leon River
Colorado River
Austin
San Antonio
Fredericksburg
Trio
FL Inge
Concho River
FORT CONCHO
Bradyville
San Saba
OLD SPANISH FORT
San Saba
Devil's River
Llano Estacado
Sulphur Springs
Big Spring
Mustang Sp. Draw
White Sand Hills
Twin Mts.
Middle Concho
Horsehead Crossing
Howard's Well
Comanche Spr.
Leon Spr.
Ft. Clark
Fort Davis
Chisos Mts.
Pecos River
Pope's Crossing
Delaware Cr.
Guadalupe Mts.
Hueco Tanks
Cornudas Mts.
Doña Ana
Las Cruces
San Elizario
Eagle Mts.
Devil's Mts.
Rio Grande
Fort Lanom
Presidio del Norte
From Chihuahua
Paso del Norte

NEW MEXICO
MEXICO

CHAPTER III

All Trails Pointed West

THE EAGER EMIGRANTS pushing at the outer and unknown borders of western Texas early in 1849 were unwilling to wait for any official report. The important thing, where reckless men scramble for gold, is not hunger and thirst, danger and death, but to get there first. Whatever might happen to life and limb, these Forty-Niners just had to "get a-going."

But those in settled business move with greater caution. The citizens of Austin were as anxious to open a route as those of San Antonio. Already parties were coming up from the coast by way of Houston and La Grange, from points south and east, and busying themselves with plans to break away to the west at once. Austin wanted to continue to draw them. So industrious citizens there sent the famous Doctor John S. Ford to join Major Robert S. Neighbors, United States Indian Agent in Texas, who was ordered to find a good wagon road to the west.

They left Austin, March 23, 1849, more than a month behind Whiting. Neighbors and old Rip Ford took along D. C. Sullivan, A. D. Neal, and the Delaware guide and interpreter, Jim Shaw. Shaw had a couple of Shawnees, a Choctaw and another Delaware under him. They packed out of Austin by way of the North Bosque Settlement, in Central Texas, on

[33]

account of the Major's Indian business. They picked up Comanche Chief Buffalo Hump whom Neighbors in his honest but as usual impractical zeal paid in advance to guide them. They turned west from the Comanche camps on the head of the Leon. By the time they reached the Colorado, Buffalo Hump had decided that traveling was not good for him, and no amount of argument could make him change his mind.

Old Rip Ford reported that "after unceasing endeavors, the services of Guadalupe, a captain of one of the upper bands, were secured." With the addition of Guadalupe and two squaws the little party pushed on by Brady's Creek, up it to its head, and across the flats to the South Concho. Instead of taking to the high and dry ridges to the left, as Whiting had done, they kept to the right, to the head of the Middle or "main Concho — called by the Indians A-hope, Ho-nope, or Blue River."

They took Connelly's Trail west. It turned to the left near Flat Rock Ponds, but they kept on by Castle Gap to Horsehead Crossing. They turned up the Pecos for twenty-eight miles and then struck southwest to Toyah Creek, a bold stream flowing forty feet wide and eighteen inches deep—"affording sufficient water power to move any sort of machinery." They continued southwest until they passed the marvelous flow of water at the base of the mountains near present Balmorhea, known then as Mescalero Springs. Ford noted that the Mescaleros had patches of corn along the Toyah, and an ancient Spanish fort at the Springs had left peach trees growing in the vicinity.

From Toyah Creek, Ford and Neighbors passed around the north end of what came to be called the Davis Mountains, and through Puerto Carrizo to the next water, sixty miles away. From there they pushed hard on their reins to reach the *Puerto del Cola Aguila*—the Eagle's Tail Door—in the Eagle Mountains, and through them to the Rio Grande. They rode up the valley, into El Paso del Norte, May 2, 1849, about two weeks after Whiting had left. In four days they started back.

[34]

From San Elizario, twenty miles below El Paso, they turned off from the river and took the route of the Old Salt Trail—out by the Hueco Tanks, by Ojo del Alamo, the Cornudas, Crow and Pine Springs, down the Delaware, across to the Pecos, and by its west bank to Horsehead.

From here they took their old trail, bearing south of the Green Mounds, across Good Spring and Dove Creeks, by what Ford called the Boiling Spring Fork of the Concho, and thence by Antelope Creek and Potato Spring to the Kickapoo. From the head of Brady Creek they turned across to and down the trail towards Fredericksburg.

On June 18, 1849, Ford reported on the routes in detail to the editor of the *Texas Democrat* in Austin recommending a course either by way of Highsmith's old camp at Enchanted Creek, or by Fredericksburg, through the Concho country and around the point of the Guadalupe Mountains. Their outward route was impractical on account of the long distances between water. Not waiting for any report, however, were trains of emigrants scrambling, pell-mell, along their blazed but not yet beaten trails.[1]

Still the army was busy. In keeping with the intent of the general order initiating Whiting's reconnaissance, Colonel Joseph E. Johnston was ordered by Brigadier-General W. S. Harney, who had taken Worth's place, to organize a couple of topographical surveys. One in command of Johnston was to direct the march and open a road to El Paso for a battalion of the Third Infantry along the route recommended by Whiting. The other, in charge of Lieutenant Francis T. Bryan, was to "examine that just reported by Major Neighbors," or the Upper Road.

For some months Lieutenant S. G. French had been fitting out a train for the purpose. In camp on the prairie nine miles out of San Antonio, he was hard at work with a crew of nearly four hundred hired men trying to hammer some sense into

[1] *Texas Democrat*, June 23, 1849, reprinted in *Southwestern Historical Quarterly*, XLVIII, 262-268, C. L. Greenwood notes; Bieber, *Southern Trails, etc.*, 38-39.

the heads of an immense herd of Spanish mules. He recalled
that for the purpose of moving the troops he had

bought one thousand one hundred and eighty oxen, and collected about
two thousand head of mules, six hundred of which were wild mules
from Mexico, and I have never had any admiration for that animal in
his native state since, for like his sire as told in the book of Job, "neither
regardeth he the crying of the driver."[2]

Colonel Johnston took Dick Howard as "surveyor" and a
party of about twenty men to open the road. Preparations
were under way before Whiting's return, but when he made
his report recommending the Lower Road on account of the
water, Johnston gave up his original plans of going by way of
Fredericksburg and the Upper Road, to take what he and the
Army generally called the Wool Road as far west as the Frio.
This road which was really that of the Mexican General Woll
—made when he marched on San Antonio by way of an old
smuggler's trail from the Rio Grande during the Texas Revolution—was quite circuitous. General John E. Wool, reversing
the route during the Mexican War, seemed to have straightened it out.[3]

Johnston left San Antonio, June 13, 1849, and with a working crew delegated by Major Jefferson Van Horne, took the
Wool Road as far as the Frio. When it bore south toward
Eagle Pass, he quit it and kept to the north, to strike the Leona
above the military post that had been established March 13,
1849, eighty-five miles west of San Antonio, which became
Fort Inge. He crossed to the San Pedro or Devils River and
turned up it, finding beaver on its headwaters and bear and
javalina in the same region. The next nearest water was at
Howard's Springs, perhaps named for the noted guide, forty-
one miles farther northwest. From there a thirty-two mile drive
put them on Live Oak Creek, which they crossed and followed

2 Samuel G. French, *Two Wars: An Autobiography*, Nashville, 1901, p. 99;
Reconnaissances, as cited, 26.

3 *Reconnaissances*, as cited, 245-246; Bieber, *A Soldier Under Kearny*, as cited,
118; Bieber, *Exploring Southwestern Trails*, 350; Ike Moore, *The Life and Diary of
Reading W. Black*, Uvalde, 1934, p. 7; M. L. Crimmins, "General John E. Wool in
Texas," West Texas Historical Association *Year Book*, XVIII, 47-53.

to the Pecos, where some enterprising but unrecorded party had put in the first ferry.

In spite of the modern improvement they damned the region about as thoroughly as Whiting had done. Wood was almost unobtainable, grass was coarse and salty, and water could be had only by dipping it up, or by digging down the sharp banks, with danger of their stock's bogging and being lost in the quicksands when they ventured in to drink.

Johnston, the noted future Confederate general, reported that "But few more places can be found more solitary, or that present a more dreary appearance, than all this region of the Pecos." [4]

Lieutenant French, who was likewise to become a general in the same cause, added a few notes of his own, interesting in view of the changes of time:

The Pecos is a remarkable stream, narrow and deep and extremely crooked in its course, and rapid in its current. Its waters are turbid and bitter, and carry, in both mechanical mixture and chemical solution, more impurities than perhaps any other river in the south. Its banks are steep, and, in a course of two hundred and forty miles, there are but a few places where an animal can approach them for water in safety. Not a tree or bush marks its course; and one may stand on its banks and not know that the stream is near. The only inhabitants of its waters are catfish; and the antelope and the wolf alone visit its dreary, silent, and desolate shores. It is avoided even by the Indians. [5]

They turned up the Pecos from the mouth of Live Oak and laid out a good road to the west by way of Escondido and Comanche Springs. Thence their trail followed Whiting's tracks across the flats to the Davis Mountains, up the Limpia, past the site of Fort Davis, by Smith's Run, twenty-six miles west, and thence by a long drive to Eagle Springs. They split the battalion into four parties, traveling a day apart because of the scanty water at the Springs, and then "got much too little." They struck the Rio Grande about 120 miles below El Paso, and followed it up on the east side to its "intersection of the Santa Fe road to the rancho opposite El Paso."

4 *Reconnaissances,* as cited, 52.   5 The same, 45-46.

[37]

Thus, in the measured movement of Joseph E. Johnston's battalion, one of the major roads that linked San Antonio with El Paso, and for that matter the southeastern United States with the West Coast, was definitely opened. As the route of sweating Forty-Niners, the way of the first southern stage, the trail for great herds of cattle, and the way of frontier military movements, this course was for over thirty years a great but always trying trail.[6]

Lieutenant Francis T. Bryan also left San Antonio in June and went out by Fredericksburg, definitely to establish the Upper Road. He struck the Llano twelve miles above the existing German settlements[7] and crossed the San Saba to Brady Creek, thence west by Kickapoo, Lipan and Antelope Creeks. He bore west by sighting for the Green Mounds, just west of the location of San Angelo. He crossed the South Concho, marched eight miles to Dove Creek and three miles farther to cross Good Spring Creek. He found the grass "only tolerable" but the water fine. On July 7, 1849, his party left the head of the Middle Concho and after about forty-five miles reached the China Ponds and found them dry. Thirteen miles from the Pecos, in the Castle Gap, through which a road had already been cleared by California emigrants, they found a little water that sufficed for their mules, though too dirty for drinking.

From Horsehead, Bryan kept to the west side of the Pecos and noted in passing that the falls were then about ten feet high. He rounded the point of the Guadalupe Mountains and proceeded to El Paso. He found the trail 638 miles in length, presenting "no obstructions to the easy passage of wagons." Except for the long dry trip across the Plains west of the Concho, he reported, travelers could camp on water and grass every night.[8] Thus it was that the Upper Road came to equal

6 *Reconnaissances*, as cited, 47-50; Bieber, *Southern Trails to California*, 39, and *Exploring Southwestern Trails*, 36; French as cited, 99-101.

7 Castell was apparently started in 1847. R. L. Biesele, *The History of the German Settlements in Texas*, 1831-1861, Austin, 1939, p. 152.

8 *Reconnaissances*, as cited, 14-24.

[38]

footing with the Lower in the eyes of the military, though the establishment of posts in the lower country was already under way.

This activity was destined to assure the Forty-Niners and the military a good road to the west. During this period, Captain R. B. Marcy had been ordered west from Fort Smith, Arkansas, to open a route through the Indian Territory to Santa Fe and explore a more southerly route upon the return.

In New Mexico, he picked up a Comanche guide, and with eighteen wagons drawn by oxen and six mule teams, left the Rio Grande at Doña Ana, about sixty miles above El Paso. He skirted the north end of the Organ range and turned southeast to strike the old Salt Road made by Mexican *carretas* creaking their way to the deposits on the Salt Flats, and took the Guadalupe route to the Pecos. From there, near the state line, he hoped to continue directly across the Staked Plains to the head of the Brazos. But his guide warned him of the lack of water, saying that "no man (not even an Indian) ever undertakes to cross the 'Llano Estacado' opposite here." But he did tell Marcy of the Indian trail that crossed through the sands some sixty miles below.[9]

Marcy traveled leisurely down the river for four days without finding a crossing. On September 21, 1849, when almost south of the site of Monahans, Texas, he stopped and built a raft by lashing his water kegs to the bed of a wagon and inverting it in the stream. Thus the party ferried supplies and equipment, dragged their unwilling mules in and across, one at a time, by ropes, and shortly headed north by east into the White Sand Hills twenty-three miles away.

There on one branch of the Great Comanche War Trail, a few miles northeast of present Monahans, they came to permanent water in several deep holes. Five miles farther east they passed the last water in that immediate belt. They kept to the Comanche Trail, out of the Sands and up on the Staked

9 *Reconnaissances*, as cited, 204. For a careful study of his route, see J. W. Williams, "Marcy's Road from Doña Ana," West Texas Historical Association *Year Book*, XIX, 1943, p. 128.

Plains, pushing hard to make the next permanent water sixty-
five miles away. Fortunately they found a lake filled by rain
along the way, and easily made it to the spring-fed hole on a
draw about ten miles east and north of the site of Midland.

Wild horse trails radiated in every direction, and they
named it Mustang Pond, though it came to be generally called
Mustang Springs. From here they passed by the salt lake now
touched by a modern highway to the east, crossed over the
ridge, and pointed their teams down the long slope, off the
Staked Plains, to where the isolated abutments miles away
marked the location of the Big Spring. This too was named
by Marcy.

On the 4th of October, 1849, he headed northwest, and
reached the Colorado two days later. After losing a man to
the Indians, he came to the Brazos near the Double Mountains. From there his course was generally a little north of
east. In the open country west of the Cross Timbers a severe
norther struck his train and froze thirty-three of his mules to
death in one night, forcing him to abandon some of his wagons
and equipment. He pushed on with a few mules and his oxen
to strike, on the Trinity, the first habitation since leaving the
Rio Grande.

Upon reaching Fort Smith, Marcy made his report to Washington. In retrospect it is plain to see that this thirty-eight-
year-old native of Massachusetts, graduate of West Point,
Mexican War veteran and observant and imaginative man,
saw the Staked Plains with prophetic eyes. He saw that

As if ... in compensation for the absence of other favors, nature, in
her wise economy, has adorned the entire face of the country with a
luxuriant verdure of different kinds of grama grass, affording the most
nutritious sustenance for animals, and rendering it one of the best
countries for grazing large flocks and herds that can be conceived.[10]

He recommended a line of forts, some of which were eventually established, across the Texas frontier to protect this
road, decidedly the best overland wagon route to California.
He saw and recommended that the future railroad to the

[10] *Reconnaissances*, as cited, 224-226.

Pacific should go this way. And so from emigrant trail to rail, from Indian wilderness to pastoral pursuit and eventual conversion to farming, Marcy saw the whole picture.[11] He was not the original boomer but he was dead sure right.

But the busy probing of the territorial mysteries of West Texas still went on. The army was on the job. Johnston had recommended that a route from Red River to the Pecos should be explored. Therefore Lieutenant Nathaniel Micheler, detailed for this job, proceeded with a party of fourteen civilians from San Antonio to Fort Washita, Indian Territory. There in the fall of '49 he increased his force to twenty-one men because of reported hostilities of the Indians. He conferred with Marcy, who had just arrived from the West, then crossed Red River back into Texas near the mouth of the Little Washita where his survey was to start.

He kept to the divide between the Big and Little Wichitas until he reached the Brazos, took up it for 120 miles to the head of the Double Mountain Fork, partly on Marcy's Trail, crossed to the head of the Colorado, and thence to the Big Spring, December 21, 1849. From there he followed Marcy's Trail into the Monahans Sands, which were, he said:

... miniature Alps of sand ... perfectly white and clean: ... summit after summit spreading out in every direction, not a sign of vegetation upon them—nothing but sand piled on sand. They form a belt two or three miles in width, and extend many miles in a northwest direction. But a matter of the greatest surprise is to find large water-holes among them: they are found at the base of the hills, are large, deep, and contain most excellent water, cool, clear, and pleasant ... young willow trees are found on their banks.[12]

Michler kept on Marcy's Trail to the Pecos, "truly a rolling mass of red mud," down it forty miles to Horsehead, and so back through the San Angelo country by Fredericksburg, to San Antonio, which he reached January 20, 1850. He found

[11] *Reconnaissances*, as cited, 196-226; West Texas Historical Association *Year Book*, vol. I, 30 ff.; and J. W. Williams, "Marcy's Road from Doña Ana," the same, XIX, 128 ff., discusses the route across Texas in competent thoroughness.

[12] *Reconnaissances*, as cited, 29-39.

the upper route excellent from Red River to the Pecos, "well watered, the greater portion, and well timbered. It stands ° unrivaled by any other portion of Texas that I have seen." [13] Rather lush appraisal of the desert by a Pennsylvania Yankee!

As the eventful year of 1849 drew to a close, the Army had mapped four great trails across the wilderness of Texas: that of Marcy along the Canadian to Santa Fe; his and Michler's route through the Brazos country to the Pecos; the Upper Road from Austin and San Antonio through the Concho country to Horsehead and the common route thence by the Guadalupes to El Paso; and the Lower Road out to the Devils River, across to Live Oak, Comanche Springs, through the present Davis and Eagle Mountains, and up the Rio Grande.

It is not to be supposed, however, that the Forty-Niners waited on the army. In their wild enthusiasm to get off, they reckoned but little with the multiple hazards. They waited not for reconnaissance and report, for established outpost or detailed escort, but rigged up as they reached the frontier. The first were long since gone.

In the winter of 1848 and 1849 they were straggling up from the coast to Austin and San Antonio. They were congregating on the edge around the neat and new German village of Zodiac and the outside settlement of Fredericksburg four miles above. They noted that these settlements, just started by inexperienced adventurers from the old world, were models of sturdy construction and commendable civic pride compared with the helter-skelter buildings of the frontier Texans. Though they may not have approved of the Mormon nature of Zodiac, they could not help but admire its "well-built houses, perfect fences, and tidy door-yards . . . such as not before seen in Texas." Others found the two thousand people of Fredericksburg "healthy and industrious" enough, though "of the lower orders."

Here many tried to restock with provisions. But the prices

[13] Michler too became a brigadier-general during the Civil War. See Cullum, *Biographical Register,* as cited, II, 347-348.

were high as the several stores were poorly stocked. Here the
Forty-Niners completed their organization into loose companies, chose their captains, formulated regulations—one known
as the "Company of Equal Rights"—and bound themselves,
but not too rigidly, to follow orders on their march across the
wilderness. As time for departure approached they attended
German balls, taking advantage of the fact that introductions
were dispensed with in the simple custom of "dance and
treat and treat and dance with whom you please." With the
rise of grass they took off in high hope.[14]

Some companies were well organized. Many were equipped
with little beyond a great zest for life and a burning desire to
gather a bag full of gold. Upon his return, Marcy warned that
little faith could be placed in maps, and that Disturnell's,
upon which he had tried to depend, was most unreliable. He
recommended that parties number seventy-five to a hundred
for proper protection against the Indians, that they post continual guards, exercise utmost vigilance over their teams, carry
only the most essential supplies, but include extra coupling
poles and felloes as little suitable timber for repairs would be
found along the way. With all this and good luck they should
"go through in four months with ease." [15]

The impatience of the bolder and better outfitted emigrants
increased as they were forced progressively to cut their pace
to accommodate the slowest part of the caravans. Dissension
flowered into disruption and companies flew apart to go their
individual ways. Restraint had no place with them while they
risked hide and hair in their mad rush toward the land of gold.
Generally, caution was thrown to the western winds.

As Major Neighbors' party straggled back in May, 1849,
they met "a solitary old man near the head of the San Saba,

14 Mabelle Eppard Martin, "From Texas to California in 1849: Diary of C. C.
Cox," *Southwestern Historical Quarterly*, XXIX, 41-42; John Russell Bartlett, *Per-
sonal Narrative of Explorations and Incidents in Texas, New Mexico, California,
Sonora and Chihuahua*, New York, 1854, vol. I, p. 58; Bieber, *Southern Trails to
California*, 260.

15 *Reconnaissances*, as cited, 225.

riding a Spanish horse with a naked saddle-tree, and leading a mule very badly packed," headed west strictly on his own. Fearful that he had fallen into outlaw company, he respectfully suggested to the five hungry men:

"Oh, Gentlemen, you certainly wouldn't hurt a poor lone man—there are seventy men just behind: go take them." [16] As they came in to report on the best route, they met others, decidedly better equipped and organized, working their way west through the Concho country.

Captain Murchison, "an old and worthy Texian" from La Grange, was on the head of the Concho with a company on the 24th of May, while just ahead of him was Captain O. B. Tong of Seguin with forty-five wagons pushing for the Pecos. Behind him a Captain Smith of Houston was progressing satisfactorily, ten miles west of the head of the San Saba, while fifteen miles below the old Spanish fort Neighbors met the Persifer F. Smith Association. This group wisely hired D. C. Sullivan from Neighbors to guide them to El Paso. Thus it is obvious that even before Neighbors and Ford could get back to report, the westward movement through the still unknown Concho country was definitely under way.

In order to catch even a fleeting glimpse of this colorful picture it might be well to rewind the reel of history and start with them at the beginning.

[16] *Southwestern Historical Quarterly*, XLVIII, 271-272, reprint from *Texas Democrat*, June 16, 1849.

During the winter of 1848-1849, they advanced by easy stages toward the stubborn but still uncertain settlements of Zodiac, Castell and Fredericksburg, there to take their choice from the apparent maze of trails that stumped the early emigrant and staggers the modern reader. Meanwhile other companies were congregating and organizing at Brownsville, Corpus Christi and San Antonio, and on the upper frontiers of Texas.[17]

The *Houston Telegraph* recorded a consequent shortage of mules, due to the emigrant demand, by the first of March—a shortage accentuated by the levies of the late war and those of the Comanches. Some mules could be bought at $35 a head,[18] but emigrants were stranded at Brownsville because of lack of mounts. At the same time an estimated 1500 emigrants and soldiers were already packed around Fredericksburg, anxious to take the Upper Road when grass rose in the spring. The reporter estimated their teams at from three to four thousand horses and mules, "besides numerous herds of cattle, which will be driven with the company for meat." Three hundred wagons were expected to start the trip West.[19]

These emigrants decided upon their own laws, voted their choice of captain, provided for their defense, wisely got some guides, and set out. Perhaps the first large train to take the trail out of Austin, March 17, 1849, was headed by a Captain Haynie. It ran into all sorts of hardships and reached El Paso in June, after having resorted to snakes and several of their horses and mules for food.[20]

Fortunately most had better luck, and, where organized under experienced Texans, embarked with greater care. Captain John Murchison of LaGrange laid his plans with precision, as the *Texas Democrat*, of Austin, noted, March 31, 1849:

[17] Ralph Bieber in *Southern Trails to California*, as cited, 32-33, gives a good summary of this early movement. See also, Martin, as cited, 132.

[18] *Houston Telegraph*, March 1 and 15, April 12, 1849.

[19] The same, March 8, 1849.

[20] Martin, "From Texas to California in 1849," Texas and Southwestern Historical *Quarterly*, XXIX, 212.

Another company is in process of organization at LaGrange for California. They will take the overland route through Texas. The company will consist of about one hundred persons, and will positively leave LaGrange on the first of May. They will have military organization. Each squad of men will be required to have a good two-horse wagon drawn by four mules or horses, with at least two extra mules for the following outfit: two sheets of sheet iron 30 inches wide and 6 feet long if possible; half dozen long handled shovels; half dozen spades; 2 spike mattocks; 1 weeding hoe; 1 chopping axe, 1 hatchet; 1 handsaw; 1 drawing knife; augurs; 1 frow; 1 iron wedge; extra horse shoes and nails; shoeing tools; 500 pounds of bacon; 200 pounds of coffee; 125 pounds of flour; 100 pounds of salt; 50 pounds of rice; the means of carrying at least 10 gallons of water; medicine, clothing, etc., in all making about 1600 pounds. Each man must be provided with a good gun, and at least one pistol, and bowie or butcher knife. Every five persons must likewise carry five pounds of powder and forty pounds of lead. 100 is the number to which the company is limited. Companies of five persons may report to Captain John Murchison at LaGrange, where they will register for the expedition.[21]

Murchison completed his arrangements and enrolled his party in the substantial village of LaGrange, April 28, 1849. Just ahead of him was one under Captain Thomas Smith, while another group under Sam Whiting came through and hurried up the road toward Austin. The *Mercantile Advertiser* of Houston noted their passage through LaGrange and recommended the route by Fredericksburg to "the gold diggings" as "altogether preferable to any other." [22] It boosted the road further, contrary to other reports, with the optimistic assertion that should horses, mules or oxen be required, "they can be had at nearly every plantation."

Murchison's party, well armed with shovels, spades and ebullient optimism, headed for the outside edge. At Fredericksburg, Thomas Smith's company reorganized with ten wagons and twenty-five packmules and left on the 17th of May. The companies of Captains Tong and Duval got started too, and the Persifer F. Smith Association, made up largely of Tennesseeans, got off with the characteristic boldness of

[21] Martin, as cited, 213.   [22] The same, 39-40.

that native breed and overcame the obstacles of travel as well as the obvious frontier handicap of their leader's given name.

Thus it was that Ford and Neighbors met them strung out from the Pecos to where the trail struck the San Saba below the Old Spanish Fort. Rip Ford observed that Duval's party was then in the lead. They met Captain Tong's "citizen train of forty-five wagons . . . getting [along] admirably well without a single case of accident or sickness." On the 24th they met Murchison on the head of the river, traveling rapidly with a "well regulated" company. As already noted, they met Captain Thomas Smith's party from Houston just beyond the head of the San Saba; and below the old fort, the Persifer Smith Association, which enlisted the experienced guidance of D. C. Sullivan.[23]

With Ford and Neighbors' report on the route by way of the Guadalupe Mountains fresh in their minds, they pushed on with renewed faith. The Thomas Smith party feasted on bear along the San Saba, and on the 28th nooned it on Good Spring Creek. The Concho country struck them as a destitute region, and C. C. Cox, of the Houston country, wrote of the prairie dogs and antelopes that night in his diary, but saw little hope for the future of the country when he observed:

"This portion of Texas is exceedingly poor, and so barren that I am of the opinion it will always remain unhabited—." Prophecy, too, is a hazardous thing.

Here Cox recorded that his party found letters left by the emigrant companies ahead for the "information of travelers generally." One of these contained the story of the accidental death of a young man named Fuller, resulting from his own pistol—perhaps the first white man killed in the immediate vicinity of San Angelo. From here the trail cut across to the Middle Concho and to the Pecos.

The emigrants met Captain Bryan on the Pecos while he was disparaging the country and condemning the route. No matter to them, hell-bent as they were for California. They

23 *Southwestern Historical Quarterly*, XLVIII, 270-272.

laughed and pushed on. While Lieutenant French commented on the first ferry across the Pecos at the mouth of Live Oak that summer, the lack of one bothered the others but little. They swam their stock and floated their plunder at Horsehead, and even one carried his ferry with him. L. B. Harris, from Harrisburg, with the Thomas Smith company, had, with commendable conservatism, provided for high water across this desert country by building his wagon bed into a scow, with "both ends turned up and constructed so as to be water tight. Oars were carried on the sides. . ." When he reached a river too deep to ford, he floated his wagon bed off the rocking bolsters and manned the raft like a bold mariner from Texas. As may be guessed, he safely navigated the Pecos.[24]

If the Concho country looked bad, Cox found the Pecos even worse, and Harris wrote back to his brother that for sixty miles up the river their road was nothing but "one steady stream of dust and sand." So far as value went, he continued that he "would not pay taxes on a league of it, if the Government would donate the ballance of it to me." This was conservative appraisal for a man risking his life for gold, for it should be recalled that the tax rate was reasonable, then.[25]

They kept up the west bank of the river from Horsehead to near the state line, and cut off northwest for thirty miles to strike the Delaware, which they at first called the Savine. At the head springs of the Delaware, June 15, 1849, in the uttermost wilderness, they were treated to a striking scene. A party of "eight or ten families from Eastern Texas" were camped there. They had set up a blacksmith shop. "Cords of children and a few Milch Cows" were scattered over the landscape

[24] "Reminiscences of C. C. Cox," *Texas State Historical Association Quarterly,* VI, 131; Martin, as cited, XXIX, 43-46.

[25] The same, XXIX, 216. The Gilbert horseback party left Dallas in April, 1849, and made its way west through the Weatherford, Abilene and Midland country, reached the Pecos May 18, continued west around the north side of the Davis Mountains and struck the Rio Grande near Isleta. A journal of this trip by C. C. Gibbs, printed in the *Northern Standard,* Clarksville, Texas, February 1850, was reprinted in the West Texas Historical Association *Year Book,* XIX, 1943, pp. 153 ff.

while the squalling of the children and the sound of the anvil seemed to reverberate from against the Guadalupe range.

This group, evidently Captain Griffin's Company from Paris, had come from north Texas through the Cross Timbers and apparently approximated Marcy's later trail to the Pecos, though several months ahead of Marcy.[26] By the time the various parties got to the Guadalupe foothills, the rugged Murchison—shovels, salt and all—was in the lead, though the Harrisburg party was poking the prow of its scow close in his dust. Taking the Ford and Neighbors horse trail, Murchison put his wagons around the precipitous point of El Capitan, dropped down the rough side of the canyon that served as a pass, and pointed his teams toward the Salt Flats. From the pure waters of Pine Spring on the southeast slope of the Guadalupes he made it to the next brackish supply out on the flat called Crow Springs, while the others straggled behind.

Thus his wagons were the first to open this road for caravan travel. It was a notable achievement and he wrote back to report that he had gotten through. The government was alleged to have set aside $50,000 for the venture, and Murchison, with a healthy skepticism toward political promise and government bonus, observed that "we think we are entitled to [it] whether we get it or not."[27]

From here to El Paso their problem was mainly one of water. Eventually they learned to meet it, but at first they had their difficulties. The day after Murchison rounded the mountains, forty-five wagons came through the pass. Murchison, meanwhile, passed Crow Spring and pushed ahead. In the eighty-mile stretch between there and the Rio Grande he wrote that he and his men "lost much time in hunting and digging for water." They knew that others were pressing close, and he noted: "My command, being in front might have got some water at one place, but like men passed it by, leaving it for others behind."[28]

[26] Martin, as cited, 49, 217.
[27] *Southwestern Historical Quarterly*, XXIX, 213.
[28] The same, 214.

Captain Billy Thompson's party was a day behind Murchison, and back of them was the Harris company from Houston. When they reached Crow Springs, June 18, 1849, Cox reported his concern in his diary, saying:

Our situation at this time is indeed precarious—No water and but little grass between this point and the Rio Grande, a distance of about eighty miles—Thompson's company got thirty miles beyond this and finding the water holes dry sent their teams back to this place, some of which have perished on the road. We will remain here a few days to allow our own exhausted animals time to recruit.[29]

Captain Tong's Delaware guide could not find the water in the Cornudas—those horn-like peaks protruding from that vast and arid plain. But Cox and Harris and the trains that followed—the two Smith parties, Duval's, Haynie's, Bryan's and Griffin's—"all reached El Paso in safety," though the Persifer Smith outfit lost one man to the Indians.[30] Thus the Upper Road was definitely opened to wagon travel by these early Forty-Niners, who stopped at El Paso del Norte to rest their stock and try to replenish their larders.

The Presidio branch of the California Trail deserves its passing notice. Travelers on either the Upper or Lower road could, and sometimes did, turn off from the Pecos to Comanche Springs and continued down the Comanche Trail into the Big Bend. From Leaton's Fort and Presidio del Norte, they followed Whiting's tough and original trail directly up the river.

Companies led by McNeal and Terry got off a month ahead of those that went up the Pecos. Along with what were called the Louisville and Mississippi Companies, they went out through the Concho country and turned Southwest to Presidio. Some kept down the Chihuahua Trail through Mexico. Others abandoned their wagons and left by pack up the Rio Grande. Terry and his party tackled the course up the river, "suffered

29 The same, 49-50.

30 *Texas Democrat*, August 4, 1849, quoted in *Southwestern Historical Quarterly*, XLVIII, 270.

considerably . . . and lost a great many of their animals," being forced to cross and recross the stream as they worked their way toward the Pass.[31]

Thus one of the most colorful characters of the West left Texas through the Concho country, down by way of Presidio del Norte and up the Rio Grande. David S. Terry was destined to sit on the California Supreme Court, to take a vigorous part against vigilante justice there, to fight and kill Senator David Broderick in a duel in 1859, to join the South and be wounded as an officer in the Civil War, and to return to California and be killed there in 1889. He too was seasoned by his experiences on the trails across Texas.[32]

By the time Terry reached the site of El Paso a great encampment of caravans was scattered up and down the river. By July there was an immense "concourse of emigrants at El Paso—upwards of four thousands," with from twelve to fifteen hundred wagons. They were camped from where the river squeezed into the mountains above the town to where the valley flowered with productive vegetable farms and vineyards clear down to San Elizario.

The noted virago, the Great Western, had moved across the river and opened her hotel on the Texas side and Ponce's Ranch, which was the extent of El Paso when the rush started, was indeed prosperous. For the weary emigrants, however, it was a prosperity built largely on a scarcity of supplies, a fact which even the potent Pass Whiskey, concocted on the spot, could hardly blot out.

In June of that year Ben Franklin Coons, a Santa Fe and Chihuahua trader, and like the rest from Missouri, bought Ponce's ranch and began to push it as a place of trade. He diverted his teams from the Santa Fe haul along the newly opened trail to San Antonio. Then Captain Billy Thompson, commanding a company for the gold fields, saw the oppor-

[31] *Southwestern Historical Quarterly*, XXIX, 214-219; XLVIII, 92; Anson Mills, *My Story*, Washington, 1918, pp. 346 ff.

[32] *Dictionary of American Biography*, XVIII, 379-380.

tunities at the Pass. He quit the trail and by July was in the mercantile business himself.

Thus the town called Coon's Ranch, which is modern El Paso, got started in the summer of 1849. Its immediate growth was encouraged by the fact that the long trip from the Texas frontier had tested the temper and the mettle of the emigrants. Many of them, relieved by the soft-eyed diversion of Mexican women and the slacking of their desert thirst, disintegrated here—some to stay. As may have been guessed, "the Company of 'Equal Rights'" likewise flew to pieces and went their individual ways.

Meanwhile, Major Jefferson Van Horne moved out of San Antonio with his troops along the Lower Road, following Colonel Johnston's lead. On September 8 he reached the Pass with his troops, his great supply train of 275 wagons, some 2500 head of cattle and a few emigrants who had attached themselves to his caravan for protection. After their march of 673 miles they located on land leased from Coons and established the military outpost which was to become Fort Bliss.

In the Santa Fe *New Mexican* that fall, Coons advertised his intention of promoting a real settlement at the site. He offered every inducement to travelers from a fine tavern to the best blacksmithing, as well as ferry service to the cool shade and warm eyes of the town of four thousand Mexicans across the river.

Meanwhile D. C. Sullivan, after seeing the Persifer Smith Association through, had been joined by others and back-tracked along the trail through the Concho country. He safely arrived at the settlements, further to recommend the Upper Road.[33] Thus at last the lesson was clear. The best way West from down in Texas was that up the gentle gradient of the Conchos and across the Staked Plains to the Pecos. It was not a sudden but it was a significant conclusion.

33 Martin, as cited, *Southwestern Historical Quarterly*, XXIX, 129-132, XLVIII, 270; Bieber, *Exploring Southwestern Trails*, 303-311; Bieber, *Southern Trails to California*, 30; M. H. Thomlinson, *The Garrison of Fort Bliss*, 1849-1916, El Paso, 1945, p. 2-4.

CHAPTER IV

ℱrontier of the ℱifties

Closely tied in with this business of opening trails to the gold fields in 1849 was the army's job of protecting the lives and the property of the scattered border people of Texas. The Indians were, and for thirty years would continue to be, the real frontier problem. Acting upon the assumption that the way to meet a savage foe was to wait behind defenses, the army was busily throwing up a line of posts across the frontier of Texas.

San Antonio was its natural depot. Fort Martin Scott, just out of Fredericksburg, became the outpost, December 5, 1848. The following spring the line was drawn. Beginning with Fort Duncan, just above the Eagle Pass, its next bastion was Fort Inge, near present Uvalde, on the trail west. From there it stretched to the north toward Red River, well outside the settlements, by way of Forts Groghan, Gates, Graham, and Worth. Westward traffic over the Wool and Lower Trails was further encouraged by Fort Lincoln, near D'Hanis, and a temporary camp at San Elizario in the El Paso Valley.[1]

[1] For this system of forts and defense, see: W. C. Holden, "Frontier Defense, 1846-1860," West Texas Historical Association *Year Book*, VI, 35 ff.; Lenora Barrett, the same, V, 87 ff.; M. L. Crimmins, the same, XIX, 121-128; J. W. Williams, the same, XVIII, 77-91.

Ostensibly this was a cordon of defense behind which the citizens of Texas should be reasonably secure. Except for infrequent spasms of peace, however, bands of Indians seeped through the frontier in the growing light of every moon to congregate, strike and scatter again, back toward their nomadic homes.

In the fall of 1849 Captain Whiting was ordered upon an inspection of the frontier. From Fort Duncan, on the Rio Grande, to Coffee's Bend, on Red River near present Denison, he noted the nature of the country and the condition of the posts. He made his first report January 21, 1850, recommending heavier garrisons and the location of additional forts. He advised that one be placed on Red River and another on the Brazos.

In view of the growing traffic through the Concho country, he urged the reinvestment of the old Spanish fort on the San Saba, and because of the seasonal raids on Mexico by Comanche, Kiowa, Apache and allied tribes along the Comanche trails, he favored two additional posts upon these routes. He urged that one be placed at the point where the Lower California Road crossed the eastern branch of the Comanche Trail, on Las Moras Creek, and one at Presidio del Norte, flanking the main trail into Mexico.

In March he made a supplemental report warning of continued border troubles, and argued his views with sound logic. More important still than the posts, however, were his recommendations as to tactics. He saw the futility of a policy of waiting in position for a fugitive foe; of static defense against a past master of movement. And so he urged outposts "where the *Indians live,* instead of where the *citizens live;*" the substitution of light cavalry for the useless infantry; and finally, not only pursuit of the raiders but "punishment of the remainder of the tribe." [2]

[2] *Reconnaissances,* as cited, 245-250; M. L. Crimmins, "The First Line of Army Posts Established in West Texas in 1849," West Texas Historical Association *Year Book,* XIX, 121-127.

It was the sage advice of a remarkably astute man. But the gods of the governmental mills grind leisurely in converting sound suggestion into settled policy, and it was not until Ranald S. Mackenzie took the saddle, more than twenty years later, that Whiting's advice was thoroughly adopted by the regular army.

Except for a post at Presidio, however, his suggestions as to fortifications met with reasonably immediate response. In 1851 Belknap and Phantom Hill were founded in the Brazos region along Marcy's Trail. The same year Fort Mason was thrown astride the Upper Road from San Antonio, and a year later Fort Clark was added to the lower line. Instead of rebuilding the Spanish Fort, McKavett was established a little farther west, on the head of the San Saba; and Camp Johnston, at the gateway to the Plains but still adjacent to the trail, was pitched along the North Concho. Chadbourne and Terrett were located to cover the space between. Instead of the recommended post at Presidio, the army, in 1854, located Fort Davis at the head of the Limpia in what became the Davis Mountains.[3]

Thus provision for the protection of the caravans of emigrants and the Texas frontier was promisingly made. Still the posts were garrisoned with considerable infantry, and Whiting's wise suggestions in tactics were largely ignored.

Yet this bustle of movement and building of forts across Texas, coupled with the healthy flow of people into the state, combined to strengthen and stabilize the frontier of the fifties. The lower end of the line of settlement was fairly fixed with the post at Eagle Pass. It was firmly tied to the settlements of old world colonists at and around Castroville and Fredericksburg, and was anchored to the Red River region by other struggling outposts that edged their way into the Western Cross Timbers. Back of this line the settled and civilized world of the period looked toward the West Coast along three great

[3] See Arrie Barrett's, "Western Frontier Forts of Texas," West Texas Historical Association *Year Book*, VII, 115, and Crimmins, as cited.

trails, the principal one of which led out through the Concho country.

The Indian troubles, while always serious and never efficiently coped with by the regular army, were in part being handled by the Texas Rangers. Still each family that ventured upon the frontier ran its own risks and looked first to its own resources to protect its lives and keep its hair. Major Robert S. Neighbors, Indian agent for the Federal government, was, with great zeal, doing his best to ameliorate the troubles, while that efficient organizer of the affairs of the German colonists, Baron John O. Meusebach, early set forth to treat with the Comanche scourges on his own. His immediate interest was the survey and the holding of the Fisher and Miller Grant, a broad tract of land that reached from the Fredericksburg region northwest beyond the Conchos.

This immense grant, extending the length of the Llano on the south, continued southwest nearly to the Rio Grande and up the Pecos to a point west of the site of San Angelo. Its uncertain boundaries then pointed northeast, again to the Colorado, and down that stream to the mouth of the Llano, thus encompassing the whole of the San Saba and Concho country.[4] The title to this land, and hence some of its history, goes back to Fisher and Miller.

Henry Francis Fisher left Germany in 1833 and made his way toward Texas. By 1838 he was in Harrisburg and the following year he was acting treasurer for what was known as "the San Saba Company," which in 1839 prepared to explore the San Saba region—far beyond the frontier of settled Texas.[5] It had official sanction, as President Mirabeau B. Lamar approved its plans, but its expedition was delayed for several years.

Then Fisher, Burchard Miller and Joseph Baker proposed to introduce a thousand families from the old world into the Republic of Texas, and settle them on the tract between the

4 R. L. Biesele, *The History of the German Settlements in Texas*, 152.

5 The same, 76-77.

[56]

Llano and the Colorado. President Sam Houston endorsed the proposal, and on June 7, 1842, a contract was made. Fisher, still agent for the San Saba Company, was active in its plans to explore this alluring section that had drawn an ill-fated Christianizing venture among the Indians during the Spanish period, and was made even more attractive by the tales of Bowie's silver mine many years later.

The plans lay dormant until the spring of 1843, when the company's expedition made its way from Houston to Washington on the Brazos. There the explorers were officially discouraged from continuing. The Republic of Texas then had Indian agents in the upper country trying to make peace with the wild tribes, and President Houston felt that the appearance of a large armed party in that section, a favorite winter resort of the Comanches, would throw a serious damper on their prospects of success. So the expedition turned back. But eventually Fisher and Miller meshed their interests and efforts with other colonizers in Germany,[6] and the settlements that soon pushed up by way of New Braunfels and Fredericksburg at last reached the lower edge of their grant along the Llano.

Then in January, 1847, the capable Meusebach, looking toward the survey of the Miller and Fisher lands in keeping with the early contract, left Fredericksburg to hunt up the Indians and make a treaty of his own. The news reached Austin and the Federal Indian Agent Neighbors was sent by the Governor to dissuade him from his venture. When Neighbors reached the struggling village, established in May the year before, he found that Meusebach had already left for the San Saba.

In keeping with his alternate instructions to join and aid if he could not stop him, Neighbors picked up the German observer and scientist, Ferdinand Roemer, who was anxious to explore the hill country of Texas, and overtook the expe-

6 Dr. Biesele, in his scholarly work, gives this background in detail. As cited, 76-82.

dition near the San Saba, February 10, 1847, just after it had met a deputation from the Comanches. Next day the combined parties met with chiefs of the tribes, arranged a later parley, and left for an exploration of the river valley and the Spanish ruins along that stream near present Menard. This accomplished to their satisfaction—Roemer making the first geological examination of the region as they rode along—they turned back to meet the Indians.

Meusebach met with several chiefs about thirty miles above the mouth of the river, March 1, 1847. He protested his peaceful designs, and asked their approval of his proposed settlement on the Llano and his survey of the lands of the San Saba. In return the Indians were to receive a lot of presents upon calling for them at Fredericksburg "when the disk of the moon has rounded twice." Thereafter they should be friends and both peoples live in peace.[7]

Rudolph L. Biesele, historian of Texas German colonization, points out that while these settlements henceforth were not exempt from depredations, they suffered but little compared with the rest of the Texas frontier as the lands were surveyed and opened to settlement.[8]

Meanwhile the beginnings of trade followed the military trails. The army called upon civilian contractors to meet the problems of supply. The hazards of hundreds of miles of wilderness trails pushed up the rates on freight to tempt the mule-skinner and the bull-whacker to risk their hair wherever there was need of corn, beans, and flour. Herds of longhorned work oxen and skittish but durable Mexican mules stirred the dust and cropped the grass around San Antonio in heavy concentrations of frontier power. Then, in patient plodding beneath the yoke and in scampering and harnessed tandems, they swung out of the crooked streets of that ancient town to deliver the supplies that maintained the isolated posts.

[7] Ferdinand Roemer, *Texas*, Translated by Oswald Mueller, San Antonio, 1935, pp. 235 ff.; Biesele, as cited, 186-187.

[8] Biesele, as cited, 187-190.

[58]

San Antonio boomed with business. Rates ran all the way from a dollar and a half per hundred pounds for every hundred miles on many hauls—such as the 1859 rates to Forts Lancaster and Stockton—up to $1.70 on the longer and still rougher trips to Fort Davis and beyond. Thus the cost of transporting a ton of corn, if corn was being hauled, from San Antonio to El Paso was approximately $230, which was stiff enough for corn either in bulk or solution. However, the rates to Fort McKavett were set at $1.75, and those to Fort Chadbourne at a flat $2.75 per hundred pounds for the entire distance.[9]

Even the Chihuahua traders were attracted by the lush rewards awaiting those who did not die on the trail, and soon their caravans were snaking their way through Presidio del Norte into Fort Davis, and thence along the Lower Road to San Antonio. Traders there, just as enterprising and alert, accepted the challenge to push their teams into Mexico. The San Antonio-Chihuahua Trail, with its regular trade, thus came into being.[10]

In between times the Indians were not idle. The war with Mexico had given them excuse as well as encouragement to depredate beyond the *Rio Bravo*. Among them were leaders of daring as well as design. The noted Wild Cat, leader of one of the smaller tribes of Seminoles, played back and forth between Mexico and the upper frontier of Texas.[11]

West of the Pecos, ranging from the cattle ranches of Durango to the Guadalupe Mountains, and particularly at home in the Big Bend, was the dreaded Gomez, whose name in 1849 was the terror of Chihuahua and a by-word in Mexico—a name

9 For an interesting discussion of this subject see Lenora Barrett, "Transportation, Supplies, and Quarters for the West Texas Frontier Under the Federal Military System, 1848-1861," West Texas Historical Association *Year Book*, V, 1929, pp. 87 ff.

For the military roads of the period and some of their extensions, see J. W. Williams, in the same publication, XVIII, 1942, pp. 77 ff.

10 August Santleben, in *A Texas Pioneer*, gives a good account of this trade immediately after the Civil War.

11 W. P. Webb, in *The Texas Rangers*, 133-136, notes the character and the operations of this notorious leader of the Seminoles, Kickapoos and free Negroes.

now perpetuated by a peak in the Davis Mountains. He was then "a well made fellow apparently about 30 or 35 years old, dressed something like a Mexican and speaking excellent Spanish, . . . hostile and insulting."[12]

Through central Texas the lesser tribes of the region were in pathetic condition, virtually having to choose between raiding and starving. But in 1853 Secretary of War Jefferson Davis brought to the office an interest in the frontier and a genuine desire to settle the Indian problem. He suggested that if Texas would establish reserves and confine the Indians upon them, it would greatly simplify the problems of protection. The response was prompt. On February 6, 1854, Texas passed a law dedicating twelve leagues of public land for this purpose. A reservation was established on the Brazos, in present Young County, for the "tame" Indians—the Caddos, Ionies, Wacos, and others—and some fifty miles west, Neighbors selected another for the wild Comanches.

Thus in the middle fifties an honest attempt at settlement of the Indians in Texas began. Hereafter, legally, theoretically, and usually as a matter of fact, those caught moving up and down the frontier were "wild" and hostile, subject to attack by the federal forces—just as they were always objects of war with the Texans.[13]

Something of the magnitude of the problem the army faced may be realized from the fact that it had to patrol "nearly 2000 miles" of Indian and foreign frontier in Texas alone. And while the Indians were estimated at 30,000, the forces of the Department of Texas in 1854 numbered only 2,886 officers and men.

The Comanches had no hankering for a settled life and no love for the reservation. Yet they found their own condition little short of hopeless. As early as 1852 the special Indian agent for the State of Texas, Horace Capron, had visited some

[12] "Whiting Diary," *Publications of the Southern History Assn.*, X, 1906, p. 11.

[13] Webb, as cited, 161-172; Richardson, *The Comanche Barrier*, 214 ff.; Haley, *Charles Goodnight, Cowman and Plainsman*, 21 ff.

Southern Comanches near Camp Johnston on the North Concho, where a chief of the hungry tribe made bitter complaint, which Capron translated to Washington:

What encouragement have we to attempt the cultivation of the soil, or raising of cattle, so long as we have no permanent home? In every attempt we have ever made to raise crops, we have been driven from them by the encroachment of the white man before they could mature.

Over this vast country where for centuries our ancestors roamed in undisputed possession, free and happy, what have we left? The game, our main dependence, is killed and driven off, and we are forced into the most sterile and barren portions of it to starve. We see nothing but extermination left for us, and we await the result with stolid indifference. Give us a country we can call our own, where we may bury our people in quiet.[14]

It was the tragic appeal of a proud and independent race that had occupied that interesting land for ages. Years were to elapse before the final verdict was written, but for the wisest heads in the buffalo-hide wigwams the decision was obvious. Nevertheless, the warlike task before the whites was still enormous.[15]

The Indians were rather quiet for a brief period after the establishment of the first forts. But peace did not last long. They were raiding with vengeance in 1853,[16] and in submitting his report that year the Secretary of War noted that while depredations were diminished, orders had been issued to set up a fort opposite El Paso del Norte. Other plans were under way to establish "A large post on the point where the great trail of the Commanche [sic] Indians crossed the Rio Grande"—an intention modified in the location of Fort Davis.[17]

The wide expanse between the forts along the Lower Road and on to the western extremity of Texas was obviously too vast for the army's protection. The passage of time and the

14 Quoted from Carl Coke Rister, *Robert E. Lee in Texas*, 25-26.

15 *Report of the Secretary of War*, 1854, pp. 5-6; the same, 1852, p. 21. For a discussion of "The Federal Indian Policy in Texas, 1845-1846," see Lena Clara Koch, *Southwestern Historical Quarterly*, XXVIII, 259 ff.

16 Froebel, *Seven Years Travel*, as cited, 420.

17 *Report of the Secretary of War*, 1853, pp. 3-4.

[61]

loss of numerous lives convinced even Washington that Whiting was right. More troops were needed; more outposts were essential.

Lieutenant Colonel Washington Seawell was already camped on the Limpia with six companies of the 8th Infantry when an order was issued, October 23, 1854, to establish a post there. It was named after Jeff Davis, then Secretary of War, and designed as a way-station on the trail to the gold fields and as a further hindrance to Indian forays into Mexico.[18]

Fort Lancaster was founded on the Lower Road just above the mouth of Live Oak Creek, to the east of the Pecos, August 20, 1855, and Fort Stockton became another comfortable station for protection and rest on the Great Indian Trail at Comanche Springs, beginning March 23, 1859. By the fifties posts could be found along the road west at convenient stages all the way across Texas.[19] They furnished encouragement to west-bound emigrants, while increasing the need and supplying the defense for the western mail, the service of which was already under way.

Early in 1854, Major J. S. Simonson, with his mounted riflemen, commanded an expedition "scouring the mountainous district north of the El Paso road, and between Fort Davis and the Rio Grande" in search of Apaches. The Indians had pulled out, apparently toward the Mescalero country to the north. He did learn, however, that the Mescaleros were in touch with the Lipans, then "established on the Nueces near Fort Inge," and that they "kept up a regular communication" with them whereby they learned "the strength and object of every party that passed that point on the road to El Paso." Simonson pushed as far north as "Marcy's Road," where he met Major Longstreet, of the 8th Infantry, working out of El Paso into the Guadalupe Mountains.

[18] *Medical History*, Fort Davis, 1869, pp. 1-2, War Records, National Archives, Washington, D. C.

[19] Arrie Barret, "Western Frontier Forts of Texas," West Texas Historical Association *Year Book*, VII, 1931, pp. 115 ff.

Major Neighbors, the zealous federal agent, kept protesting the expeditions against the Indians as an injustice to the tribes. Instead of agreeing, General Smith asked specific authority to keep the Mescaleros away from the El Paso road. To make matters worse, he claimed that a tribe of Lipans and three bands of Mescaleros had crossed into Mexico where they were under protection of the state. But even with these protective measures supply was a serious problem.

The summer season had been an uncommonly dry one, and Simonson, reporting from his camp on the Limpia in the Davis Mountains, lamented the fact that the Governor of Chihuahua had put an embargo on corn shipments from that state "solely to annoy us...." Since no corn was raised on the north side of the river, this, he continued—with the shortage of water and grass due to drouth—would "embarrass our supplies of forage towards Fort Davis...." [20]

Just as the wily Apaches harried the west-bound emigrants and wagon trains, so the bold Comanches and the Kiowas continued to plague the luckless travelers to the north of the Concho country. Still there were some bright spots in the drab picture. As if to give tone to the rugged life of the frontier posts, and as further emphasis of the genuine character of the leaders of the army at this time, Robert E. Lee was sent to the frontiers of Texas. He came by way of San Antonio north to Fort Mason, and thence to his command of four companies of the Second Cavalry at Camp Cooper, on the Clear Fork of the Brazos, where the government was attempting to locate the Comanche tribes.

He inspected his command with a magnanimous but military eye, studied his indifferent Indian charges with little hope for their reform, and contrasted the rough environment of the frontier post with the gentle background of his life in Virginia. No more significant conclusion of this place and period emerges than the fact that the borders of Texas were

[20] *Report of the Secretary of War*, 1855, pp. 5, 52-53.

the proving and seasoning grounds for the army's great leaders in the impending Civil War. To hold fast to discipline and order, to ideal and honor, to patriotism 'and purpose in an obscure command at a remote and apparently forgotten frontier post—in what Lee himself called "a desert of dullness"— called for manhood of the highest nature. Anyone thinking that it was lacking in Texas at this time should read the obscure reports of lieutenants, captains, majors and colonels buried in the War Department Records in Washington. Enshrined there is a virtual roster of the generals who commanded the Northern and Southern armies in the War between the States.

Lee, the real aristocrat, reached his shoddy outpost on the Brazos in April, 1856. As the season progressed familiar but unwelcome drouth laid its blighting hand upon the land, accentuating the hard contrast between this wilderness and his gracious home.

Upon May 27, 1856, he received a special order from headquarters at San Antonio, following Comanche forays against the border settlements, to take two companies from his post, draw two more from Mason, rendezvous near Fort Chadbourne, and make an extensive reconnaissance through the Colorado and Concho country. With a party of Delaware Indians as scouts and trailers under Jim Shaw,[21] furnished from the nearby Comanche reserve by Agent Neighbors, Lee struck out by way of Fort Phantom Hill, and down the military road to Chadbourne in what is now Coke County.

There he picked up the companies from Fort Mason on June 17. He made his plans while the expectant troopers pondered the significance of broad curtains of white smoke, obviously marking the firing of the prairie grass, far to the south and west towards present San Angelo. Lee pushed out toward the Colorado while his scouts brought word that the entire country south of the river was afire. He turned and scouted upstream for some twenty miles, kept northwest to

21 For the story of this unusual Indian, see R. N. Richardson, West Texas Historical Association *Year Book*, III, 3.

Marcy's trail, took the right hand course back toward the
Brazos, and pitched camp on the evening of June 28 at the
foot of the Double Mountains.

After scouting as far as the Wichita, he sent his captain,
Earl Van Dorn, toward the head of the Double Mountain
Fork to prowl for Indians. Then he dropped back to the Clear
Fork, where, with worn, sick and tired men, he spent the
fourth of July, 1856, under a blanket propped up on four
sticks for shade, in an attempt to alleviate the heat of that
drouth-stricken, glaringly red and eroded land.

Van Dorn fell upon a small Indian camp and killed a
couple of warriors and captured a squaw. She told his in-
terpreters that the party had been on a raid into Mexico and
upon their return had camped at the Big Spring. When Van
Dorn rejoined the command, the news greatly heartened the
troops, and Lee decided to head back to the Big Spring in
hope of intercepting other bands coming back up the war trail
from Mexico. He sent his wagon train and his sick men south
to Chadbourne and marched directly for the Spring himself.

He found no Indians there, though old signs of the raiders
from Mexico were abundant. From there he sent Van Dorn
south to the head of the Concho, with orders to scout down
its right hand slope to the Chadbourne-Mason crossing, while
a detail under Captain Theodore O'Hara, who became the
noted author of "The Bivouac of the Dead," was to take the
left-hand bank. Lee turned east to scout the Colorado valley
down to the point of rendezvous.

Most of the Comanches had followed the buffalo north, and
all that the soldiers discovered were abandoned camp-sites.
Lee, now thoroughly convinced the Indians were gone, re-
assembled his command at the military crossing of the Colorado, July 9, 1856, and decided to return to his post. One
company from Mason was ordered in by way of Brady's Creek;
the other set out to scout the Kickapoo region, cross to the
San Saba, and thence continue back to its billets.

Dr. Carl Coke Rister, author of *Robert E. Lee in Texas,* sums up the results of the expedition:

The troopers had been absent for forty days. The separate columns had traversed eleven hundred miles of drought-stricken country and had found only uninhabited wastes, thirst, severe heat, and sickness—and a small band of Indians. They had brought back only a lone captive Indian woman, and when Lee learned that her father and mother lived on the Brazos reservation, he sent her to them without delay.[22]

But the troops had added much to the military knowledge of the Concho country, and despite drouth, fatigue, illness and dreary disappointment, Lee had demonstrated again that the finest soldier tempers death with compassion when the campaign comes to an end.

His original impression that the civilizing effort for the Comanches on the Brazos was a futile venture demonstrated again his good sound sense. Lee left the frontier of Texas for more responsible service, while his able subordinate, Earl Van Dorn, rose to vigorous military stature through his devastating campaigns against the Comanches north of Red River, on their home range, in 1858 and 1859. The hostile Texas settlers, agreeing in principle with Lee's appraisal while lacking his magnanimity and tolerance, broke up the reservations on the Brazos in guerilla fashion, and pushed the Indian agencies beyond Red River.

Thus, by the end of the decade of the fifties, General Twiggs, then commander of the Department of Texas, was able to report with some satisfaction that the efforts of Van Dorn and the operations of the regular army were "giving the Indians something to do at home in taking care of their families," which "might possibly" result in their letting "Texas alone."

At last the army had moved, in a measure, to adopt the sensible tactics recommended by Whiting a decade before. But Twiggs' optimistic hope that Texas might be left alone

22 Carl Coke Rister, *Robert E. Lee in Texas;* M. L. Crimmins, "Robert E. Lee in Texas; Letters and Diary," West Texas Historical Association *Year Book,* VIII, 3 ff.

reckoned not with the stubborn resistance and the tenacity of the warlike Comanche nature.[23]

Fortunately, however, the industrious enterprise of free people waits not on peace and security. Vital expansion rests not on military tactic or federal plan, but on the uninhibited hopes and impulses of vigorous men. Settlements were pushing westward because men were free, and being free they were hopeful, and being hopeful they were daring. They rationalized their action no more than they suffered the futility induced by sophistication. They discounted the hazards of drouth; they forgot the distance and danger. Through the rosy haze of imagination the outer limits of unsettled Texas resembled the promised land. And so men ventured to settle in wild and lonely, and hence intriguing spots, along the Colorado and out toward the Concho country.

With this regional migration marked by new and fragrant cedar picket houses at springs in the hills, and cabins of twisted and durable pecan logs in the shaded valleys of the Llano and San Saba, was other vital activity flowing into Texas from older portions of the country.

Further explorations of the frontier, experimentation with camels, opening of transcontinental mail lines, plans and surveys for a Pacific railroad, and even a subterranean search —optimistic as always—for a permanent and sufficient supply of water for the arid Staked Plains were under way in spite of the warfare with the Indians.

In 1850 Captain John Love explored the Rio Grande in a fifty-foot boat for over a thousand miles—almost to Presidio del Norte. This as a navigation feat was really something, considering the abundance of rocks and shortage of water.[24]

23 For Van Dorn's work, see Richardson, *The Comanche Barrier*, as cited, 238-242, and *Report of the Secretary of War*, 1858, pp. 258 ff.; and 1859, pp. 365 ff.

24 M. L. Crimmins, "Two Thousand Miles by Boat in the Rio Grande in 1850," West Texas Historical and Scientific Society *Publications*, 1933, pp. 44 ff. and Lenora Barrett, "Transportation, Supplies, and Quarters for the West Texas Frontier Under the Federal Military System, 1848-1861," in West Texas Historical Association *Year Book*, V, 90.

Two years later at the other extremity, on the northern boundary of Texas, Captain Randolph B. Marcy explored Red River to its source, while numerous minor parties were poking into the nooks if not the crannies of most of the land between. At the same time the country generally was hoping to bridge the wilderness gulf between the Atlantic and the Pacific coasts with lines of steel. In pursuit thereof, the federal government appropriated money for the survey, by army engineers, of four different routes across the country, one of which—along the thirty-second parallel—lay across Texas. Captain John Pope was assigned the job between the Rio Grande and Red River.

His party made its way down the river from Albuquerque to Doña Ana, assembled help, rigged up eight wagons with six-mule teams, and pulled out east through the pass of the Organ range, February 12, 1854. They headed south to strike Marcy's emigrant trail, and after numerous delays hunting mules and water and repairing broken down wagons, eventually reached the Pecos, where on the morning of March 8, 1854, they came to camp at the mouth of the Delaware, just above the state line.[25]

Pope sent a reconnoitering party of twelve men up the river, another back toward the Salt Lakes, and another under Captain C. L. Taplin through the Sands and across the Staked Plains. Taplin found the route tough going. He abandoned his wagons, used up his water, and pushed on for about a hundred and forty miles before he found another supply, five days later, in Sulphur Draw, northwest of Big Spring. He turned down the draw to Marcy's Trail, headed back west, and re-joined Pope near the site of Midland, March 29, 1854.

Pope had taken the road down the Pecos, followed Marcy's

[25] Pope's Crossing became a noted landmark. The original crossing was about a hundred yards from the mouth of the Delaware. The Crossing which bore his name until the building of the Red Bluff Dam was several miles downstream, just below the Texas line. Pope's survey is detailed in *Reports of Explorations and Surveys to Ascertain the Most Practicable and Economical Route for a Railroad from the Mississippi River to the Pacific Ocean, 1853-1854,* Washington, 1855, Sen. Ex. Doc. 78, 33rd Cong., 2nd Sess., hereafter called Pope's *Report.*

Trail through the Sands, and had wasted precious time and mule flesh hunting for water along the route east—to push on at last, in great anxiety, for the welcome holes called Mustang Springs. From there the combined command proceeded to the Big Spring. From camp there it scouted out the country to Sulphur Springs, and sent another party back with a light wagon and kegs of water to run the levels across the *Llano Estacado* direct to their old camp at the mouth of Delaware Creek. Pope sent a detail into Fort Chadbourne, and headed east to come again into Marcy's Trail before reaching the Brazos.

On April 21, 1854, he came to the first sign of settlement since leaving the Rio Grande—the farm and log cabin of Indian Agent Jefferson Stem—about thirty-five miles up the Brazos from Belknap. And though Stem had been killed by Indians in February before, the place, nevertheless, looked like civilization to Pope's party. From here their course lay by Belknap, through the Cross Timbers to Gainesville, and into Fort Washita, Indian Territory, where "the expedition was closed." [26] Pope and his men had scouted out the heads of the North Concho draws, and had crossed the Staked Plains by a route that Marcy had figured was the best course for a railroad. Twenty-seven years later it was the route approximated by the Texas and Pacific Railway.

At the same time a private party was running its prospective lines. The Texas Western Railway, with offices in New York City, was chartered, February 16, 1852. Its engineers set out under A. B. Gray with the idea of building across the state from the "eastern boundary line . . . to El Paso . . ." Gray reached San Antonio by way of Indianola in December, 1853, organized his party, and was on the extreme frontier at Fort Chadbourne, January 13, 1854. He marched northwest to Marcy's Trail and ran the levels across the *Llano Estacado* and into El Paso by the Guadalupe Mountain route. His report of the survey, published in 1855, urged the economic

26 Pope, *Report*, 59-93.

wisdom as well as the physical advantages of the proposed road.[27]

Captain Pope insisted upon the thirty-second parallel as the proper course to the Pacific. He pointed out that its comparatively level terrain meant that grading would be held to a minimum. And as for the obvious shortage of water he was obsessed with the idea that drilling would produce an artesian supply sufficient for every need of the railroad, and that such wells were "indispensable" in the region for military purposes.[28]

This imaginative idea germinated interest in the humid air of official Washington. In January, 1855, he was sent back to try it out, and in 1857 and 1858 he kept hopefully at the work. Some miles east of Pope's Crossing, on the state line, is still to be seen the rusty, alkali-eaten boiler of the steam engine that poked down a hole for 1050 feet in search of water that flowed. But an artesian flow was never found, and it is still a thirsty land where the dried-up cowboy, casually riding by this relic of the past, would be satisfied with just enough to drink.[29]

This period of the fifties cannot be passed without mention of Jefferson Davis' bold plan to solve the problem of frontier transportation with a herd of camels. Their use on the southwestern deserts was not original with him, but he did press it to practical application. Congress provided an item for their importation in March, 1855, and on the 15th of February, 1856, a cargo of thirty-three camels pulled out of Smyrna for the United States. After a tempestuous voyage of three months they were landed at Indianola, then the gateway of the Gulf to

[27] *Texas Western Railroad. Survey of Route, Its Cost and Probable Revenue*, etc., Cincinnati, 1855, pp. 2 ff.

[28] Pope, *Report*, 14.

[29] His party of 102 men, under Pope and Lt. Geo. B. Cosby, were still on the Pecos, November 30, 1857, as shown by Company Returns, Detachments of 2nd Cavalry and 8th Infantry, of that date, *War Records*, Washington, D. C. See Sen. Ex. Doc., 2nd Sess., 35th Cong., vol. 2, 1858-1859, pp. 582-583. *The Clarksville Standard*, November 1, 1856, and Lenora Barrett, "Transportation, Supplies," etc., as cited, 93; Conkling, *The Butterfield Trail*, I, 382-386.

San Antonio. They threw a regular wall-eyed fit of joy upon again getting their feet on the ground, while the ship turned back after another load of forty-four, which were delivered at the same point, February 10, 1857.[30]

Major Henry C. Wayne, who was in charge of the importation, had his Arab caretakers drift the first load up the road to San Antonio. Their progress was marked by broken bridle reins at every hitching rack along the way as surprised horses awoke to snort in terror, set back on their haunches, break loose, and "take to the tall uncut." In their wildest dreams they

had never seen or smelled anything to compare with this. Thus the army and the camels had the right of way into San Antonio, and beyond into the Texas hills. On August 28, 1856, they were driven into their new home at Camp Verde, an attractive military post in a broken and lovely land south of the site of Kerrville.

There the noted army officer, Edward Fitzgerald Beale, came to pack off a train of the animals for use in laying out his wagon road from Fort Defiance, Arizona, to the Colorado

---

30 Lewis B. Lesley, *Uncle Sam's Camels*, Cambridge, 1929, pp. 4-11; Chris Emmett, *Texas Camel Tales*, San Antonio, 1932, pp. 1-16; and Sen. Ex. Doc. 63, 34th Cong., 3rd Sess., *Report of the Secretary of War ... Respecting the Purchase of Camels*, 1857, pp. 13-49, 95-102; George P. Marsh, *The Camel, His Organization Habits and Uses*, Boston, 1859, pp. 210-217.

River of the West. He left San Antonio June 25, 1857, with 25 camels packed with an average weight of 576 pounds, mainly of shelled corn for his mules. He watched the camels live on bitter brush along the Devils River, and marvelled to see them cover that rocky course and drop off the caprock into Fort Lancaster—over roads that "act like a rasp"—without the "slightest distress or soreness." They padded along in patience upon an apparently resilient foot that "yielded sufficiently without wearing off," which enabled them to travel continuously in a country where no other barefooted beast would last a week.[31]

The expedition crossed the Pecos, camped at Comanche Springs, plumbed the "bottomless" Leon Holes and found them twenty-five feet deep, and broke bread with the hospitable officers at Fort Davis. They reached Fort Bliss late in July, and camped just out of Albuquerque, August 9, 1857. After being hardened to the trail and waxing strong on screwbean and mesquite brush, the camels were loaded there with 700 pound packs for their trip west to Zuni, and so on to the Colorado. At the conclusion of his survey Beale reported on their staying powers with great enthusiasm.[32]

Meanwhile other tests were being made in Texas. Lieutenant Edward L. Hartz was sent on an extended trip into the rougher part of the Trans-Pecos country. He packed his camels with loads ranging from three to six hundred pounds, kept them moving without water for as long as five days, traversed some of the roughest regions in the Davis and Stockton country, and pronounced his expedition a decided success despite the severe suffering of his men.

Again acting under similar instructions in 1860, Lieutenant W. H. Echols was sent out with a herd of camels from Camp Verde to test them on the same rough terrain. The party was reinforced at Camp Hudson, and with twenty camels and fifteen mules Echols headed for the other side of the Pecos

31 Beale's *Journal*, as reprinted in *Uncle Sam's Camels*, 144, 156, 199.
32 The same, 78, 83, 144, 191, 199.

River. He packed the camels with grain and kegs of water for men and mules, and with a party of thirty-one men pushed into the Big Bend by a tortuous course. He then turned back to Fort Davis, dropped over to Presidio, and went down the river to the Comanche Trail. He wandered, twisted and turned through the Chisos country, and made his way back to Camp Hudson, August 5, 1860, some forty-two days after departure.[33]

The general verdict was favorable. The animals were gentle, docile, amiable creatures. Without water they traveled 110 miles through rough country in less than four days, each packing a load of 350 pounds. Admittedly, nobody with the party knew how to pack them. But in spite of sore-backs and the scanty browse and grass of the country—for they got no other feed—they came to the end of the portage in good shape. Then they were loaded with 600 pounds each and pushed for days on end over the worst country Echols could find.

The Civil War broke before the results of the tests could be translated into a broader field of action, and the camels were scattered to the winds in the confusion that followed. Reconstruction brought a revival of interest in the extension of the rails, and the patient, lumbering ruminants from the Levant were forgotten. But not in history, for they belonged to a period in Texas when men practiced the techniques of the past in new forms, hopefully and ingeniously, as they pushed their trails more deeply into the Concho country.

33 E. E. Townsend, M.S., "Notes on the Camel Expedition Led by Lt. Echols in 1860," 6 pp., in files of author; Lenora Barrett, "Transportation, Supplies," etc., as cited, 93-94. The intimate recollections of Texans upon the camel experiment are found in Emett's *Texas Camel Tales*, 180-183.

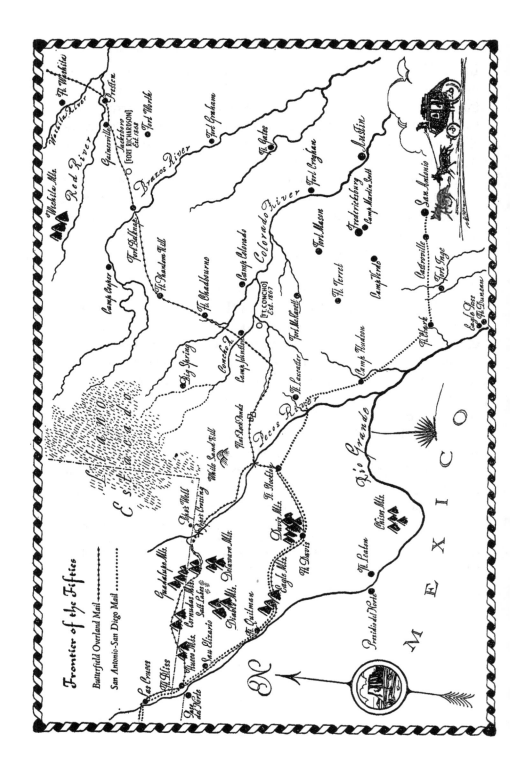

Frontier of the Fifties

Butterfield Overland Mail ⟶
San Antonio–San Diego Mail ⋯⋯⋯⋯

(Map labels, reading across the image:)

Red River · Wichita River · Ft. Washita · Preston · Fort Worth · Fort Graham · Gainesville · Jacksboro [FORT RICHARDSON] Est. 1868 · Wichita Mts. · Brazos River · Ft. Belknap · Camp Cooper · Ft. Phantom Hill · Ft. Chadbourne · Camp Colorado · Ft. Gates · Fort Croghan · Fort Mason · Austin · Fredericksburg · Camp Martin Scott · San Antonio · Castroville · Fort Inge · Ft. Terrett · Camp Verde · Eagle Pass · Ft. Duncan · Ft. Clark · Big Spring · Concho 2 · [FT. CONCHO] Est. 1867 · Camp Johnston · Ft. McKavett · Ft. Lancaster · Colorado River · Camp Hudson · Rio Grande · Estacado Llano · Flat Rock Ponds · White Sand Hill · Pecos River · Howard's Well · Hogue's Crossing · Ft. Stockton · M E X I C O · Guadalupe Mts. · Cornudas Mts. · Salt Flats · Delaware Mts. · Davis Mts. · Eagle Mts. · Ft. Davis · Chinos Mts. · Ft. Leaton · Hueco Mts. · San Elizario · Diablo Mts. · Ft. Quitman · Eagle Mts. · Las Cruces · Ft. Bliss · Frontera del Norte · Presidio del Norte

CHAPTER V

The Stage-Coach Mail

IT IS DOUBTFUL if any western trail so stirred the imagination of people generally as that which brought the mail. In distant isolation men waited with whetted expectation, with curiosity and suspense, for the coming of the mail. It alone brought the news and maintained that tenuous tie between rough and lonely men on the outer edges, and civilized life and the home folks back in the settlements. The winged speed of later years may have dulled the response. It has not altered that intimate association of affectionate and devoted people that is maintained by the mail.

Thus the Concord coachman's horn announcing the arrival of the first scheduled mail at the little fort of Chadbourne, Thursday afternoon, September 23, 1858, was an epic blast in West Texas. It was the beginning of the Butterfield Overland Mail. And though Chadbourne was just a way station on the longest stage route in the world, and though the line was to last only until the outbreak of the Civil War, the Butterfield story is significant in the annals of America.

By persistent account the first mail service was opened through western Texas from San Antonio to El Paso in 1851 by the bold and resourceful Henry Skillman. The Postmaster General advertised for bids for such a route, with bi-monthly stages by way of Eagle Pass and Presidio to El Paso, Texas, and Doña Aña, New Mexico. He received a bid from Wallace and Howard. They, with more knowledge than the Department as to the tremendous physical difficulties and risks, proposed to carry the mail once every "two months, through in thirty days," for $25,000 annually. As an alternate proposal they would leave out Eagle Pass and Presidio and carry it for $18,000. The Postmaster General disallowed the bid, April 14, 1851, as "extravagant and not according to advertisement."

Yet the account that service was established that year persists with the story that the first stage, a Concord Coach pulled by six mules, was driven by Big Foot Wallace. No relief stations had been provided along the way, the story continues, and so the same team was used throughout the trip. Understandably, thirty days were required for the first "run." [1]

At any rate Skillman—whose memory is kept green by a grove in the Davis Mountains—soon had a contract. He carried the mail west along the Lower Road through present Uvalde, up by Howard's Wells, across the Pecos, thence west through the Forts Stockton and Davis country, and across by Van Horn's Well and Eagle Springs to the Rio Grande. The service he initiated ran for years on a monthly schedule.

Julius Froebel, crossing by way of the San Antonio trail to Chihuahua in 1853, noted that he passed the mail from El Paso at the Pecos River, near the mouth of Live Oak:

Two carriages, each with four mules, coachmen, guard and passengers all fully armed. One of the passengers was a little girl of three or four years old, who—entrusted to the coachman, and with no other companion—was thus sent the 700 miles from El Paso to San Antonio. The other passengers, however, joined him in taking care of her; and it was touching to see how these rough bearded men, with their pistols and daggers, supplied the place of a mother's care to the tender little crea-

[1] Original records of the Postal Department are almost non-existent. The few that have been preserved are in the National Archives, Washington, D. C. For this period in Texas, see Sen. Ex. Doc. No. 56, 32nd Cong., 1st Sess., p. 391; Bieber, *Exploring Southwest Trails*, VII, footnote p. 312; Carlyle Graham Raht, *The Romance of Davis Mountains and Big Bend Country*, 127-128.

ture. It was a true picture of wild American life, where the highest qualities in human nature are often found, united with the roughest externals.[2]

In 1854 another noted traveler, Frederick Law Olmstead, reached the frontier near Castroville and observed that the mail then went west to El Paso and Santa Fe. Olmstead talked with the driver and guards while they were camped on the trail on their third night out of San Antonio. This indicates that the runs were still being made without sufficient way-stations. Olmstead wrote that the mail "train" then consisted of "two heavy wagons, and an ambulance for passengers, who are carried through to El Paso, seven hundred miles, for one hundred dollars, and found. 'Passengers,' the contractors advertise, 'are allowed forty pounds of baggage, and not required to stand guard.'"

At that time there were four mules to each team, besides a spare mule that was led behind for emergency. The mounted guard of six men were armed with Sharp's rifles and Colt's sixshooters. Perhaps the fact that "a man is lost on nearly every trip out and back," as Olmstead observed, had something to do with the munificent pay of forty dollars a month.

The system was obviously designed to accommodate the mules instead of the passengers. Success depended on the teams. After passing Fort Inge there was "no change of team for more than five hundred miles." The drivers usually camped from ten at night until four in the mornings, when they rigged up and again started. They stopped about eight for breakfast and grazed their mules for an hour, and stopped again in the afternoon for the same purpose.

No government agent accompanied the "train," Olmstead continued, but the guard, under an old Ranger captain, had "so much the appearance of drunken ruffians" to the Eastern travelers that they discouraged them from using the service. At this time a mail route that branched off from Fort Inge to Eagle Pass was carried by pack, and its agents regularly

[2] Froebel, *Seven Years in Central America*, etc., as cited, 416-417, 451, 466; Ike Moore, *The Life and Diary of Reading W. Black*, Uvalde, 1934, p. 37.

played hide-and-seek with the Indians for wages of thirty dollars a month.[3]

Even then the service was scarcely satisfactory. But a new day for the western mail was definitely in the offing. Most of that to the West Coast was finding its way south through the Gulf, across the Isthmus, and thence north in slow and sluggish vessels. Congressmen were actively promoting a direct service, though the obstacles to such were manifest. Heavy outlays of capital were necessary to span the wilderness and protect the line. Time passed as the idea germinated and grew with proper political cultivation.

Meanwhile Skillman continued his monthly mail until the great overland route from San Antonio to San Diego was made possible by legislation passed on August 18, 1856. It was put into effect the following year when James E. Birch, an experienced and driving enterpriser, swung on to the scene. The Postal Department had advertised for bids for semi-monthly service out of San Antonio and San Diego on the ninth and twenty-fourth of each month, to arrive at the other end thirty days later. The contract was to cover a period of four years.

Seven firms, among whom were G. H. Giddings and F. P. Sawyer, bid on the contract. Sawyer, who failed to get it but did acquire other Texas routes, was later to reach the Concho country in connection with the mail. The San Antonio-San Diego route was let to one N. P. Cook, who transferred his interest to James E. Birch, of Swansea, Massachusetts. Birch had learned the business by extensive staging in California during and after the gold rush, and, being eternally on his business toes, came out of Washington in June, 1857, to open service at once.[4]

Mail steamers already touched at Indianola to feed a segment from the coast that connected with San Antonio, while

3 Frederick Law Olmstead, *A Journey through Texas*, New York, 1857, 286-288.

4 *Contracts for Carrying the Mails*, House Ex. Doc. No. 92, 35th Cong., 1st Sess., p. 430; *Texas Almanac*, 1859, p. 139; George Hugh Banning, *Six Horses*, New York, 1930, pp. 8, 91 ff.

Skillman's line pointed the way by the Lower Trail to El Paso, and thence up the old Spanish road to Santa Fe. Birch placed his plans in the hands of Major J. C. Woods, his agent and general manager in New York, and left by ship for California to launch the enterprise there.

Thirty days were to be allowed for each trip. Bi-monthly mails were to be carried from either end. Birch was to be paid $149,800 annually for the service. Passengers were to be taken at a fare of $200 for the trip, with a luggage limit of thirty pounds, and a charge of a dollar a pound for over-weight. Birch and his crew of some sixty-five men contracted for corn, built stations along the route, bought about fifty coaches and four hundred mules, and left San Antonio with the first mail in keeping with their contract date, July 9, 1857, but by saddle instead of stage.

Major Woods reached San Antonio from New York on the 11th, and when the second of the monthly mails, and their first by stage, pulled out, apparently on August 1, though scheduled for July 24, Woods mounted to ride it through. In spite of delays along the way incident to the opening of the long line, he reached San Diego amid great rejoicing by the town thirty-eight days later. Meanwhile Birch had taken passage on the steamship Central America, by way of the Cape, on his return to New York. Soon after Woods arrived at San Diego he got the distressing news that the ship had been lost on the high seas and that Birch had gone down with it.[5]

Woods had incurred heavy debts in opening the long line. He was at a loss as to the status of the business, but continued at the job until he learned through advertisements in the San Antonio papers, picked up as he made his return trip, that Birch's widow had sold the properties to Otis H. Kelton of Charleston, South Carolina. Still his authority had not been revoked. When stranded by financial uncertainty at El Paso, he might have been forced to abandon the service had not

5 *Texas Almanac*, 1859, p. 139; Banning, as cited, 98; LeRoy R. Hafen, *The Overland Mail*, Cleveland, 1926, p. 105.

Simeon Hart, owner of the mill there, given him financial help.

Thus relieved he reached San Antonio, January 18, 1858, where he received his revocation of authority from Mrs. Birch. He turned over the properties to his successor and proceeded to Washington to make his report to the Department, while the State of Texas was modestly congratulating him and itself on the "remarkable fact that not a single failure has yet taken place under this important mail contract."

With the partisans of the North and South eyeing each other with increasing suspicion, there had been bitter political controversy as to the location of the route. The results were enough to impress the enthusiastic Texans that the southern route to the West Coast was preferable to all others, and indubitably the proper railroad course to the Pacific. This, with its obvious convenience to cowmen, and its stimulus to business along the line, seemed to mean that manifest destiny, reaching across the route for 1475 miles, was shaking West Texans by the hand.[6]

The conveniences were costly but obvious. Edward Fitzgerald Beale, heading west with his camels, July 7, 1857, spoke of being passed by the westbound "monthly El Paso mail" as he worked his way north from Howard's Well toward Fort Lancaster. The stage carried express for those who could afford the fee. A box was aboard for Beale from friends in San Antonio, "a box about two feet square," for which, he recorded, "the moderate charge of twenty dollars was made," but he added generously that "the dangers of this road . . . justified any price for such matters."

Scarcely a mile of it but has its story of Indian murder and plunder [he wrote in his diary]; in fact from El Paso to San Antonio is but one long battle ground—a surprise here, robbery of animals there. Every spring and watering-place has its history or anecdote connected with Indian violence and bloodshed.[7]

This appraisal of a real army officer exploring roads and wrangling camels on the frontier was not echoed, however,

6 *Texas Almanac*, 1859, pp. 139 ff.

7 Lesley, *Uncle Sam's Camels*, as cited, 154-155.

by the politicians determining policy in Washington. Properly enough, the Postmaster General looked at his budget and had his opinions too. In October, 1858, this service, then semi-monthly, had been changed to a weekly line from San Antonio to El Paso, and into Fort Yuma, connecting with the San Diego segment. The annual compensation to the contractor was now $196,000, and the deficit to the department was $601.

These figures were taken as "conclusive" evidence that the weekly service was not needed, and the Postmaster General ordered the line back to its "original footing" as a semi-monthly, with a compensation of $120,000 to the contractors. Before writing him down for immortality as Washington's prize bulldog of the budget, it is well to note his own bias as he sharply reprimanded Congress in his report:

Whatever objects, political or otherwise, may have been contemplated by the government in establishing this route through an almost unbroken wilderness and desert, it is clear that its continuance at the present rate of compensation is an injustice to the department.[8]

Thus it may be seen that the antipathies leading to the Civil War were brought to bear upon the overland mail. There is no end of politics, and in the broad and generous sense there should be none. But the objections would have carried more weight if the loss had been serious, and especially if any course to the Pacific could have been found except through "an almost unbroken wilderness and desert." The really valid argument against its continuance was the opening of the Butterfield mail, and not the loss of $601 to the Federal government.

Under legislation that had been approved March 3, 1857, A. V. Brown, then Postmaster General, had advertised "for bids for a semi-weekly mail service from some point on the Mississippi to San Francisco." Birch was among those who bid on a proposed route from Memphis by Little Rock, Gainesville, and Fort Chadbourne, to the head of the Concho River,

[8] *"Report of the Postmaster General, 1859,"* Sen. Ex. Doc. No. 2, 36th Cong., 1st Sess., pp. 1410-1411.

and from there by the old trail to El Paso, Yuma and San Francisco. The allotted cost was to be $600,000 a year. But this line was not established. At the discretion of the Postmaster General, however, the contract was let to John Butterfield, William G. Fargo and others, July 2, 1857, for a similar line along the southern route for a term of four years at the same cost.

This contract provided for two eastern branches beginning at St. Louis and Memphis and converging at Little Rock. The line was to be made up of nine divisions for its thrust of 2650 miles across the Southwestern wilderness. Actual operation was to start within a year.

The skeptics said it could not be done. In length as well as in natural hazard, nothing like it had ever been attempted before. The first division was to consist of the Pacific railroad for 160 miles from St. Louis to its terminus at Tipton, Missouri. Here the horse-drawn stages were to take over and point their tongues south to Fort Smith, Arkansas, to complete the next division of the line. The next segment in this great arc, to be cut through the resilient native sod by the spinning wheels of heavy stages, terminated at Colbert's Ferry, in the Denison section, on Red River. Another great sweep carried it across northern and western Texas to Fort Chadbourne.

The fifth division, one of the most severe of the entire route, was to cross 458 trying miles of glaring, open country, noted for hostile men and sterile land, between there and Franklin—now El Paso, Texas—across the Rio Grande from El Paso del Norte, which is now Juarez, Mexico. Then it was to bend north, up the river to Fort Fillmore. From there it would turn west to Tucson, Yuma, Los Angeles and San Francisco—a rough, and dangerous road that would boldly point the way through a desert wilderness.[9]

But it was done. The first mail left St. Louis, September 16,

9 R. N. Richardson, "Some Details of the Southern Overland Mail," *The Southwestern Historical Quarterly*, XXIX, 1-3; Hafen, as cited, 86-93; Roscoe P. and Margaret B. Conkling, *The Butterfield Overland Mail, 1857-1859*, I, 103 ff.; *Postmaster General's Report*, 1858, Sen. Ex. Doc., 35th Cong., 2nd Sess., IV, 739 ff.

1858, to connect with the Memphis branch at Fort Smith. With four-horse teams and frequent changes at stations that had been quickly erected along the line, it passed Fort Smith and reached Colbert's Ferry in good time. From here it swung out through the Cross Timbers to Fort Belknap, on west to Phantom Hill, and, by keeping on the move day and night, it reached Chadbourne September 23, "nearly twenty-four hours ahead of table time." Beyond this point across the desert the stops were few and far between, and mindful of the fact that wiry Spanish mules carried plenty of "bottom," the operators shifted from horses to them. And here trouble really started.

The only through passenger on that first stage was W. L. Ormsby, special correspondent of the *New York Herald*, who en route was writing a remarkable series of articles about that killing trip.[10] His courage had never faltered until he faced the business end of these bronc mules on that stretch of wild road from Chadbourne to the Middle Concho. Mindful of the reportorial tradition that the news must be made and written, he stuck it out in spite of his misgivings, as well as the fact that most of what those mule-skinners said was decidedly not "fit to print."

Fort Chadbourne then consisted of only one company of the Second Cavalry, the balance of the command being out on scout. Ormsby noted in his dispatch to the *Herald*, October 24, 1858, that:

There are few houses besides the government buildings, and few inhabitants besides the soldiers. The place is almost surrounded by a sort of barricade which was built a few years since in anticipation of a sweeping attack by the Indians—which did not come off. Some of the buildings look unusually neat for this section of the country.

10 Ormsby, then twenty-three years old, realized that he was witnessing a genuine historic event. His articles, printed in the *Herald* between September 26 and November 16, 1858, furnish the best picture of the Overland Mail. They were edited by Lyle H. Wright and Josephine M. Bynum and reprinted by the Huntington Library, 1942, in an attractive volume called *The Butterfield Overland Mail*. Besides R. N. Richardson's article, see R. C. Crane, West Texas Historical Association *Year Book*, pp. 58 ff.; Hybernia Grace, the same., VIII, 62; W. A. Riney, the same, IX,

It was a vexatious matter to this young man, with the pulse of history and the deadline for news urgently throbbing beneath his hand, to see the stage lose several hours at Chadbourne while the helpers man-handled the Mexican mules. To make matters worse the stage hands were celebrating the occasion in that ancient fashion Texans still think proper, and it took them longer than usual to rope, snub-up, choke-down, and harness their completely uncooperative mules. But at last they got the team hooked up, Ormsby climbed inside, an outrider mounted, and the celebrants began shouting farewell. But instead of taking to the trail, Ormsby said:

> The mules reared, pitched, twisted, whirled, wheeled, ran, stood still, and cut up all sorts of capers. The stage wagon performed so many evolutions that I, in fear of my life, abandoned it and took to my heels, fully confident that I could make more progress in a straight line, with much less risk of breaking my neck.

At last the mules ran away into the woods, tore the top off the stage and scattered drivers and helpers across the grass. The teams tangled themselves up in the harness, until, at last, the leaders broke loose from the gear, curled their tails, and took to the "tall uncut."

Ormsby "thought it the most ludicrous scene" he had ever witnessed, but what the Texas stage hands said and thought should not be quoted.

The mounted attendant swore that all could go to the devil. Ormsby wanted to wait over. Nichols, the driver, already imbued with a superior sense of responsibility, implied that he could wait and be damned, but swore that the mail "should go" through. Ormsby, wishing he had "made a hasty will," climbed back into the stage, and at last they were off at a long lope with only the wheelers still in harness.

97; A. D. Richardson, *Beyond the Mississippi*, New York, 1867, pp. 228 ff., and especially that monumental miscellaney and careful retracing of the trail in three volumes by Roscoe P. and Margaret B. Conkling, *The Butterfield Overland Mail, 1857-1869*, Glendale, Calif., 1947, vol. I, pp. 227-412, which traces its course across Texas with exact location in relation to the life today, and with much added related history.

Ormsby sat on the uneasy seat thinking the two mules would never make it at the killing pace, and tried to reassure himself in the darkness by talking to the driver:

"How far is it to the next station?" he inquired of Nichols.

"I believe it is thirty miles."

"Do you know the road?"

"No."

"How do you expect to get there?"

"There's only one road; we can't miss it."

"Have you any arms?"

"No, I don't want any; there's no danger."

Away they went across a wide stretch of prairie grass, sere with the season and "glistening in the light of the moon." At two in the morning they came to a steep and rocky hill. Here one of their mules balked and kept them there until sun-up. Then the mule agreed to be led up the incline. In all God's wondrous Creation, there is nothing quite like a mule.[11]

After topping the mesa they could see the welcome smoke from the campfire of the next station, miles away, and Ormsby reported:

We soon reached it and found it to be a corral, or yard, for the mules, and tents erected inside for the men, under charge of Mr. Henry Roylan. They had seen us coming and were herding the mules as we drove up. Their corral was built of upright rough timber, planted in the ground. They had pitched their tents inside, for fear of the Indians, and took turns standing guard, two hours on and two hours off. . . .

The station was near Grape Creek, a fine stream, and also near some fine timber—two desirable things not to be found everywhere in Texas. The distance from this point to the head of the Concho River being fifty-six miles, and there being no inhabited station between, we had to take, in addition to our own team of four mules, a *cavellado,* or drove, of as many more, for a change at intervals along the route. The change of teams was soon made, and, Mr. Roylan taking the reins, we were off once more at a good pace. Our road lay over the rolling prairies

---

[11] This account appears in the *New York Herald,* October 24, 1858, and is reprinted in Wright and Bynum's book, pp. 53-57. For details of the route, see Conkling, as cited, vol. I, 347-348.

studded with mesquite timber. A few miles from Grape creek we cross the [North] Concho, and then, leaving the old road, which follows its winding course, we took a new road, across the country, which has been made under the supervision of the company—a ride of about thirty miles, the new road being very passable. We strike the [Middle] Concho again at a station about twenty-five miles [away].[12]

After crossing the North Concho "the new road" led out of the valley through a depression in the hills, by a southwest course across the divide to the Middle Concho. It crossed Annie's Creek one mile east of the site of the little village of Arden, continued to the river and up it to the station at the head waters, as Ormsby recorded, fifty-six miles by mule team from Chadbourne. Later, relief from the excessively long drive was provided by the building of Johnson's Station on the Middle Concho, a little over three miles southwest of Arden.

On Saturday morning, September 25, 1858, the first mail reached the Head of the River, "a most comfortable camp," consisting of tents and a brush corral for the large stock of mules already on hand. Superintendent Glover, in charge of the division from Chadbourne to El Paso, had just pulled out on the road west, as nobody knew the stage was due. There was a scampering to rustle the teams, while the Dutchman acting as cook set out tin platés and cups and served "broiled bacon, shortcake, and coffee, which was considered quite an aristocratic meal for so early a settlement. . . ."

Again there was an hour's delay. The mules "ran in terror round the corral, the greasy Mexicans wielded their larrettos and frightened them still more, so that by the time a mule was caught and harnessed, often nearly choked to death, he was almost always nearly tired out before his work commenced." Then they were off "over a well weeded plain," with an outrider driving another change of mules before them—since the seventy-five miles across "the desert" between there and the Pecos still held no station for relief. Their last water was at the Mustang Holes, about eleven miles east of the site of Stiles, and from there across the Plains, through Castle Gap and

12 Ormsby, as cited, 54 ff.

down to the Pecos at Horsehead Crossing, they traveled dry—on stamina, nerve and mule flesh.

Upon the Plains their road "was hard and smooth." The country was covered with mesquite brush. The bear grass, Spanish daggers and cacti were a source of interest to the New York observer. Remarkably, he thought, there was "an abundance of animal life on the desert." He saw "droves of antelope," quail, snipe and other birds, and plenty of "dog towns." "It seemed impossible that so much life could exist without a constant, never failing supply of water." And yet the evidence of "the terrible exactions of the desert," of that long drive across the Staked Plains, of the cost to herds that had been pointed from Texas to California and its gold fields, was all around them,

strewn along the road, and far as the eye could reach along the plain—decayed and decaying animals, the bones of cattle and sometimes of men (the hide drying on the skin in the arid atmosphere), all told a fearful story of anguish and terrific death from the pangs of thirst. For miles and miles these bones strew the plain—the silent witnesses of the eternal laws of nature, which, in the hope of gain, man hesitates not to brave. They are silent but speaking monuments of undeviating fate.[13]

It took nearly twenty-four hours for the first stage to cross from the head of the Concho to Horsehead on the Pecos. Glover had arrived with the mules and had employed here, as Ormsby reported, "fifteen Mexicans, or 'greasers' as they are more commonly called—and a more miserable looking set of fellows I never saw." At the time of the arrival of the stage at about 3:30 on the morning of the 26th, the crew was hovered over a fire "and had to be fairly driven off" to hook up the relief team. After another hour's struggle with the mules the stage was off again, up the east side of the Pecos.

A fresh driver was in the seat. The lines were gathered in the firm and confident hands of one of the most noted men in Southwestern staging, Henry Skillman, "a Kentuckian . . . of magnificent physique, over six feet tall," with sandy hair and

[13] Ormsby, as cited, 66.

beard. He was then in his middle forties and much resembled "the portrait of the Wandering Jew" except that he carried "several revolvers and bowie knives," was dressed in buckskin, "hated Injuns" and knew the frontier like a mustang knows his range.

Sometime before the Mexican War Skillman had engaged in the Santa Fe and Chihuahua trade. During the War he had served with gallantry and distinction as captain of one of Doniphan's companies of scouts and spies on the march to Chihuahua. He had won the utmost respect of Whiting by taking the toughest assignments available on Whiting's return from Paso del Norte, in 1849, and then in 1851 he again turned his wild and enterprising nature to business account by taking a contract to carry the mail and maintain a stage from San Antonio to Santa Fe. Now he was helping Butterfield get a-going across one of the worst segments of the line.[14]

For one hundred and twenty miles from Horsehead up the Pecos the Butterfield stage took what was then called Pope's new road—made by the well-drilling expeditions—to Pope's Crossing. A *caballado* of mules was driven with the stage to furnish change of teams along that dusty, glaring and alkaline trail. They scampered away from Horsehead at 4:30 in the morning, and at 10:00 that night they drove into a station at Emigrant's Crossing, on Marcy's Trail—nearly sixty miles from their starting point. This was, at one time, a well-known ford of the Pecos, about twenty-four miles above the site of Grand Falls in present Ward County. Here three Americans in charge of the station had, with the help of a half dozen Mexicans, built an adobe corral and started a house of the same durable dirt.[15]

14 The best sketch of Skillman has been compiled by Ralph P. Bieber, *Exploring Southwestern Trails*, 311-312. See also Bieber's *Southwest Historical Series*, Glendale, 1936, III, 332, 343, and IV, 335, 340; W. W. Mills, *Forty Years at El Paso*, 1901, pp. 82-84; Ormsby, as cited, 68-69; Raht, *Romance of the Davis Mountains and Big Bend Country*, 151; Owen White, *Out of the Desert: The Romance of El Paso*, El Paso, 1923, pp. 36, 65; Connelley, *Doniphan's Expedition*, as cited, 89, 203, 398, 402, 407, 419, 440, and 590.

15 Ormsby, as cited, 69-70; Conkling, as cited, I, 375-378.

From here Skillman pushed on the lines to Pope's camp—commodious quarters of stone and adobe three miles below Pope's Crossing. It had been abandoned by the well drillers in July, 1858, and occupied by Butterfield's men in August to serve as a station for the line. It was the only substantial habitation in the 436 miles between Fort Chadbourne and the first settlements below El Paso.

At Pope's Station the party ate a late supper and pushed on. Next morning they stopped to cook their breakfast with cow chips near the head of Delaware Creek. It was a slow and weary uphill pull to the log corrals at the Pinery—the station close in the afternoon shade of the Guadalupes. Then with a fresh team they went over the pass, and with set brakes, ground their lasting ruts into the canyon now followed by the Carlsbad-El Paso Highway below El Capitan peak. Here in the darkness they met the first east-bound stage, which had left San Francisco, September 15. It was then eight hours ahead of schedule.

Thence their trail led on by a station out in the flat at Crow Spring, thirty miles farther to another at the Cornudas, and so to the natural Hueco Tanks in the mountains of the same name thirty-six miles farther toward the *Rio Bravo*. At the Huecos the company had built a good corral and house, but, as is habitual with that vast land, a drouth was on. The station keeper pointed carefully at a couple of eight-gallon kegs, saying:

"That is all the water we have left for a dozen men and as many head of cattle."

Nevertheless, a little dry and dreadfully weary, they rolled on in good time to Franklin—a place then noted for its onions, grapes, and wine—with the rugged Captain Skillman still on the wagon seat and manfully playing the lines. He had cracked the whip across the alkali flats and plateaus, and on the darkest nights "whirled along on the very brink of the precipices with perfect safety," from the time of their departure at Horsehead at 4:30 on Sunday morning, until they arrived at Franklin at

5:00 on Thursday morning, September 30, 1858, without relief or rest, ninety-six hours later. Even in the brave annals of Texas, Skillman ranks as quite a man.[16]

From Franklin the Overland Mail took its way up the Rio Grande and west from Fort Fillmore to the coast. During the next few months other stations were built along the line through Texas. Twenty-five miles below Pope's, and about seven miles north of the site of Porterville, in Loving County, was one called Skillman's Station. Upon that dry stretch west of San Angelo, another known as the *Llano Estacado* station was built forty-five miles east of the Pecos and ten miles west of the present town of Texon.[17]

In June, 1860, a talented English Quaker named William Tallack was on the stage as he returned from Australia by way of the States. He too left an account of his trip—"the longest

16 Conkling, *The Butterfield Overland Mail*, II, 61; Ormsby, as cited, 75-78.

17 Roscoe P. Conkling, authority on the detailed route of the Butterfield Mail, states that this stand on the property of Mrs. James Belcher, "though in ruins, has suffered less from destruction, due to its remoteness, than any other along the route." Like so many of the other stands, it was of the *posada* type, with corral walls of heavy limestone slabs perhaps ten feet high. Its two rooms were built inside the thirty by sixty foot enclosure, fortress fashion, with the doors opening inside. Conkling, as cited, I, 367-368. Conkling regrets that William Tallack, passing that way June 30, 1860, did not leave a record of the name of the station, and says that "as no name has been found for this lost and forgotten station . . ." he had "taken the liberty to designate it by the appropriate name of 'Llano Estacado'." The same, 369. Mr. Conkling may be pleased to know that this was actually its contemporary name, for an account in that noted northeast Texas newspaper, *The Standard*, Clarksville, Texas, July 20, 1861, refers to the *Llano Estacado* station, thirty-five miles west of the Head of the Concho.

stage ride in the world." But the route from El Paso by way of Pope's Crossing had been abandoned by Butterfield in favor of the Lower Road as laid out by Whiting. It led down the Rio Grande from El Paso, turned east through the Eagle Mountains to Van Horn's Well, by Deadman's Hole, Forts Davis and Stockton, and thence to the Pecos at Horsehead.

Here the Company had established a ferry boat, and passengers crossed the river to another stage wagon which met them on the opposite side. A conductor usually accompanied the driver, and Tallack observed that the approach to a station was announced by "a long blast from the conductor's horn, often heard far away in the silence of the wilds, and serving to economize time by enabling the station-keepers to prepare the requirements both of hungry passengers and jaded mules. Never was the sound more welcome," he wrote, upon crossing the Staked Plains, "than . . . after sixteen hours' fasting during an airy ride in these clear upland regions. On dismounting at the [*Llano Estacado*] station we found a good dish of dried apples stewed, fried steaks, and hot coffee, and never ate a breakfast with keener relish." [18]

Towards evening [Tallack continued] we reached a more fertile region of prairie vegetation, and traversed long undulations clothed with the deep leafage and bright blossoms of asters, red and blue verbenas, golden rod, the milk-plant and convolvulus, the wild cherry, and with miles of sunflowers—the latter alike turning as with faithful glance to the great luminary from which they derive their name, and affording to a lover of symbolism a beautiful emblem of spiritual and moral allegiance.

Amongst this vegetation we observed herds of antelopes, several red deer (the white-tailed prairie species), many mule-eared hares, a wild turkey, and several venemous [sic] smaller creatures, as the tarantula and the long brown centiped, also large ant-hills . . .

After sundown one of the passengers exclaimed, "Lightning Bugs!" and, on turning to see what these were, we found them to be fire-flies, a number of which were gliding in beautiful curves across the stream,

18 William Tallack, *The California Overland Express*, with introduction by Carl I. Wheat, Los Angeles, 1935, pp. 48-50. This narrative was first published in an English magazine, *The Leisure Hour*, in 1865.

like silently floating stars of bright green fire amongst the deepening shades of the surrounding foliage.... They are one of the principal ornaments of an American landscape after sunset.[19]

The stage had reached the head of the Concho. And at last in this English Quaker it brought a sensitive and appreciative observer who could look through the dust and thirst, and past the struggles with mules and Indians, to see and record the distinct beauty of the Concho country.

Here Tallack's party met the west-bound stage, eight days out, and here, just a week before, a man had been scalped by the Indians. A little way down the Middle Concho they met a party of "Texan Rangers proceeding in search of the offenders." At Fort Chadbourne they saw "the first inclosed farm ... since leaving California," as well as the first evidence of slavery "as a regular institution," and ate at a table of "food ... black with clustering flies, which crowded even into our tea, and had to be spooned out by wholesale."

Still it was an intriguing trip enlivened by the appearance of a mounted Indian on the trail near Chadbourne. He was put to flight by the conductor who took a shot at him with his sixshooter and lamented the fact that he missed his aim because he had "promised ... his wife an Indian scalp 'to keep her combs in'," and as a gentleman he meant to keep his promise.[20]

The incident was significant. For of all the troubles that plagued the Overland Mail the Indians were the worst. The country west and north of present day San Angelo had its full share. The region around Grape Creek Station, where the first driver assured the *New York Herald* reporter that they needed no arms for there was "no danger," was about as hazardous as any on the road. When another writer, J. M. Farwell, special correspondent for the *Daily Alta California* of San Francisco, reached this station, November 1, 1860, he was told that the Indians had just stampeded and stolen seven horses and a

[19] The same, 50-51.
[20] The same, 52.

mule "in open day . . . the three men at the station looking on unable to prevent it." [21] In February, 1861 some thirty Indians laid seige to the place and took the stock, while the chief, in broken but insolent English, shouted to Joe Pennington, who kept the station, that they would be back in a month and kill them all if they did not have better horses.

When the Civil War broke and the Overland was abandoned, the station keepers generally pulled out for the settlements. Pennington, his wife, his brother-in-law, Charles Cox, and a man named Elijah Helms were about to leave when the same Indians again came, attacked their split-log house, and set it on fire. As the whites fought their way out, Pennington was knocked down by a load of slugs from a shotgun that tore away part of his face. Helms and Cox fought the Indians off and carried the wounded man into a thicket. Helms left him to be tended by his wife and guarded by Cox, and struck out for Fort Chadbourne. An ambulance was sent, and Pennington was treated in the post hospital by the surgeon, miraculously recovered, and later made his way to the refuge of his home at Fort Mason. [22]

Meanwhile the Indians were giving the line trouble on the Staked Plains where an experienced frontiersman, Adam R. Johnson, operated the stands. He had come from Kentucky to settle in Burnet County and had hunted, surveyed, and fought Indians on the outer edge with the best. He bought the Staked Plains Station, "the most dangerous point on the line," [23] and contracted to keep some of the other stations. In his autobiography he recorded that he and a party reached the line one night to find "that the redskins had stripped several stations of their stock and killed all of my own oxen that had been kept for supplying the people of the several plains' stations . . . we drove the team night and day and reached our

[21] Lang, as cited, 124.

[22] Conkling, as cited, I, 349-350.

[23] H. H. Bancroft, *North Mexican States and Texas*, II, 569, says he bought it in 1855; an obvious error, as it was not built until 1858 or later.

men in their little forts in time to relieve their necessities and re-establish our line."

Not long afterward [Johnson continued], the Indians attacked the station at the head of the Concho and slew the station agent. A twelve-year-old boy, who was with the mules belonging to the station, was cut off from the house, but saved his life by his coolness and courage. They pursued him a long way and he perceived that when he rode over rough ground his pony, being well shod, forged ahead, leaving them further behind. So he sought out in his flight the rocky ridges and, by circling around the Indians, finally got in the rear and reached the house in safety.[24]

The Indians then turned down the Concho and charged and captured the stock of the station immediately below. From there they pushed up the trail to attack the station on the North Concho, and cut Bob Cavaness off from the stand. But he held his fire and charged right through them to reach the door of his house, from where he successfully stood them off.[25]

Johnson complained of "the constant raids of this band of Indians; a band that made it exceedingly dangerous and very difficult to obtain supplies." The Staked Plains station had no water except that which was hauled for miles from the Mustang Ponds—some holes about ten miles west of the Middle Concho.

For nearly seventy miles from the Mustang Ponds to the Pecos River there was no water. Hence the Overland had built "a little storehouse" at the water holes, and here a large band of Indians once jumped two of Johnson's water haulers who took refuge in the storehouse while the Indians killed, dressed and in plain sight coolly barbecued their oxen and threw an immense feast. The west-bound stage, which passed after dark, reached the Staked Plains station and reported the Indians. As it was impossible at that distance to keep the stock supplied from the Pecos, Johnson took a mail line wagon, loaded some empty barrels and several men in it, and struck out for the

[24] Adam R. Johnson, *The Partisan Rangers of the Confederate States Army*, edited by William J. Davis, Louisville, 1904, pp. 6-7.

[25] The same, 7-8.

holes. When he got there it was still dark, but the Indian fires were burning and the feast was under way.

In his determination to gain the storehouse he adopted the stratagem of getting near the place as quietly as possible. Then, after telling his men to rattle the barrels, let out their war-whoops, and make as much racket as possible, he whipped his horses into a run. It worked! The Indians, thinking a command was charging them, smothered their fires with blankets, and decamped at once. Before daylight crept out on shafts of light across the ridges along Centralia Draw to disclose the weakness of Johnson's force, the Indians were far away and the whites had "watered out." [26]

It became an old story along the Conchos. On October 1, 1859, Albert D. Richardson, another newspaper correspondent with a passion for the West, reached Johnson's Station three weeks after Indians had bottled up the station hands and laid seige to the place. They had driven off all the mules and cattle and had left a dozen of "their iron-pointed feather-tipped arrows . . . still sticking in the cottonwood logs" as their calling cards.

Upon the morning of Richardson's arrival, another bunch of Comanches shot an arrow through the station keeper's hat and chased him into the barricades. He told the story with huge amusement. His wife, instead of thinking it funny, was outraged "declaring vehemently that they would not be driven out of the country by worthless Red-skins." After all it was certainly the spirit that counted. [27]

And so hazardous life went its way on that section of the Butterfield Trail that passed through the Concho country. In spite of the hardships and the dangers of that long ride, people continued to use it. Yet the mail and the passengers carried were of little moment compared with the traffic which still went by boat to cross the Isthmus of Tehuantepec.

The only mail upon the Butterfield line was first class letters,

[26] The same, 9-10. See Conkling, as cited, I, 360-362.

[27] Albert D. Richardson, *Beyond the Mississippi*, New York, 1867, p. 231.

though a few leading newspapers were admitted in courtesy, and some express was allowed. While the average outbound letter mail from San Francisco by stage in November, 1859, was about 5000 pieces, that for December 10, 1859, numbered but 1143. Meanwhile the steamer mails were averaging about 25,000 letters.

There was some complaint against crowding on the stages, where through passengers traveled continuously for almost twenty-four days without rest. The only stops were for meals and a change of mules. With a capacity of only six persons, and rarely full at that, it is not surprising to learn that only a "few hundred persons . . . availed themselves of the stage, while they were using the steamers by the thousands . . ."[28]

The costs of the line were heavy while the income was light. The postal receipts in 1859 amounted only to $27,229.94, but in 1860 they jumped to $119,766.77. Still this left a sizeable deficit, even by government figures, in the contract cost of $600,000 annually to Butterfield and his associates. It is remarkable to record that in spite of the manifold handicaps—[29] drouth, floods, runaways, Indians and shortage of supplies— the mail usually came through two or three days ahead of schedule. News from the West Coast reached the East a few days quicker than by boat, but only by resort to the telegraph at the end of the line. But there was a challenge in the business that was vital and bold and truly American.

Nevertheless the new Postmaster General fretted over the deficit. With the tensions between the sections growing on the eve of the Civil War, he vigorously charged the choice of the southern route to the bias of the previous administration. While the Legislature of Texas was chartering toll bridges across the Pecos on both the Butterfield and the San Antonio-San Diego routes in January, 1860, and urging service from Austin, he was charging that the mail was a piece of Southern

[28] Rupert N. Richardson, "Some Details of the Southern Overland Mail," *The Southwestern Historical Quarterly*, XXIX, 8-9.

[29] The same, 9.

[96]

intrigue to favor that section, and should not be paid by the Federal treasury. And so he discontinued "that portion of the route between San Diego and Fort Yuma ... [on the San Antonio run] as entirely useless," and modified the service from El Paso into San Antonio to effect considerable economies. Yet when the contract was again let, the lack of bidding proved that it was not a money-making venture, for the Southwestern enterprisers were even less interested than he.[30]

Then the tie broke and Texas joined the movement out of the Union. While the state's policy was apparently that of leaving the line alone, private buccaneers were not so considerate and depredations started at once. On March 2, 1861, Congress authorized the Postmaster General to discontinue the line.[31]

Ten days later the last stage from the west passed through Fort Chadbourne with Anson Mills—a surveyor from El Paso who would later return as commander of Fort Concho—as one of a very crowded load of eight passengers, scurrying back to the North before hostilities broke in earnest. Near Chadbourne they ran into a party of Texas troops under Colonel McCulloch. The passengers advised the driver to tell the rebels that he "was carrying the United States mail," as it had been rumored that the Texans would seize the stage teams for the Confederate cavalry. Mills and the others sat on nervous seats as the Texans reined out their horses on either side for the stage to pass between, while the driver, talking fast, invoked the prestige of those once magic words—"carrying the United States mail."

The rebels laughed in his face. Four jumped off to grab the left-hand wheels, and four more did the same on the right, and shouted at him to drive on. But as Mills recalled in his quaint style, this driver "could not, with the greatest whipping,

30 *Report of Postmaster General*, Sen. Ex. Doc., No. 1, 36th Cong., 2nd Sess., pp. 435 and 437; *Offers and Contracts for Carrying the Mails*, House Ex. Doc., No. 86, 36th Cong., 1st Sess., pp. 341-345; R. C. Crane, "Stage Coaching in the Concho Country," West Texas Historical Association *Year Book*, X, 62-63.

31 R. N. Richardson, as cited, 18.

induce the horses to proceed." Again the Texans laughed at the dismay of the passengers, and recalling that the fervid abolitionist, Horace Greeley, had been lecturing on the West Coast, and had announced his intention of returning by the Butterfield route, they roared: "Is Horace Greeley aboard?" Skeptical of the answers, they looked the passengers over, as they would know him from his pictures, and not seeing the sententious apostle of western migration of youth, and the long-winded agitator of the slavery question among them, they let the stage pass. Greeley, though an ardent humanitarian with a heart burning for the other man, was a sober realist when it came to taking care of himself. He had wisely detoured Texas by taking a steamer for the Isthmus.[32]

The shadows of civil war were falling over Texas as the last of the Butterfield stages rolled out of the state around the middle of March, 1861. Its dusts settled as a gray shroud over the high hopes of the men whose boldly imaginative minds had conceived the line, and whose strong hearts had carried it into execution against manifold odds. In part its grass-grown ruts would be broken again by other stages during Reconstruction. Yet the great Butterfield Southern Mail, with its relatively insignificant traffic, but its wildly imaginative stimulus to a virile race, was gone.

[32] Anson Mills, *My Story*, Washington, 1918, p. 64; Conkling, as cited, 306, 342; *Dictionary of American Biography*, 528-534.

CHAPTER VI

Conflict and Confusion

THEN THE WAR BROKE. In the approaches to the Concho country it was a time of desultory conflict and considerable confusion. The Secession Convention came together at Austin to vote disunion, and at San Antonio General D. E. Twiggs, commander of the Military Department, wavered on the horns of a dilemma between resistance to rebel demands to surrender his posts and supplies, and the easier course of decamping from Texas in peace. He resolved the problem by pulling out in peace, to the violent, retributive recollections of partisan Yankees at a safer period and distance ever since, though he is sometimes accidentally recalled by Texans with greater tolerance.

The problem of frontier defense, serious even with the help of the federal army, remained essentially unchanged. The ready supply of provisions from a section that made them, backed up by the largess of the federal treasury, became a thing of the past. Lack of supply was woeful. Insufficient arms and meager powder were jealously saved and guarded. But firm resolve reckons not the hazard.

Throughout the state the valiant flocked to join the fight. Young men fired with hot blood and strong heads, middle-aged men with the strong convictions that go with great character, and old men with worn muscles but powerful traditions, trickled from the fringes to join the stream of warriors pouring into points of concentration. They soon rode off with Hood's Brigade, Terry's Texas Rangers, and many another command, to glory, honor and death in what has been sadly called the "lost cause."

But the frontiers, well beyond the plantation regions of Texas, were assuming a different character. Here slavery was not and would never have been an especially profitable institution. Here men were primarily engaged in the risky pursuit of ranching, and neither the character of the Negro nor the institution of slavery was adaptable to such a fluid and hazardous undertaking. Upon these hinterlands there was little fervor for war. Yet with the exception of the German settlers sentiment was still decidedly with the South.

People here had their own vital problems of keeping back the Indians and supplying their meager larders, even though killing crusading Yankees struck them as a commendable pursuit. But since pleasure then gave way to business they were inclined to stay at home. At first some who did not believe the Union should be broken, and who were unwilling to support their state in what they considered a wrong and tragic course, scurried to loyal land beyond its borders. Caravans headed for the West Coast, while uneasy German settlers moved toward Mexico. As the war progressed the confusion of the frontier was aggravated by deserters from the Confederate service and fugitives from conscription. Some built the first huts on the head of the South Concho to form what was called Cole's Settlement.

The Texans quickly moved to take over the military supplies and posts which the federal troops abandoned. The Secession Convention met at Austin, January 28, 1861, and two days later a Committee of Public Safety was appointed. Three commissioners named by this committee called on General Twiggs to surrender the arms, posts and other properties of the federal military department. He complied on February 18, 1861, and prepared to pull out of Texas.

The Convention divided the frontier into three military districts. Old Rip Ford, as colonel, was placed in command of the first, which reached from the lower Rio Grande almost to Fort Duncan. Ben McCulloch, as a colonel of cavalry, was placed in charge of the second, which extended from the upper limits of the first into Fort Chadbourne, and his brother, Henry McCulloch, was in charge from there to Red River. Each was responsible to the Committee of Public Safety.[1]

Meanwhile the upper frontier of Texas was rife with Indian troubles. The *Dallas Herald*, January 9, 1861, reported that the region was "depopulated and the women and children all concentrated in the towns." Already Minute Men and special ranging companies under such leaders as Sul Ross, Captains E. W. Rogers, Jack Cureton, Buck Barry and the hell-raising John R. Baylor were in the field lusting for blood and hair. Governor Sam Houston had commissioned his aide-de-camp, Colonel W. C. Dalrymple as commander of the Texas Volunteers, to wage war against the hostiles. And while the country caught its breath and wondered whether secession would bring armed conflict with the North, there was much to engage the fighting propensities of the Texans on the west.[2]

In December before, a committee for frontier relief had been organized at Houston. Hot-blooded Hempstead was raising men to help, and the ladies of Dallas gave a "most elegant" supper, where the guests "enjoyed themselves hugely" raising money to buy guns to be used in killing Indians.[3]

[1] Caroline S. Ruckman, "The Frontier of Texas During the Civil War," ms. thesis, University of Texas, pp. 30-32. W. C. Holden, "Frontier Defense in Texas During the Civil War," West Texas Historical Association *Year Book*, IV, 1928, p. 16; J. Evetts Haley, *Charles Goodnight, Cowman and Plainsman*, Boston, 1936, pp. 62-63.

[2] *Dallas Herald*, January 9 and 23, 1861; *The Standard* (Clarksville), March 23 and June 15, 1861.

[3] *Dallas Herald*, January 6, 1861.

These incongruous but warlike preparations were well under way when Henry McCulloch, with his commission from the Convention, left Austin and picked up five companies of mounted men as he headed for the federal forts upon the periphery of his territory. He moved first against Camp Colorado in Brown County. After two days' parley the Yankees there surrendered, February 22, 1861, and were allowed to depart for the coast with their side-arms intact. McCulloch left a detachment at the Camp and headed for Fort Chadbourne.[4]

In the field Houston's commander, Colonel Dalrymple, had gotten word of the action of the Convention and marched against Camp Cooper on the Clear Fork of the Brazos. With a generous helping of volunteers from the country around Dallas, Fort Worth, Weatherford, and Palo Pinto, his men marched into the post with the Texas flag flying before them, and notwithstanding its alleged garrison of 270 regulars, demanded its immediate and abject surrender. The commander looked them over and agreed. The rebels took possession on February 21, gave three cheers for the Lone Star, and in typical frontier fashion immediately dispersed. Colonel Dalrymple, however, left Captain E. W. Rogers, of Ellis County, in command, and again gave his attention to the Indians.[5]

As the disconsolate Federal troops from Camp Cooper moved down the military road toward Chadbourne, McCulloch was marching west from Camp Colorado to take that post. On February 28, Lieutenant Colonel Gouverneur Morris, the commander at Chadbourne, received the general orders from Twiggs, issued on the 19th, to evacuate all the posts, and with his eighty-three men, was "awaiting transportation to leave the soil of Texas by way of the coast."[6]

Morris peacefully acceded to McCulloch's demand, who then prepared to move on Cooper, still under a detail of Dal-

4 James K. Greer, *A Texas Ranger and Frontiersman: The Days of Buck Barry in Texas,* 1932, p. 127; Holden, as cited, 17.

5 *Dallas Herald,* February 27 and March 6 and 20, 1861. J. B. Barry papers, U. of T. Archives, March 11, 1861; Ruckman, as cited, 19-20.

6 *Post Returns,* Fort Chadbourne, February, 1861.

rymple's command, but whose authority McCulloch did not recognize since he was commissioned by Houston, instead of by the rebellious Convention. On the way McCulloch met the Federal forces en route south and made them surrender all over again to him, a bloodless ceremony which scarcely enhanced their pride, but did give them official passage south.

Still ahead of McCulloch were Dalrymple's men. Conflict in authority was feared, as Houston had bitterly fought secession and resented the break. Dalrymple himself was ranging after Indians, but when McCulloch arrived and demanded the post by the authority vested in him by the Convention, Captain Rogers, Dalrymple's subordinate, readily agreed. McCulloch called Captain Buck Barry from Fort Phantom Hill and placed him in charge, and upon his return Dalrymple sensibly recognized McCulloch's authority.[7]

In the meantime attempts were being made to harmonize the Texas military effort with that of the Confederacy. The Legislature of Texas took steps of its own to meet the frontier problem by authorizing each of the thirty-seven frontier counties to organize companies of Minute Men, of not over forty volunteers each, to provide constant patrols. Colonel Earl Van Dorn took over as commander of the Texas Department, and in May established two military lines across the frontier so far-flung as to be impossible of defense. One reached from Forts Cobb and Arbuckle, in Indian Territory, to the junction of the Conchos, below Fort Chadbourne; the second from Fort Bliss, at El Paso, east by way of Forts Quitman, Davis, Stockton, Lancaster, Clark and Inge to Camp Wood. Small detachments of Texans occupied the old posts.[8]

Late in February an election ratified Secession and Houston was deposed. By the middle of March a measure of quiet had returned to the upper frontier, shaken for two years by the

7 *Dallas Herald,* March 20, 1861; Holden, as cited, 18; H. E. McCulloch to J. B. Barry, March 7, 1861, Barry Papers, University of Texas; Ruckman, as cited, 19-20.

8 Ruckman, as cited, 30-32; Holden, as cited, 18; *The Standard,* June 15, 1861; Haley, as cited, 63.

violence of its Indian troubles. Hundreds of settlers started back to rebuild their cabins, gather their scattered stock and tend their little fields. Meanwhile the casual attitude of many toward the impending struggle had changed to one of dire concern, and caravans of wagons wormed their way west out of Texas. Typical of this movement was that of Noah Smithwick—one of the most zestful Texans ever to kill an Indian or "gut a buck."

He sold his farm and sacrificed his mill on the Colorado, west of Austin, rounded up a bunch of longhorned steers, broke them to the yoke and in the spring of 1861 headed for the West Coast. Of the thirty-five people in his wagon train, "thirteen were men, all armed with revolvers." In his autobiography, a remarkable frontier chronicle called *The Evolution of a State,* he recorded his exodus from the land he had served since 1827:

At Fort Chadbourne we encountered the first visible effects of the impending war in the absence of the American flag from the fort where it had fanned the breeze so long. There were a few Texan rangers there. ... we struck the United States overland mail route to California, and in the dismantled and deserted stations thenceforward were constantly reminded of the disturbed relations between the two sections of the country. The road paralleled the Concho river many miles. Through all that fine fertile country there was not even a stock ranch. The Comanche was lord there. At the head of the Concho a protracted rain came on and, availing ourselves of the deserted station buildings, we awaited fair weather.

And there they were joined by another large train of refugees fleeing from Dallas.

The caravans passed out through the Concho country, camping at abandoned mail stations on the way. They were made up of citizens either loyal to the Union or simply anxious to avoid the fight, all bent on escaping the violent passions engendered by war. The San Antonio-El Paso Mail was still in operation, though the Butterfield was out of commission. Emigrants were already tearing out the station stand doors and other woodwork, often hauled for hundreds of miles, and

[104]

using them for firewood. Forts Stockton and Davis were occupied by small contingents of Texans who were trying to hold the line. There was some attempt at communication, but already the disintegration of war was moving apace.[9]

While frontiersmen made up the companies of Minute Men, the garrisons of the posts were drawn, at least in part, from the older settled sections of the state. Characteristic of these was a company of mounted volunteers sworn in at Marshall in April, 1861, as the W. F. Lane Rangers, for a year's service in the Confederate cause. They left for Austin in gala fashion, were forwarded to San Antonio, and there—against their wills, for they were out for Yankees—were sworn into the frontier service as Company F, Second Regiment of Texas Mounted Rifles. On June 5, 1861, this company was ordered west to Camp Wood.[10]

Details of the company were kept scouting up and down the frontier looking for raiding bands. They were shifted back and forth along the line from Fort Inge, through Camp Hudson to Fort Lancaster, to the west. They took over this latter outpost during the fall, just as the dusts of the Lower El Paso Road were stirred by Sibley's troops hurrying west to join John R. Baylor, then on the Rio Grande, above El Paso, bent on the conquest of New Mexico for the Confederacy.

General Sibley himself stopped at Lancaster, and on November 28, the company in uniform, fully mounted and armed, was ordered to the parade ground for review at seven in the morning. Sibley took over to see how well they were drilled. When they passed in twos at a brisk trot, and the General commanded "File Left!" the order went unheard in the general clatter, and the company proceeded on its direct course, off the parade ground, across the mountains and out of sight. As they disappeared the General turned and snorted in disgust,

9 Noah Smithwick, *The Evolution of a State or Recollections of Old Texas Days*, Austin, 1900, pp. 335-339.

10 The source is that remarkable journal kept by W. W. Heartsill, and printed, a page at a time, at Marshall, 1874 and 1876, called *Fourteen Hundred and 91 Days in the Confederate Army*, pp. 1-14.

[105]

"Gone to hell!" But it was a quick trip. Even soldiers awaken to logic at last. They eventually stopped and returned to camp that evening, to find to their relief that Sibley had left for New Mexico.[11]

Remarkably, the El Paso mail stage was still running from San Antonio to Santa Fe that winter. The driver, in mid-January, reported that smallpox had broken out at Fort Davis. Elsewhere, mumps among the men were common. Forces in support of Sibley kept passing to the west, while the captain of Lane's Rangers, Sam J. Richardson, was busily working his way back and forth from the frontier to San Antonio in an attempt to get his men paid and to maintain their supplies. Life was tolerable but not sumptuous.

While the detachment to the south at Camp Hudson, on the Devils River, was varying its diet with javelinas or musk hogs, the men at Fort Lancaster, early in December, were, after traffic with a Mexican freight train, really living high off the hog with "a first rate dinner [of] . . . Corn-bread, El Passo onions and Dried apples." W. W. Heartsill, one of the rangers, wrote that at night "kiota's . . . collect in hundreds around our quarters . . ." and no little sport was had in hunting them, though the obvious lack of dead Indians is no credit to their record.

This is not to disparage their fighting qualities. The disadvantages of waiting for an elusive, guerilla foe in static defense, over that of punitive expeditions into his homeland, were well known. These men were from the plantation zone, in close accord with the Confederacy, and would fight. When their time was up in the spring, they were called into San Antonio to be mustered out, and were dined at the splendid Menger by their captain. Of the hundred men who had fretted through this first year, ninety volunteered for reenlistment for the period of the War.[12] Such loyalty to the cause, however,

[11] The same, 48-49. For the story of his campaign and defeat there, see Daniel A. Connor, "Military Operations in the Southwest, 1861-1865," Thesis, Texas Western College, El Paso; and W. A. Keleher, *Turmoil in New Mexico*, Santa Fe, 1952.

[12] Heartsill, as cited, 77-79.

was not evident among those living upon the frontier. Reorganization of defense there had long been under way.

During the fall of 1861 numerous complaints of Indian depredations piled up on Governor Clark's desk. Lack of discipline in the State forces was a problem. The frontier aversion to military discipline was noted in regimental orders which "earnestly pressed upon all officers alike to lay aside their prejudices ... against drill." Daily guards were prescribed at the posts. Horse racing and gambling were prohibited, as well as the sale of liquor by the sutlers. Some attempts at manufacture of ordnance were under way in Texas, but by November ammunition was scarce, and as there was none "coming to replace it" an order was issued that not "a single round" was to be used "except in case of actual necessity."[13] Its observance would have contributed no little to the peace of the prairie dogs and coyotes.

On December 21, 1861, the Legislature passed the law setting up the Frontier Regiment of ten companies of rangers. They were to cover the frontier from Brownsville to Red River, supplanting the Minute Men, who were to be mustered out after the first of March, 1862. Francis R. Lubbock, then governor, appointed Colonel James M. Norris to command. In the early spring Norris made his way along the frontier, sewing up his line of defense along a shorter seam. In rough outline it reached from the Red River south through old Fort Belknap, in Young County, past the site of Breckenridge, and almost due south through Callahan and Brown Counties to a camp at the head of Richland Creek, in San Saba County. It continued by way of Camp Verde, in Kerr County, on south to the San Antonio-Eagle Pass road at the crossing of the Nueces, and finally to Fort Duncan on the Rio Grande. And while it was still an extended and tiresome patrol, it was not over half as long as the Van Dorn line laid out in May, the year before.

It became the first genuine line of defense since the regular

13 Barry Papers, Regimental Orders No. 10, May 11; Special Orders No. 40, June 18; and Circular No. 3, November 9, 1861.

army had withdrawn. But it represented a wide and definite retreat of the entire frontier in the face of Indian warfare from without, plus the contraction of the economy to feed the fires of war from within.

The Regiment enlisted over a thousand men. Every other day regular patrols between the camps were covered by jogging horsemen cutting for sign of Indians. When trails were discovered, alarms were sounded up and down the line, and the scattered rangers converged upon the raiders. The system was the most effective that had been devised, but far from perfect, for the Indians began splitting into small bunches and filtering through the line a-foot, leaving no trail for horsemen to follow. They then congregated at an appointed place, raided settlements and ranches, stole horses to suit their needs, and headed for the country west of the line at a high lope. With a good head start when the news broke, they were extremely hard to catch.[14]

Within a year Norris left the service, and Colonel J. E. McCord, his successor, with headquarters at Camp Colorado, took over with efficiency. The year 1863 was one of drouth and shortage of grass, and consequently poor and jaded horses. McCord abandoned the patrols and substituted a system of scouts and expeditions into the Indian country in search of their camps. During the year depredations again became serious, but McCord's men did effective service. In the fall of 1863 Governor Lubbock issued a draft against the state militia, and evaders began drifting out of the settlements to the frontier, complicating the situation there.

Reorganization of frontier defense came again that fall. The state asked the Confederacy to take over the Frontier Regiment, principally to escape the costs of its maintenance. The Confederate officials agreed upon condition that Texas submit to their right of removal of the Regiment from the state. Lubbock opposed this bitter concession. But it became known that the Governor-elect, Pendleton Murrah, favored it. Then the

14 Holden, as cited, 19-20; Haley, as cited, 66-67.

[108]

Texas Legislature passed a law reorganizing frontier defense in December, 1863, to provide for militia made up from the frontier counties, to be administered through three military districts.[15]

The war rocked on to the obvious disintegration and impending defeat of the South, while along this general line as established by the Frontier Regiment, Texas maintained a measure of stability on her borders. Life here was hard. Service was attended by the barest standards of subsistence, dependent, at last, on the natural bounty of meat. There was suffering and bloodshed a-plenty, not in mass movements, but in the effective fighting of guerilla bands and in heroic individual combat. The Regiment did not stick to its barren and inhospitable billets, but ranged far into the Indian country hunting the home camps of the Comanche and Kiowa Indians.[16] Its work was complicated by the fact that the frontier became the refuge for bands of deserters, draft evaders, Jayhawkers, Union sympathizers, and outlaws generally. The Concho country, favored with plenty of wood, water, game and shelter, had its undue share.

Charles Goodnight, observant scout and guide for Captain Cureton's company out of Belknap, summed up the situation when he expressed his belief that "fully half of Jack Cureton's rangers were in fact Union sympathizers. I know positively that Captain Cureton, while a slave-holder in a way and a Southern man all his life, as were his ancestors, believed the war to be cruel, wrong and uncalled for."[17] Captain Barry noted the seriousness of the problem in the spring of 1864, when the Regiment itself had to divert its attention from fighting Indians to chasing deserters, many of whom had gathered "in the Concho country."

Colonel McCord was determined to drive them out or bring them back as prisoners. To the north Colonel Bourland sent a

15 Holden, as cited, 26-27.
16 See Greer, *Buck Barry*, as cited; Holden, as cited; and R. N. Richardson, *The Comanche Barrier*, 265 ff.
17 Haley, as cited, 98.

force against those in the settlements near Red River, "where Union sentiment was strong." The plan to attack them leaked out, and "over a hundred . . . fled to the southwest to the Concho country and thence made their way toward New Mexico." Buck Barry took after those who were hiding farther west along the Wichita.

"In some instances," Barry said, "men with their families had moved above the line with the idea of emigrating to California with their stock and belongings. Deserters were flocking to them. . . ."

Captain Henry Fossett, from Camp Colorado, moved up the Middle Concho late in May, 1864 and estimated that "five hundred deserters, some families, and forty loaded wagons" had, in a great train, left just a week before upon the trail across the Staked Plains to the west. During this period Cole's settlement was founded.[18] Several substantial cabins were built on Cole Creek, about three miles below the site of Christoval, but it was abandoned, apparently when the Texas troops moved against the deserters.

Courts-martial of captured deserters were held up and down the line. Sentences ranged from mildly disciplinary measures to stiff commitments to Confederate headquarters at Houston. High feeling, which resulted in killings throughout the Upper Cross Timbers, came to a climax in Duff's massacre of the Germans in southwest Texas, and the wholesale hangings at Gainesville. It was a bitter period. But the measures, suited to the times, though often unjust, had their effect.[19]

As the war dragged out, there was a fortunate lull in Indian fighting. But late in December, 1864, this violent period, during which the Texans had maintained their frontier defense with some measure of success, moved to a tragic anti-climax. It began with the discovery of an immense Indian trail on the upper Brazos. It culminated in the decisive defeat of about

[18] Greer, as cited, 172-174.

[19] Greer, as cited; Goodnight mss., in files of author. Eugene McCrohan file, *San Angelo Standard*, San Angelo. See issue May 3, 1924.

three hundred Texans by some five to six hundred Kickapoo Indians, perhaps assisted by renegade Jayhawkers, on Dove Creek, tributary to the South Concho, southwest of the site of San Angelo.

In addition to being the most tragic incident in Texas frontier defense it became the most controversial. This Indian band, making its way toward Mexico, was actually on friendly terms with the whites. With a little judgment the fight could and should have been avoided. But the fact that it was not is easily understandable in view of the passions and violence of the times, since all Indians found in Texas were considered hostile.

Thus it was that when Captain N. M. Gillintine and his scouting party of twenty-three men out of Erath County discovered the trail of this great body on the upper Brazos, he was genuinely concerned. At a point about thirty miles west of abandoned Fort Phantom Hill, in present Jones County, he came upon their camp-site just two days after they had left. He estimated the force at "five hundred or more Indians." Their wigwams and other sign that a finished plainsman would have read with ease, should have told him they were not Comanches or Kiowas.

Nevertheless Gillintine classed them as hostiles and drew back to report to Captain Barry, still in command at Camp Cooper. It then occurred to him, in view of the size of the force, that it would be sensible to return to the settlements, spread a general alarm, and attempt to raise enough men to whip the intruders. Since Major George B. Erath, who was then commander of the second military district, which encompassed this region, was in Austin, plans for the expedition were made by Captain S. S. Totten of Bosque County.[20]

Totten ordered the militia to Meridian by December 19, 1864, and rushed off to Waco to pick up Tonkawa Indian

[20] The background and the story of this engagement have been explored and ably treated by William C. Pool in "The Battle of Dove Creek," *Southwestern Historical Quarterly*, LIII, 366 ff.

scouts and 6000 percussion caps that would fire, to replace the "worthless . . . caps furnished by the state . . ." Companies from surrounding counties rendezvoused at Camp Salmon, in Callahan County, apparently on Christmas day, and duly organized the battalion of "325 men rank and file."

Word reached them here that Captain Henry Fossett, with a command of Confederate troops, had already gone to Camp Colorado, and wished the militia to meet them at Chadbourne. Totten decided, instead, to strike out for the point where Gillintine had picked up the trail, and follow it independently from there. The weather, which had been bad enough on men and horses in open camp, continued to be mean with rain and snow. By January 1, 1865, Totten's battalion was close to the old camp on the Clear Fork.

Meanwhile Fossett had moved to Chadbourne, where his command of fifty men had been swelled to 161 by arrivals from other companies. Here he waited impatiently while Totten was slowly picking his way along the old Indian trail all but obliterated by rain and snow. Upon January 13, 1865, Fossett, tired of waiting, "set out up the Colorado to find the Indian trail" himself. Next day he cut the sign ahead of Totten, and turned down the trail toward the North Concho, where, at an abandoned camp, he counted the location of "150 wigwams." On January 7, Fossett sent scouts ahead and went into camp to await the state militia.

When his scouts returned to report the Indian encampment on Dove Creek, southwest of the site of San Angelo, Fossett, still not having heard from the militia, moved up the Middle Concho and began making plans to engage in battle. At this juncture scouts from Totten's command caught up with him, and being advised of the impending fight, rushed back to hurry the militia to the scene.

Totten left his pack-train, and by a forced march, for he was far behind, joined the Confederate soldiers at a point three miles north of the Indian camp by nine o'clock on the morning of January 8, 1865. When he arrived, Fossett's men

were in the saddle ready to attack. All too hurriedly the final
plans were made.

Brigadier General J. D. McAdoo, who investigated the affair
afterward, was critical of the obvious lack of preparation.
When they met, he said:

The two commands halted but a few minutes, during which a brief
conversation was had between the two commanders, after which, without any council of war, without any distribution of orders, without any
formation of a line of battle, without any preparation, without any inspection of the camp, without any communications with the Indians or
inquiry as to what tribe or party they belonged, without any knowledge
of their strength or position, the command "forward" was given, and a
pell-mell charge was made for three miles.[21]

That their action was rash to the point of suicide soon became obvious. That it was in keeping with Texas frontier
character, noted more for fighters than generals, is likewise
obvious. With many competent frontiersmen in their forces,
the commanders were bound to have known that the camp
was not made up of their deadly enemies—Comanche, Kiowa
or Apache. But as was generally known, and as Fossett frankly
made plain, later, they recognized no friendly Indians in Texas.
In the war these Texans had waged so long, surprise in attack
was often half the battle. Hence, in view of their attitude
toward all redskins, McAdoo's criticism of their failure to get
in touch with the Indian camp rings hollow if not absurd.
And so the charge was made.

A small hill obscured the command from the Indians. Totten
took his men to the left of the hill, dismounted, and charged
the camp from that side. Fossett's mounted men circled the
hill to the right, and came in from the opposite side, cut off
the Indian horse herd grazing there, and then attacked the
camp. But the camp-site was well chosen, and Totten later
explained the Kickapoos' obvious advantage:

The Indians were camped on the south side of Dove Creek in a dense
thicket of green briars and live oak, containing about 100 acres, with

[21] J. D. McAdoo to John Burke, February 20, 1865, *War of the Rebellion Records*, Series I, vol. 28, chap. LX, 27.

the creek in front and a high bluff with heavy timber at its base; in their rear there were two dry branches in the thicket that were completely concealed by brush and briars, forming the very best of rifle pits . . . their position was such that it was impossible to ascertain its strength until the attack was made.[22]

Fossett later estimated the Indians to have numbered between four and six hundred fighters, while Totten figured there were "about 600 Indians and Jayhawkers," or Union renegades, who had joined them. The Texans, having left part of their forces with the camp equipage, were outnumbered two to one. Totten's men on foot charged through the open upon the heavy force of Indians, who were armed with Enfield rifles. These, hidden in the ravines and thickets, picked off the Texans as they rushed into the camp "with but little risk to themselves." The initial slaughter resembled an ambush at almost point-blank range. The early volleys killed Captains Barnes and Collier, wounded Captain Gillintine, and killed "sixteen other men." For awhile the fighting was intense, but heavy losses threw Totten's militia into a panic and it fled the field with about a hundred Indians in pursuit.

Totten fell back to the junction of Spring and Dove Creeks, about three miles to the north, still out of communication with Fossett, whose men were yet on the field. They had taken position among the live oaks on the right-hand ridge as they went up Dove Creek, facing the Indian camp to their south. Those who were wounded in the early part of the fight were sent, for protection, to Captain Cureton, who held the Indian horse herd to the rear.

Back of the ridge on which Totten's men were newly deployed was a tributary of Dove Creek. During the day the Indians worked their way up this little stream to place his men in a cross-fire, and to imperil him in his new position. And so the fight raged throughout the day with the odds definitely against the Texans.

When the sun was only half an hour high, Totten's command

[22] From the *Houston Daily Telegraph*, n.d., quoted by Pool, as cited, 13.

moved to abandon its position, and Cureton's scouts, with the wounded and the horse herd, started east to cross Dove Creek. The Indians, noting the plan, came up under cover of the stream bed, and from the brush tore them to pieces at the crossing, throwing this veteran's men into confusion and re-capturing the horses. The command effected the crossing, but with "great disorder." Then they rallied at a "long dry branch" while the wounded were carried ahead. Here again the Indians dislodged them in utter rout and "wild panic." Night alone brought relief and the welcome sight of Totten's campfires on Spring Creek—the first seen of him since he had quit the field early that morning.[23]

The straggling forces made dismal camp on the south bank of Spring Creek. Their dead lay where they had fallen. Their pack-trains and provisions were still a long way behind, and as the forces re-gathered, weary and hungry, about their camp-fires on the night of January 8, 1865, it began to rain. The rain turned to snow, which continued until twelve inches, or more, lay on the ground by the morning of the 10th.

Still out of supplies, the troops began eating their horses, and suffered through the nights in their single blankets, while the wounded were dying from lack of care, terrible exposure and starvation. Yet a check-up on casualties showed that Fossett had only four killed and five wounded, while Totten's militia suffered eighteen killed and fourteen wounded.

Totten's generous estimate, in reporting to Major Erath, was that the Indians had suffered a hundred killed, but from Eagle Pass, where the Kickapoos crossed into Mexico nearly a month later, they reported their loss as twelve killed and eight wounded. Meanwhile, through snow and slush, the dis-organized frontier and Confederate forces straggled down the Concho toward the settlements. One named I. D. Ferguson told how they carried their wounded.

Men were put to chopping and trimming up pecan poles to make litters for the wounded men. We constructed litters by cutting notches

23 William C. Pool, as cited.

[115]

in the end of the poles; then took a rope and tied across from one pole to the other, like a bed cord, placing the pole far enough apart for a man to lay between them. When this was made we spread blankets over them and put the wounded men on the litters. We then backed a horse up with a saddle on, between the two poles of the litter; placed the ends of the poles in the stirrup leathers and tied them so they could not come out. We then led another horse forward with his breast between the rear ends of poles, and fastened . . . [them] into the stirrup leathers, and tied the bridle reins forward to the litter pole.

The wounded were thus loaded, and with one man leading the horse in front and another driving the horse behind, they painfully moved down the Concho toward the settlements.[24]

They passed Tankersley's ranch, the extreme outpost, some fifteen miles from the battle site, and finally reached John Chisum's, near the mouth of the river, while tragic incident, and a little civilized sentiment, marked their weary way. Among the wounded was Jim Dyer, who had been shot through the stomach. The torture on that trip, without food and proper care, gradually killed him and a number of the others. At last Dyer called his friend, Ferguson, to say that he did not expect to get home, adding: "I want you to always remember me, and this wild country in which they lay me to rest."

Years later Judge Ferguson, then of Denton, wrote:

I left him with the assurance that I would never forget him, and went away in sorrow. Late that evening as we went into camp again, I learned he was dead. . . . on the banks of the Concho by the bright moonlight,

24 I. D. Ferguson, in *Hunter's Magazine,* June, 1911, and reprinted in the *Brady Standard,* June 27, 1939.

[116]

we dug his grave. We wrapped him in his blanket and gently laid him to rest, firing a volley of twelve guns over his grave. Here by ... this beautiful river, sleeps the remains of this heroic boy who 'did not live to get home.' I still remember him. I remember the wild country in which we laid him away to rest. I hope the wild flowers will still spring up and grow over his unmarked grave; that the birds may ... cheer his silent abode, somewhere on the Concho.[25]

At Chisum's Ranch the disorganized forces picked up some flour and a number of beeves. The main force scattered to its frontier homes, while Totten, writing to Major Erath from "the settlements on the Concho," January 15, stated that he would take a scout of twelve men and go back in an attempt to find out what had become of the Indians.

He found that they had precipitately abandoned their camp, leaving their equipage — "extra clothing, cooking utensils, buffalo hides" — in their flight. They had hidden their dead in the brush and had struck across the Plains toward the Pecos. Totten then turned back to meet the wrath of his superiors, while the Kickapoos crossed into Mexico near Eagle Pass, still professing their friendship for the whites as well as their peaceful intentions. There is little reason to doubt them.

By report from the same place they claimed that in advance of the battle, they sent a woman and child with a white flag to meet the Texans and to assure them of their friendly intent. In his official investigation General McAdoo could find no one who saw it. However, he did claim that the Indians were taken by surprise, "were generally in their wigwams" when the charge was made, and that the women were screaming about the camp, some of them in plain English "declaring they were friendly." And he did report that "an Indian went out from the encampment with two children to Captain Fossett ... with his hand raised" and told Fossett they were friendly, and if he would but see their "principal chief" "all things would be made satisfactory." [26]

Fossett denied seeing any flag of truce, but readily admitted

[25] I. D. Ferguson, as cited.
[26] War of the Rebellion Records, series I, vol. 48, chap. LX, 26-27.

the capture of the man with two children. In forthright explanation he said:

> After the fight had gone on for an hour or more a party of men came to me with an Indian man, and two children from 10 to 12 years old, saying they had some prisoners and asking what should be done with them. They told me that they had cut them off while attempting to get to the Indian camp. I had no conversation with the Indian myself. The fighting going on all around and there was little time for that. I remarked that in Indian fighting it was not customary to take prisoners. One of the men then shot the grown Indian. The men who captured the Indian state that he had been herding the horses. He said that perhaps the fight might be stopped by seeing the chief. . . . The Indian had no flag.[27]

After all their suffering at the hands of the warlike tribes, it was an understandable action on the part of the Texans. Still it was an unnecessary one that could easily have been avoided by the exercise of better scouting, plainscraft, generalship, and a little restraint. It was the worst tragedy of the long warfare that marked the history of the Indian border of Texas. As such it augured the outcome of the great civil conflict in the South.

The breakup was at hand. But the end of the War did not bring an end to struggle and confusion on the frontiers of Texas.

[27] Fossett to J. B. Barry, March 12, 1865 (published in the *Texas State Gazette*, April 5, 1865) quoted from Pool, as cited, 19.

CHAPTER VII

Founding of Fort Concho

LEE'S SURRENDER threw the state of Texas into confusion. General E. Kirby Smith briefly tried to rally the Trans-Mississippi Confederacy to further resistance. But the people were tired of war, and in Texas the army began to fly to pieces. Desertions took place by wholesale, discipline was forgotten, and supplies were openly plundered by the soldiers in the presence of their officers in a state of quiet but dangerous and thorough mutiny. The break-up was complete and Texas too sued for peace.[1]

In an attempt to bring some semblance of order out of the general anarchy, President Andrew Johnson, on June 17, 1865, appointed A. J. Hamilton as provisional governor of Texas. Hamilton, a sturdy man who had opposed secession along with Houston and had then fled the state for safety, eventually had gone into the Federal army as a brigadier general. He came back to Texas late in July to the loud acclaim of other Unionists who now emerged from hiding to become either political leaders or public parasites.

Hamilton moved on to Austin and took over the rudder of the uncertain ship of state. It was a real job. No political

[1] This period is treated with clarity and compassion by that late great historian of the South, Charles W. Ramsdell, in *Reconstruction in Texas*, New York, 1910, pp. 27-51.

[119]

organization, no public fund, no recognized authority and no semblance of order existed at the seat of the government. It was little better elsewhere, though local officials were trying to hold the line against outlawry and general moral disintegration.

Texas fell under the immediate military jurisdiction of General P. H. Sheridan, who ordered General Gordon Granger to Galveston to take over the situation. Granger arrived on June 19, 1865, and immediately issued the order that marks the day for the colored race, putting into effect the President's proclamation for the freedom of slaves. An attempt by the Federal forces to confiscate Confederate supplies followed, but the rebellious soldiery of Texas had left little to their levies. Then began the Federal scandal over the disposition of cotton, the cash crop upon which the immediate revival of the Southern economy depended. Conflict over the problem of the free Negro, childlike and confused, who, suddenly in power, sat down to enjoy the leisure and bounty that demagogues always promise, tended to complete the anarchy.

The new government was launched with great difficulty but with commendable moderation. But moderation did not last long. As the white troops were discharged from the regular army, Negro soldiers were brought in during the late summer and fall to take their place. These, guilty of widespread outrages, compounded the resentment of the defeated Texans and added to the passions of the time. After this the radicals took over and the blackest period in Texas history was marked by widespread violence and blood.

General Sheridan had attained great success on the military field. But military ability is no guarantee of statesmanship. He showed little sympathy for the Texans and little aptitude as a civil administrator. His misrule was amplified by the fact that the baser part of human nature, working toward the ascendancy in war, relishes the imposition of arbitrary authority and the exaction of vengeance upon and retribution from a conquered people. Time and again history records that civilized tolerance leavens the mass but slowly. And so it was in Texas.

Through General Charles Griffin, who became commander of the Texas District, Sheridan pursued his punitive measures to the eternal damnation of his name in Texas. Griffin fell in with the radical element that took control. The moderates among the Unionists were ruthlessly pushed out and as the decent citizens who had fought for the Confederacy were virtually outlawed, they resorted more and more to personal rectification of indignities. Texas was swamped with killings. Federal authority became not only onerous but oppressive, and the Ku Klux Klan came into extra-legal existence to right the wrongs of men who had no standing in court.[2]

The frontier was largely left to its own meager resources, which meant simply to the resourcefulness of its lion-hearted and iron-jawed men. Indian depredations became more frequent and violent, and again the line of settlement was bent and broken in reaction. Throughout 1865 and 1866 petitions for aid piled up on the desk of the Governor. As Texas was under virtual military dictatorship he passed them on to the army. Sheridan refused aid because, he claimed, the troops were needed in the interior for the protection of the Negroes. It was a bitter period, but in general outline is essential to an understanding of the times in which the settlement of the Concho country actually began.

But at last arbitrary power must submit to the force and logic of nature, and in the spring of 1867 Captain E. J. Strang, Quartermaster General, was ordered to put the frontier posts of Texas "in proper order for the reception of troops." Plans from Washington were received at San Antonio. Laborers were to be hired. Camp Verde, near present Kerrville, was to become the headquarters for the 4th Cavalry, and posts farther north, including Chadbourne, were to be reinvested with life. In April, 1867, the report went out that "Shortly all the posts along the El Paso route from San Antonio will be re-established."[3]

[2] Dr. Ramsdell traced this period in detail. See pp. 145 ff.

[3] *San Antonio Express*, April 20, 1867.

And so at last the military turned a little of its attention from policing the conquered whites to their protection. On May 25, Fort Chadbourne was reoccupied by Company G of the 4th Cavalry, and by the end of June 331 men were at the post. Lieutenant Colonel Eugene B. Beaumont was ordered up from Fort Mason to take command, with Major Michael J. Kelly to assist him. Then Captain G. G. Huntt, of 4th Cavalry, was sent with reinforcements from Camp Verde, in July, and took over the post.[4]

To the west Fort Stockton was reoccupied for the protection of the El Paso mail, as well as the guarding of trail herds and the encouragement of the California emigrants. But the army did not move back to Fort McKavett, at the head of the San Saba, where Mr. Robinson, the only inhabitant and the "owner" of the land, still held lonely vigil until a year later.[5] As the country adjacent to the three Concho Rivers was again patrolled by Federal troops, plans were being made to quarter them closer. Just why this vital section should have been neglected so long in view of its strategic position at the virtual junction of two great trails is difficult to understand. A fort established at first here might have taken the place of both McKavett and Chadbourne.

The strategic advantages of the Conchos had been recognized fifteen years earlier, when, on March 15, 1852, Camp Joseph E. Johnston was established by four companies of the 8th Infantry on the south bank of the North Concho. Dr. Ebenezer Swift, when ordered to that remote outpost, understood that it "was considered the most important on the frontier . . ." though it was "150 miles beyond the last white settlement." But when Fort Chadbourne was established thirty-five miles away, a few months later, Camp Johnston

4 *Post Returns*, Fort Chadbourne, Texas, June and July, 1867, Records of the War Department, National Archives, Washington.

5 Fort McKavett was reoccupied April 1, 1868. *Medical History*, Fort Stockton, 1869, pp. 1-5; *Medical History*, Fort McKavett, 9-12; Circular No. 8, May 1, 1875, *A Report on the Hygiene of the U. S. Army, with Descriptions of Military Posts*, p. 240—all in the National Archives.

was abandoned, November 18, 1852, and the garrison was removed.[6]

Yet much activity across the frontier of Texas at this time was up and down the valley of the Middle Concho, by the Butterfield Trail and the San Antonio roads, instead of by Fort Chadbourne. The Goodnight Trail, laid out from the Palo Pinto region of Texas to New Mexico and Colorado in 1866, was being followed through the same region by reckless drivers hunting markets for their longhorned herds. The Comanches were depredating upon them, and after the war the first work of the army out of Fort Chadbourne was to protect the trail west. On June 9, 1867, Lieutenant Peter M. Boehm, with fifty men, reported upon "a scout on the main Concho River, to protect trains and droves of cattle crossing *El Llano Estacado. . . ."* [7]

Obviously a reappraisal of the defense needs of Texas was in order, and that summer General Sheridan named a board of inspection, made up of General Alexander McD. McCook, Major John P. Hatch, Major John S. Mason and Captain D. W. Porter, for the selection of post sites. McCook and Mason were Ohioans of considerable frontier experience. Hatch, a native of New York, had seen distinguished service in the Mexican War and on the frontiers in Texas and New Mexico. Porter was another New Yorker of less distinction. All, of course, had seen service in the Civil War.[8] This experienced group made a tour of the frontier late in the fall.

During the spring and summer of 1867, however, the movement of herds upon the Goodnight Trail was considerable,

---

6 The exact location is not known. For Camp Joseph E. Johnston see Arrie Barrett, "Western Frontier Forts of Texas," West Texas Historical Association *Year Book*, VII, 130-131; *Post Returns*, Camp Johnston, Texas, War Records, National Archives, March to October, 1852; E. G. Campbell to O. C. Fisher, October 4, 1946; M. L. Crimmins, West Texas Historical Association *Year Book*, XV, 35-37.

7 *Post Returns*, Fort Chadbourne, June, 1867.

8 *Medical History*, vol. 401, Fort Concho, 1-2; Cullum, *Biographical Register of the Officers and Graduates of the United States Military Academy*, vol. 2, for McCook, Hatch and Mason; Heitman, *Historical Register and Dictionary of the United States Army*, vol. 1, for Porter.

and the depredations of the Comanches were correspondingly bad.[9] Following these early raids, the War Department, in May, ordered a "permanent camp" of cavalry to be set up on the "head waters of the Main"—which meant the Middle Concho.[10]

Acting under special orders issued June 8, 1867, from Fort Chadbourne, Lieutenant Boehm, a New Yorker who had come to Texas with the army of occupation, left with a detachment for that purpose. On the 12th he reached the point where the old Butterfield Mail came to the Middle Concho, and there, some eighteen miles above the junction of the North and South Rivers, established what came to be called the Permanent Camp. It was forty-five to fifty miles from his home post of Fort Chadbourne.[11] Leaving a corporal and nine men there as a guard, he made his first report:

I proceeded with the balance of my command to escort three herds of cattle to the Pecos River. At the head of the Main Concho thirty-five miles from the Permanent Camp I sent back two non-commissioned officers, and eight men to the camp as an additional guard. With thirty men I continued to march to the Pecos River, where I arrived on the 18th. Water and grass was abundant from the head of the Concho to Middle Station, there having been heavy rains, but from Middle Station to the Pecos neither grass nor water was found. On the 19th marched up the River with ten men, six miles above the Horsehead crossing to the Salt Lake, and returned to camp at the crossing the same day. No Indians were seen but signs were abundant and from citizens I learned that the droves which had crossed within a month had been broken up and scattered by the Indians. On the 20th of June I started on the return to the permanent Camp. . . . I arrived on the 24th. On the 25th I sent the Sergeant and twenty men left as a Camp guard to the Pecos with a herd. This party returned on the 5th of July, having encountered no Indians. Brev't Major M. J. Kelly, with Company "G" 4th U. S. Cavalry,

9 Haley, *Charles Goodnight*, as cited, 148-149 and 157-161.

10 *San Antonio Express*, May 27, 1867.

11 John P. Lee, veteran ranchman of this section, calculates the Camp must have been near the mouth of East Rocky Creek, probably just west of the Irion County line within two miles of present Arden.

relieved me on the 8th of July, and I returned to Fort Chadbourne on the 11th, having lost during the scout two men of company "M" deserted and three mules strayed.[12]

Thus again in routine patrol the regular army returned to the Concho country, to a camp that proved not so permanent, but in a military association and capacity that was to be permanent for the next twenty-two years.

In anticipation of increased activity the garrison at Chadbourne had grown to 423 men. The outpost on the Concho was kept garrisoned with one commissioned officer and fifty men, with monthly relief details. Its primary function was that of "looking out for Indians and affording protection to drovers, emigrants and trains crossing the plains."[13]

In keeping with the decision to reoccupy the frontier posts, Colonel J. G. C. Lee, Assistant Quartermaster General, organized a "large train of mechanics" at San Antonio for the building of permanent barracks. On August 1, 1867, the detail of civilian help assigned to Fort Chadbourne left San Antonio for the frontier post, where it arrived on the 15th.[14] It was organized and put on the payroll at what was then handsome wages: a superintendent of mechanics at $125 a month, 2 engineers at $150, 2 sawyers at $100, a stone mason at $100, 41 masons at $75, 42 carpenters at $75, and 8 quarry men,

[12] P. M. Boehm to Chas. A. Vernon, July 19, 1867, Records of the War Department, Fort Concho, Texas.

[13] *Post Returns*, Fort Chadbourne, July, 1867; G. G. Huntt to Adjt. Gen., August 15, 1867.

[14] *San Antonio Express*, June 13, 1867.

4 blacksmiths, 1 wheelwright and 1 lime burner at $75 each, 1 guide at $60, and two cooks at $30. A new post was planned; Chadbourne was not being rebuilt.[15] These hands were destined, with the usual government waste and delay, for service on the Concho.

The water on Oak Creek, at Fort Chadbourne, was in short supply and decidedly bad. Major Kelly, but lately detailed to the Permanent Camp, came down with typhoid fever. He was relieved on account of his illness and sent back to Chadbourne for treatment on August 3, but died August 13. Captain Huntt, commanding officer at the post, reported his death to headquarters, particularly regretting his passing since he was the first Union officer "to reoccupy the Post since its evacuation on the treachery of the traitor Twiggs," he added, in compound damnation of the former commander of Texas.[16]

The same month, steam sawmills were sent from Chadbourne to the North Concho "where there was an abundance of water at all times . . . where it was presumed the new post would be located," and where there was "a sufficiency of pecan timber (the only kind in the section of the country available for building purposes)", as Quartermaster E. J. Strang observed in his report for that year. For some reason, he continued, "the mills did not get into operation until the middle of October and first part of November. The mechanics were kept employed in quarrying stone, felling trees, constructing temporary shelters, &." [17]

Nevertheless August of 1867 was a busy month. On August 22 a detail of ten men, after escorting the paymaster up the military road to Fort Belknap, was upon its return attacked by Indians at Mountain Pass, forty miles north of Chadbourne. Two soldiers were killed and two of their horses captured. Another detail on the road to San Antonio was held

15 *Post Returns,* Fort Chadbourne, August, 1867.

16 G. G. Huntt to Adjt. Gen., August 15, 1867. Huntt seems to be in error as to Kelly's being the first, but his feeling for Twiggs is understandable.

17 E. J. Strang, Annual Report, June 30, 1868, pp. 10-11. The Saw Mill Camp was just above the river crossing west of present Carlsbad.

up five days by high water at the crossing of the Colorado. A relief for Kelly's men was sent to Permanent Camp and another detail of thirty was sent up the road to bury the bodies at Mountain Pass. Report then came that a man had been killed at Permanent Camp,[18] and upon "official information having been received that Indians were concentrating in force in that vicinity," an officer and eighteen men were sent as reinforcements. Others were ordered after the Indians, while details were kept moving as guards for civilian employees and for haying contractors. Two men deserted, and another deserter was killed while attempting to escape his guards "at the crossing of the San Saba."[19] Thus summer passed and fall came on. Meanwhile the money for the post in the Concho country was being wasted, while not a mud-sill had been laid, and not even the site had been chosen.

In October Sheridan's committee on locations left San Antonio upon a "Military Tour of Inspection" while the *San Antonio Express,* spokesman for the military and vocal organ of policy, criticized the old idea of a "cordon of posts" from the Rio Grande to the Red River. It had been a good plan but had failed, the *Express* continued, primarily because the posts were so widely scattered. Now it contended that the great need was for intermediate garrisons connected by a military telegraph, so that news of raids could be flashed up and down the line, and army pursuers could get a-going without delay. As the committee proceeded up the military road they had time to consider their problem.

Colonel Strang had passed through Chadbourne on an inspection in July. He had recommended the removal of the post to "a more favorable and convenient locality" on account of the "insufficiency and unhealthy quality of the water . . . together with the distance of the post from the most frequented routes of travel."[20]

18 This was Hugh Collins. His tombstone is still to be seen on the North Concho. See Conkling, as cited, I, 352.

19 *Post Returns,* Fort Chadbourne, August and September, 1867.

20 Strang, as cited; *Post Returns,* Fort Chadbourne, August, 1867.

[127]

Mason, Hatch and others of the inspection party made their way north. On November 5, 1867, Captain George G. Huntt, commanding officer at Chadbourne, left the fort with an escort of eighteen men to meet them, since they were to determine "the permanent location of the new post. . . ." Huntt was back on the 9th, while one commissioned officer and forty men accompanied the board on its way. Thus, allowing two days for the march each way from the post to the junction of the Conchos, it would appear that in all probability the location of the site of Fort Concho, and thus San Angelo, was made November 7, 1867. Anyway, according to the official records, thirteen men left Chadbourne on November 13 "to explore and establish a new road from this Post to the site of New Post on the Rio Concho. . . ." They were back four days later and their road was put to immediate use.

The next mail to Fort Mason went out that way, and on the 23rd Captain Huntt and an escort left for the site "to lay out" the new camp. Then the first garrison, a detachment of Company H of the 4th Cavalry, under the command of Captain James Callahan, marched off from Chadbourne for the site on the 27th, while Company M, except for details out with the trail herds, left Permanent Camp on the 25th "and marched to the same place." Thus the camp which was to become Fort Concho was established late in November, instead of in December, as the authorities usually show.

Mason and his board pushed their inspection clear to Red River and returned to San Antonio on December 2. They recommended the removal of the post from Buffalo Springs, in Clay County, to Jacksboro, where it became Fort Richardson; they wanted Belknap moved to a "better location," and it eventually became Camp Wilson, on the Clear Fork. But their most important recommendation was for the removal of Fort Chadbourne to the forks of the Conchos—a suggestion that determined the permanent development of the Concho country.[21]

21 *San Antonio Express,* December 4, 1867.

[128]

Captain Huntt officially transferred his headquarters company on December 4, thereby making "*permanent* occupation of the post," which was designated as Camp Hatch, in honor of the New Yorker who had helped select its site. Thereafter Chadbourne simply became a picket post, garrisoned from the Conchos, until the commanding officer asked authority to discontinue it, about a year later.[22]

Obviously the new post at first was simply an open camp. Huntt was immediately in charge of construction. For two months a large crew of men had been busy cutting and sawing pecan timber on the North Concho and taking out rock in anticipation of the job. Even though the cost had mounted to $28,218.93 by November 10, the work was lost. Colonel Strang dismissed the matter by saying that "The stones, logs and material prepared were not available owing to the distance of transportation."[23] The sawmills, however, were subsequently moved to the junction of the rivers, near the new location, where plenty of pecan—"a peculiarly intractable wood for building purposes," they recorded with commendable restraint—was available.[24] Shortly Captain D. W. Porter, assistant quartermaster and a member of the board on sites, was placed in charge of construction, December 10, 1867.

In spite of the large crew of mechanics, building progress was distressingly slow, due in part to the extreme isolation of the post. Transport of supply was a mean job—"most of it being brought 600 miles in ox carts, from the coast . . ." When work was not bogged down with the problems of transportation, it was hindered by the stubborn and uncooperative nature of green pecan timber, or the admitted inability of the Quartermaster's Department to superintend simultaneous con-

---

[22] *Post Returns*, Fort Chadbourne, November, 1867; Memo. 3962, A.G.O., 1879; General Order 74, Reservation File, A.G.O.; G. A. Gordon, *Letters Received*, Fort Concho, October 25, 1868. Captain Huntt's first camp "occupied the ground adjoining and south of the present site of Fort Concho, on the west bank of the Main Concho river." *Medical History*, vol. 401, pp. 1-2.

[23] Strang, as cited, 11.

[24] The same, and *Medical History*, as cited.

struction of posts at three widely separated points across
Texas. And last, but hardly least, was the lack of coordination
and cooperation between the civilian help and the military
authorities. Apparently it has ever been thus.

Even though there were ninety-six civilian employees on
the payroll just before the move started, and 137 in December,
the foundation of only one building had been laid by the end
of January, 1868. At that time the officers and men were under
canvas; "the horses simply corralled . . ." The hospital consisted of three crowded tents, poorly warmed by open fire-
places. The only "permanent building" at the post was the
sutler's store, of picket poles set in the ground, covered after
a fashion "with a green pecan board roof." But the advocates
of equalitarianism could have taken comfort from the fact that
the accommodations for the officers were "inferior if possible
to that of the men." [25]

Yet from the beginning, Camp Hatch was a considerable
post. In December, 1867, it had a total garrison of sixteen
commissioned officers and 372 enlisted men. Captain George
G. Huntt, the first commanding officer, a native of the District
of Columbia and then thirty-two years of age, had seen service
in the Civil War. Another officer to become noted in West
Texas, Captain Joseph Rendlebrock, was on his staff.[26]

The civilian employees consisted principally of artisans, for
some reason a couple of lawyers, a saddler, a crew of teamsters,
ox drivers, and a wagon master and his assistant. The masonry
foreman got $125, the lawyers $100, and the cooks were still
fussing over open fires on $30 a month.[27]

Major Hatch, with commendable modesty, objected to the
post's being named in his honor, and "in deference to his
wishes" it was changed to Camp Kelly in memory of the
officer who had fallen victim to malaria while in Permanent
Camp along the stream that emptied there from the west.

[25] *Medical History,* as cited; Strang, as cited.
[26] Heitman, as cited, vol. I, 559; Powell, Wm. H., *Records of Living Officers of the United States Army,* 303-304.
[27] *Post Returns,* Camp Hatch, Texas, December, 1867.

[130]

Richard Kelly, brother of the deceased officer, came from Washington to take the body home for reburial in Mount Olive Cemetery. He proceeded to the frontier from San Antonio, and on the 14th of January, 1867, a detail was sent with him from Camp Kelly to Chadbourne "to disinter and escort the remains" to the post named in the Major's honor. From the Conchos the funeral procession led out by Mason and reached San Antonio a week later.[28]

It was not until February 6, 1868 that the name of the new post "was finally fixed as Fort Concho," though during the course of early construction the Department had, to further the confusion, referred to it as Fort Griffin in spite of the fact that there was another post on the Clear Fork by the same name. At last, and appropriately, "it was given the name applied to the three rivers that formed their junction beside the fort."

It is interesting to note that a memorandum prepared by the War Department in July, 1889, for publication in the San Angelo *Enterprise* of that period, commented upon the origin of the name of the rivers. The anonymous author speculated as to whether it came from the Spanish *concha*, meaning shell, and obviously in this case the mussel shell which abounded upon the streams, or whether it was "from its Mexican derivative, the shell-shaped cover of the spike of Indian corn." Logic, however, still favors "the river of pearls"—based on the limestone *concha* secretions of the lowly mussel shells.[29]

During the month of February, 1868, there was a little progress toward stability. A remarkable character, Dr. William Notson, arrived as the first post surgeon; the sawmills were relocated near uncut timber around the fort; and a corporal and five privates left Camp as "an escort exploring for timber and to select a new site for a saw mill." Forty men were at

[28] Memo. on History Ft. Concho, n.d., A.G.O., Reservation File, prepared by W. M. Feagle, published in *San Angelo Enterprise*, and mailed July 5, 1889; *Post Returns*, Camp Kelly, Texas, January, 1868; *San Antonio Express*, December 24, 1867, January 24, 1868.

[29] *Memo*, as cited above.

work on the quartermaster's depot and a detail was out after rock lime and poles.[30] In a leisurely sort of way this sounded like business, though a 600 mile haul from Indianola on the coast, a 306 mile trip to the nearest railroad station at Denison, and 100 miles to the nearest post office at Fort Mason were obvious handicaps when the usual transportation was by mule and ox team.

As the officers and men proceeded with some ambition in their plans to erect a really permanent post, Quartermaster General Strang emphasized economy in construction. In his annual report, issued in June, he simply pointed out that

It is a common remark among troops, that as soon as they make their quarters comfortable and convenient, they have to leave them. I am inclined to believe that the same results attend Frontier Posts; by the time they are made habitable and comfortable, the necessity that caused their construction has passed away,—a new line of defence is adopted, new posts are constructed at more remote points, and the old ones abandoned. Military Posts are matured villages planted in the wilderness to decline and decay as other villages of more permanent character steadily grow up around them. It would seem unwise then, to say the least, to attempt the construction of permanent buildings, whose stone walls and chimnies a few years hence will serve as monuments to mark the waste of money, as those of Forts Phantom Hill and Belknap now do.[31]

But human nature—being what it is in its thirst for easy money—decreed otherwise. His voice was indeed one crying in the wilderness. This sort of notion was rank reaction. Those most directly concerned felt that a handsome and substantial post should be built. In the years required for its completion Strang's prophecy was forgotten, but it proved completely true.

30 *Post Returns*, Camp Kelly, Texas, January and February, 1868.
31 Strang, as cited, June 30, 1868, pp. 18-19.

CHAPTER VIII

Building the Post

THE SITE CHOSEN for the location of Fort Concho was little short of perfect. At this point the North Concho emerges from the hills or the abutments of the Staked Plains and bends sharply to the east. The Middle Concho, its modest waters swelled by the more abundant flow of Spring Creek and the South Concho, cuts through the valley from the west, almost parallels the North Concho for a mile or more, and then loops back to the north to form the junction. In the late 1860's the land immediately between was an open tableland almost surrounded by the rivers and gentle enough in its contour to give good drainage without serious threat of erosion. It was covered with grass and scattered mesquite. On three sides the native pecan shaded the long deep holes of both streams, intermittently broken, as if for convenient fords, by shoals of gravel and solid rock.

Since Texas owned the public domain, the acquisition of sites became a vexing problem for the army wherever camps were pitched. Locations were often grabbed by alert individuals who saw the chance to profit. In time the owners naturally expected the government to rent or buy the lands from them, and if and when the posts were abandoned the improvements usually reverted to the individual for their questionable worth.

The matter of private ownership was an old sore for the military by the time Fort Concho was located. An object lesson could be read in Fort Chadbourne, where the site had been acquired by Sam Maverick of San Antonio, and after bothersome negotiation, was leased by the government for twenty years at twenty-five dollars per month.

In his report for 1867 the Secretary of War noted that "Difficulty as well as expense attends the renting of land for military sites in Texas. . . ." Therefore he recommended the purchase of sites, and suggested that officers be prohibited from erecting "any but the most temporary buildings on the lands of private individuals." [1] The same year Quartermaster Strang recommended economical, troop-built posts "of logs, adobes or frame" that should, he thought, be "as comfortable as the stone buildings ordered, and for one-half the cost. . . ." [2] But Fort Concho was designed in substantial proportions while title to the land was apparently forgotten.

Yet the *San Antonio Express*, representing the radicals of Reconstruction and equally voluble, had warned against the policy well before the camp was founded. Charging that the frontier fattened on the federal government, and that land should not be rented, it contended that "In most instances the yearly rents paid on lands on which Posts were located, were greater than the land could be sold for in the open market." [3]

Therefore, it could not have been much of a surprise when surveyors showed up in April 1870 for persons "claiming the land in the vicinity of the post," and began running their lines. In the meantime the fort was simply perched, more or less at sea, out in the state of Texas. More than a year later the Department Commander, General J. J. Reynolds, established the reservation of 1640 acres by special order, and an attempt was made to lease the ground then privately owned.

From the first the government and its contractors had been

[1] MSS., "Historical Data, Fort Chadbourne," War Records, n.d., *Report of Secretary of War*, Sen. Ex. Doc. No. 1, 34th Cong., 1st Sess., 22.

[2] Strang, as cited, 19.

[3] *San Antonio Express*, May 4, 1867.

cutting timber off this and adjoining lands. On February 14, 1872, Gustave Schleicher, acting for Granville H. Sherwood, of Galveston, sold to E. D. L. Wickes, a contractor and freighter of San Antonio, the right to all the timber on 21,440 acres of land on the "southwest bank" of the north river "in the neighborhood of Fort Concho." They had figured out that even in West Texas timber was valuable, and the deal was made for the specific purpose of letting Wickes prosecute Schleicher's claims against the government for timber cut upon the lands.[4]

The ownership of the reservation, however, seemed to rest with a group—with Mrs. M. G. Schleicher, Wickes and Trainer, Adams and Wickes, and E. D. L. Wickes and James Trainer, individually. The Schleichers were extensive land-owners; Wickes and Adams, contractors of government freight; and James Trainer, a New Yorker who came to Texas with the army, was the first post trader at Fort Concho. All knew the speculative value that government work implies for land. They had simply got there first. An attempt was made, as already observed, upon May 16, 1871, to lease the site. Two years later Congress set up a board for the purchase of sites. It did not immediately get a price out of Adams and Wickes, who were by then the owners of the reservation, but it valued the land at $6400 under the impression that such an offer, if and when made, would be accepted.

Negotiations dragged on until July 1, 1873, when Colonel S. B. Holabird, Deputy Quartermaster General, leased 1350 acres from the San Antonio owners at $640 a year.[5]

Eventually Adams and Wickes offered to sell at $15,000 and General E. O. C. Ord, then commanding the Department of Texas, recommended the purchase. But the deal was disallowed by his superior, who ordered leasing, as usual. Eleven years after the founding of the fort the Secretary of War

4 *Medical History*, as cited, vol. 401, p. 167; J. J. Reynolds, Order No. 97, May 16, 1871, in *Letters Received*, Fort Concho; *Deed Records*, Bexar County, vol. W1, 420, 582-583.

5 Memo. No. 4998, A.G.O., 1872; *The Purchase of Military Sites in Texas*, House Ex. Doc. No. 282, 43rd Cong., 1st Sess., 22-23.

decided that he would "urgently present the subject of purchasing sites" in Texas. Fort Concho was included. By the time the papers got out of the pigeon-hole and were sent to the owners, Adams and Wickes answered by ". . . offering tracts of 690 acres for $20,000."

The matter went up through the military hierarchy to General W. T. Sherman, who wrote the Secretary of War that the outrageous price should not be paid, and furthermore suggested that they "should refuse to expend another cent in Texas until that State provides by law some equitable method of acquiring sites for present and prospective military stations." Texas Senator Maxey replied that a law providing for condemnation by the state had already been passed.[6] And there the matter rested while the army continued to occupy Fort Concho at a new lease of $94.50 a month. Considering the surplus space in Texas, Adams and Wickes were well paid.[7]

During the decade of the 1870's, the army was nettled over the ownership of land by sutlers within the military reservation. These lands, diverted to the lush trade and easy virtue that traditionally follow the camp, gave considerable trouble.

Lack of title did not stop construction of the post. Building proceeded at a provoking pace, though there was a fortunate source of artisans. German workmen swarmed from the settlements around Fredericksburg — woodcutters, hay-makers, butchers, tinners, saddlers, lime-burners, carpenters and rock masons.[8] These were augmented by tempestuous Irish, frontier bull-whackers, mule-skinners, scouts and hunters, to make up the motley civilian crew that came to help at the fort.

The sawmills were moved from their original locations up the North Concho to timber nearer the post and kept at work.

[6] 1767 A.G.O., 1879, "Memo Relative to Fort Concho, Texas, March 25, 1879"; W. T. Sherman to Sec. of War, March 26, 1879; Adams & Wickes to Gen. E. O. C. Cord, January 14, 1879; Reservation File, A.G.O., *War Records.*

[7] Reservation File, A.G.O., *War Records*, National Archives.

[8] Esther Mueller, in a series of articles called "Old Fort Concho," *Fredericksburg Standard*, February 22 to March 22, 1934, gives an excellent account of this migration of skilled labor. See also, Kubela, "History of Fort Concho, Texas," thesis, U. of T., p. 31.

Late in 1867 an observant young German named Rudolph Runge began work at one twelve miles up the river. Suitable timber was scarce and there was talk of moving a mill to the Guadalupe River, where cypress grew. Runge worried over the expense involved and wrote to his mother, February 2, 1868:

> I am afraid the timber has cost the government as much as 15 cents a foot, and unless we get more timber from some other source, we will be here four or five years building the post. Our second sawmill exploded and wounded five of the workmen, and so it is out of commission.[9]

By April 1868, lumber was being freighted from Fredericksburg, though an escort to guard against the Indians was necessary. The local search for timber had resulted in moving one of the portable sawmills to Home Creek, on the Colorado, where a permanent guard against Indians was posted.[10]

Gradually a little lumber was piled on the site, but progress was unbelievably slow. On September 15, 1868, Major Rendlebrock[11] was placed in charge of construction. The approach of winter discouraged operations. By December the garrison consisted of twenty-six commissioned officers and 338 enlisted men. The large civilian building force had been cut off completely, though little work had been done.[12]

A post office had been established, April 30, 1868, and the sutler James Trainer was named as postmaster. The usual scouts after Indians were being undertaken. Escorts were furnished to emigrants and trail herds upon their way west, hay had been put up from the natural meadows on contract, and corn had been freighted at great expense from the settlements. The post, though barely on its way toward construction, was operating on routine.

9 Quoted by Kubela, as cited, 35-36.

10 *Post Returns*, Fort Concho, March and April, 1868.

11 The name, even in military records, is often spelled Rendelbrook, and was corrupted, in the naming of some springs in Mitchell County, to Renderbrook. Rendlebrock was a Prussian who entered the army in the fifties, served during the Civil War and was sent to Texas with the army of occupation. He died March 13, 1889. See Heitman, as cited, vol. 1, 823.

12 *Post Returns*, Fort Concho, December, 1868.

A heavy loss of horses resulted from some undiagnosed epidemic during the first winter. About 400 head died throughout the district and "post-mortem examination showed softening of the brain and swelling of the head." General Strang, suspecting the trouble "was due in great measure to feeding on corn alone," recommended a half-ration of oats after observing that the officers' horses, which had been fed on oats, "were free from the epidemic." He had seen the same trouble on the Tehuantepec Mail Route in the tropics, where he had bought local corn at twenty-five cents a bushel "and yet imported oats from New York."[13]

Still another winter passed without appreciable progress in construction. In April, 1869, Captain George H. Gamble, commander of the post, brought in another big crew of civilian hands. Again the freighters were busy. Forty-four teamsters and three herders of work stock swelled the ranks of artisans who pottered about the site. By fall the number was again greatly reduced and only eight men remained in December.[14]

Meanwhile colored troops were quartered at Concho. Dr. Notson, the remarkably intelligent and critical observer of the post and its lack of progress, noted in his official record, the *Medical History of Fort Concho,* that a change of construction policy had been made in keeping with Colonel Strang's recommendation for the use of soldier labor. This experiment, Notson wrote, in view of the mixture of colors in the garrison, made it "interesting as an ethnological as well as a military experiment." But he suspended judgment upon its wisdom.[15]

The hospital building for twenty-four beds—a box-like structure surmounted by a cupola for adornment and observation—was then well along. Workmen dug a hole beside it for a cistern to hold rain water for the sick. Water-proof cement for plastering it was freighted from the settlements at great expense. Then the post surgeon learned to his great

13 Jas. A. Ekin to General J. J. Reynolds, September 23, 1868, *Letters Received.*
14 *Post Returns,* Fort Concho, April and December, 1869.
15 *Medical History,* vol. 401, p. 129.

disgust that this cement, "so carefully guarded from the weather, under the portico of the hospital, was used by the quartermaster to make the floor of the men's quarters. . . ."

And so the summer of 1869 passed with the cistern still incomplete. Dr. Notson complained that "the yawning cavern blasted out at so much expense, is likely to remain another half year or longer, an eyesore to the beauty and tidiness of the Hospital, and a dangerous pitfall to the inmates, instead of the reservoir of health it was intended to be." The apologist for government mistakes might take comfort from the fact that the season was dry and it probably would not have been filled anyway.

The country about Fort Concho was so droughty that grass fires seriously imperiled the operation of the post, and Dr. Notson, surveying the prairie with skeptical eye, believed they were set by "malicious persons." Grass fires were the frequent resort of Indians to baffle pursuers and to concentrate game for their kills, but what other purpose of malice might have prompted the firings is a little vague. Anyway, Dr. Notson wrote that round about "in every direction" the country was burned bare of grass as the officers made efforts

to detect or arrest persons guilty of this offense, considered so grave by the statutes of the State, and by the unwritten law of the prairie. . . . The wide circle of flame, often entirely complete, visible from the belvedere of the hospital, of a dark night, was a sight long to be remembered. This devastation has lasted all of the present and a greater part of the preceding month [August and September]. The direct question of supply of hay, for the horses and stock of the garrison, is involved, both as to the quantity and quality to be supplied, and either way, probably brings ruin to the contractor.[16]

Captain Gamble resigned from the army that fall and in December Brevet Colonel William R. Shafter was named to take the place of Captain C. C. Hood, temporarily in charge. The Post Surgeon, closing his *Medical History* for that year,

[16] The same, 129-139.

noted that at last the buildings were barely habitable, and expressed a hope that Shafter would inject "new life and fresh inspiration . . . into the garrison and officers here. . . ."

Shafter arrived January 7, 1870, and in his own words "found this post . . . in what I consider a very bad condition in every respect. Animals were in bad condition and insufficiently guarded, men apparently knowing but little of drill, camp and quarters filthy and officers seemingly taking but little interest in their duties."[17]

He applied himself to the care and feeding of the horses and soon had them on the mend. He attempted to relieve the congestion in quarters by reducing the space held by commissioned officers. Four days after his arrival either Indians or white thieves showed their contempt by raiding the quartermaster's corral to stampede and steal eighteen horses and four mules right off the military reservation. None of them was recovered and the culprits were never caught. Shafter did, however, take hold with vigor.

Corrals were genuinely needed and ten days after his arrival he commented upon the impossible conditions under which the teams were being kept.

I find at this post no stables for the animals of the Qr Ms Dept. The team mules stand in all weather tied to the wagon tongues and the loose animals are turned into a brush pen.

The horses of the Companies of Cavalry are slightly protected by paulins nailed over the temporary frame work of a stable. Genl Meigs after looking at the Corral and stables advised me to build a corral of stone large enough to hold all the public animals at the post and have a shed roof put around the inside. The stone can be taken out here by the enlisted men in any quantity desired. There is also a fine lime kiln where all the lime required can be burned by the same labor. All the shingles necessary to cover the roof are also here so that all the lumber required will be for the rafters, sheathing and what will be needed for making mangers &c. I hope to get cedar poles on the Llano that will do for rafters and thus do away with the necessity for sawed ones. . . .

[17] W. R. Shafter to Gen'l Com'd'g 5th District, February 19th, 1870, *Orders*, vol. 24.

Shafter had only eight civilian employees, a guide, clerk, wagon master, forage master, carpenter, wheelwright, blacksmith and one saddler, but he expected to replace them with suitable enlisted men except for the clerk and guide.[18]

Discord among the officers over reduction of their quarters broke out at once. Two were placed under arrest while others were threatened with the same punishment. Charges and countercharges flew between them "destructive of much of that social relation," Dr. Notson gently recorded, "almost essential to families upon the frontier."

"On the other hand," he continued, "much license has been allowed the soldiers in their festivities. Music, dancing and exhibitions in the quarters of the men, once or twice during each week through the month" had been common. Shafter, however, was busy with Colonel Ranald S. Mackenzie, in from the south, inspecting the frontier "with a view to stationing pickets and sending scouts in the direction of the Colorado. . . ."[19]

Just as Shafter got well under way, he was moved and Major John P. Hatch, of the 4th Cavalry, assumed command, June 9, 1870. Hatch conceived the idea that the sun-dried adobe brick of the Mexicans, instead of quarried rock, was best for building, and set forth with such enthusiasm that he acquired the nickname of "Dobe" Hatch. He barely had time to get started when he was relieved, less than a month after assuming command, by Colonel Alvan C. Gillem, of the 11th Cavalry. Gillem got down to work at once.

The barracks were floored and at last "made fit for occupancy." Another set of quarters was started and a yard for the making of adobe was laid out, even though it had been found unsatisfactory at the Ben Ficklin mail station about two miles from the post because it would not stick together.

Colonel Gillem pushed his men at the work of quarrying stone, seeking sand beds and cutting timber. Dr. Notson was

[18] W. R. Shafter to H. Clay Wood, January 14, 1870, *Letters Received*, Fifth Military District.

[19] *Medical History*, as cited, 149-158.

placed in charge of the bakery in an attempt to improve it, dependent as it was on a "broken, worn out, mud and rubble oven, entirely unfitted for the purposes of the present garrison," where "the bread has not been made satisfactorily even to the baker," to say nothing of the satisfaction of the men. The limestone oven, which cracked from the heat, eventually was rebuilt with soapstone cut by German workmen from a pit near Fredericksburg.[20]

Work on the adobe bricks went forward. Instead of being Mexicans, to whom the art is native, soldiers puddled the mud and filled the moulds. But it took a commissioned officer to keep a squad at work, and even then they moved so slowly that Gillem found it faster to quarry and dress stone instead. Other men were put to dressing lumber. The old guardhouse of pecan boards was torn down to make room for additional quarters. Two more buildings for the enlisted men were soon well along, though the heavy rains of August, 1870, slowed the work, stopped the lime burning and forced the abandonment of adobe by beating "to pieces" the bricks on hand. By the end of the year stone work for the barracks for all eight companies at the post was complete, and at last all but two companies were able to get from under canvas and into permanent quarters.[21]

Colonel Gillem congratulated himself that the rate of construction had been "without precedent" in the life of the post,

20 The same, 179: Esther Mueller, "Old Fort Concho," as cited.

21 Medical History, as cited, 181, 185, 193, 199.

and at least two things had been learned. Adobe had been discarded as too soft and expensive, and stone was found to be "cheaper and more easily obtained than wood of any quality." Thus at last the pattern for the completion of Fort Concho had been evolved by costly trial and error. There was a feeling of optimism as the end of the year approached, though a brand new guardhouse, "commodious" if not comfortable, stood as a sort of damper upon undue outbursts of the Christmas spirit among the enlisted men.

On January 21, 1871, less than seven months after he had arrived, Gillem was relieved of the command as the headquarters for the 11th Infantry was moved north to Fort Griffin. Concho again became the home of the 4th Cavalry, and again under Hatch, who started work on the stable which was to be the "best and largest known in the state." He barely had time to tear down the corral built by Shafter the year before when Colonel Mackenzie came in to take command, about a month later. Thus the continual shifting of commands, in view of no settled policy of construction, enhanced the cost and delayed the completion of Fort Concho for many years.

It is a sorry story to relate but in June, 1871, three and a half years after its founding, the Department of Texas called for estimates for the completion of the post for the accommodation of six companies of men. Again the army turned to the settlements for materials, and Wm. H. Hicks of San Antonio offered to deliver 55,000 good shingles to Fort Concho from the cypress streams of the Hill Country at $13.75 a thousand.[22] Nor were lumber and shingles the only items in short supply. Details scoured the country in search of proper sand for mortar and concrete work until a source of sandstone rock was discovered on the north side of the river just a hundred yards from the post. Here workmen began crushing the soft stone and sifting out the sand. By October, 1871, there seemed some hope for completion of additional quarters. But the zealous Dr. Notson almost gave up in despair.

22 Wm. H. Hicks to John Walton, March 19, 1871, *Letters Received*.

With fatalistic regularity "the wrong articles are invariably delivered first," he wrote. To begin with the "mechanics, or what are called mechanics," were on hand without materials. And then in October, with orders for construction of six sets of officers quarters, "the articles first delivered are shingles." [23] It is an ancient but oft-forgotten story—the impatience of free men with the sloth and inefficiency of bureaucratic government in the business field.

Meanwhile Colonel Mackenzie had been busy with plans for settling the Indian problem in Texas instead of providing comforts for officers in post. He was a leader of great capacity, ambition and zeal, and planned to carry the fight against the marauders into their own camps. In pursuit of his plan he shifted the headquarters of the 4th Cavalry from Concho northeast to Fort Richardson in Jack County, nearer Indian Territory and the hostile region between the Cross Timbers and the Staked Plains. When he rode out of Fort Concho in March, 1871, he so depleted its heavy garrison that plenty of room was left in its quarters as Hatch again assumed command.

In September speculation upon resort to a new type of construction came with a noted French visitor, Jules Poinsard, then a resident of San Antonio. He had "long been known to many army officers from the interest he has taken in the use of that kind of concrete called pise," a rubble mixture that he had used years before in building Camp Verde and Camp Colorado. He made some suggestions for expediting construction at Fort Concho, and left for Fort Griffin, where, it was understood, he was "about to exercise his talents." [24]

Hatch was left in charge for nearly four and a half months, to be followed by Captain Joseph Conrad for a month and a half, who in turn was succeeded by Captain Napoleon B. McLaughlen for less than a month. Then "Dobe" Hatch was

[23] *Medical History*, as cited, 237.

[24] *Medical History*, as cited, 234. Chris Emmett, in his book, *Texas Camel Tales*, 104-106, refers to this construction and records a rock tablet in the masonry at Camp Verde inscribed: "Jules Poinsard, 1857—Pise Work."

sent back for an extended service of seven months, ending December 30, 1872. Small wonder that slow progress in building was made.[25] Dr. Notson, after four years of fretting, drearily recorded his observations and convictions:

Viewing the buildings upon the posts of the western frontier of Texas, an officer compelled to pass the vigorous years of his life away from civilization, and its advantages, may well feel the indignation he dares not express, at the waste, not necessity, that compels him to live his years of durance in quarters reduced 'pro rata', and on commissary supplies that have been culled, before leaving the region of hotels, stores and boarding houses. From the photographs of the posts of the Rio Grande line, and from the ruined, unfinished, and abandoned buildings the Post Surgeon has seen at Mason, Concho, Griffin, Chadbourne, Phantom Hill, Belknap and Richardson, it is safe to say that there are the fragments of twenty buildings upon which government money has been expended upon this line, for every one it now occupies. Forty ghostly chimneys at Phantom Hill, a dozen houses whose trimmings have been robbed at Belknap, as many more at each Chadbourne, and Mason, are not the provocatives to zeal in duty, or desire in ornamentation, to men who are restricted in their home lives, for want of houses and room, and all through the want of foresight of the wise acres who are supposed to provide for the government themselves. Up to the middle of the month [of February, 1872] the work of construction went on with rapidity and under more favorable auspices than it ever had before ... when the misguided policy of the holder of the purse strings, caused the issue of the order for the suspension of work, or at least its equivalent in the discharge of the citizen mechanics. With the small garrison, and that in prospect of reduction, with strong outstanding pickets and frequent scouts, barely men can be obtained for the necessary military duties ... (and those that could be spared were disheartened by the lack of progress in the work). It is partly to the pound foolish policy, that the opprobrium of extravagance is fastened upon the Army. Mechanics have been collected from far and wide in the country, at great trouble and expense, they have been kept but half employed during the winter, in preparation for the more favorable building season, and yet, as that season opens, they are discharged and scattered, for the want of a small appropriation.

Work might be resumed in a few months, he continued, but then the hands would be back in the settlements,

[25] The same, 209, 213; General E. S. Adams, memo. on Fort Concho, March 8, 1939, Adjt. Gen. Office, Washington.

far from where they are needed, the material will have deteriorated, the favorable season have been wasted, and the stigma of waste and extravagance fastened stronger upon the army.... And yet the subject is beyond any control. Yet through all these errors [he noted at last with a ray of hope] work goes steadily on. Harmony prevails amongst the officers....[26]

And so it went throughout the years, tearing out here and adding there, until the lovely post of durable stone built in the fork of the Conchos came to completion and was then, as Colonel Strang had anticipated, shortly abandoned.[27]

[26] Dr. Wm. M. Notson in *Medical History*, vol. 401, pp. 253-254.

[27] Circular No. 8, War Department, Surgeon-General's Office, Washington, May 1, 1875, *Report on the Hygiene of the United States Army*, 195-196: REPORTS *of* ASSISTANT SURGEONS W.M. NOTSON *and* W.F. BUCHANAN
Officer's quarters are five cottage buildings of stone ... two rooms facing parade, separated by a broad hall; in rear of west room is a kitchen. Rooms are commodious, about 15 feet square, well lighted, without closets or shutters.... Storehouses are built about the same plan, ... flooring is large irregular slabs of stone cemented with ordinary mortar. Woodwork.... of pecan, a particularly intractable variety of our northern hickory, which by its twisting, curling, and shrinking hardly promises a permanence of symmetry ...
The barracks are two stone buildings, 180 by 27 and 100 by 27 feet to the ridge, with piazza, 9 feet wide around each. Each dormitory unceiled, with ridge and eaves ventilation—fitted with iron bedsteads, and for a full company gives 368 cubic feet of air space per man.
... Tarantulas and lesser spiders lurk under every cactus shrub, and the centipede brings forth its interesting brood in every pile of chips or lumber about one's quarters. Small scorpions, from two to three inches in length are found, though less frequently than either the centipede or the tarantula. Indians, believed to be chiefly Comanches and Kiowas, commit frequent depredations in the vicinity.

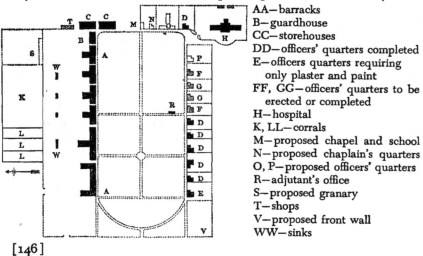

AA—barracks
B—guardhouse
CC—storehouses
DD—officers' quarters completed
E—officers quarters requiring
  only plaster and paint
FF, GG—officers' quarters to be
  erected or completed
H—hospital
K, LL—corrals
M—proposed chapel and school
N—proposed chaplain's quarters
O, P—proposed officers' quarters
R—adjutant's office
S—proposed granary
T—shops
V—proposed front wall
WW—sinks

[146]

After eight more changes of commanding officers, Colonel Benjamin H. Grierson of the 10th Colored Cavalry took over the post, April 30, 1875. In May he made known to headquarters that he wanted additional buildings—a forage house, a new headquarters, and so on. His recommendations were approved contingent upon the appropriation for the following year, and with a tart reminder from the Department that his requests for special items were not specific enough:

Lime and hair for plastering, Putty for Puttying, paint for painting the Commanding General retorted is no more of an explanation than is wood for sawing, or a horse for riding. . . . These estimates indicate great haste and want of regard for the limited character of the appropriation. . . .

Grierson was informed, as the special items were disallowed.[28]

When the recommendations on building reached the headquarters of the Military Division of the Missouri, as they worked their way toward Washington, General P. H. Sheridan stamped his disapproval upon the whole business in no uncertain terms by returning them to the Adjutant General, saying:

The usefulness of Ft. Concho as a post will cease before long and as the troops there are now as comfortable as they could well be anywhere in Texas, I must decline to spend any more money upon that post, except what is necessary to keep the buildings in decent repair.[29]

Obviously however, hay sheds are not primarily for human comfort. Therefore the forage house was constructed early in 1876 to the "north of the blacksmith and wheelwright shop," and a large building was put up on the east line of the post opposite the parade ground as offices for the commander, post adjutant, quartermaster and commissary. Two extensions to the rear were turned over to the clerical force and the post library, and in 1878 an ordinance storehouse and a post schoolhouse were built.

For years the proud little fort, in the intervals when it did feel pride, worried just a little over the fact that it had no

28 *Letter Book*, I, Fort Concho, 476-477.

29 P. H. Sheridan to Adjt. Gen., December 2, 1875.

flagstaff. Two that had been cut in the Fredericksburg country were so long that freighters refused to haul them in fear of breaking their wagons down.

Upon June 18, 1874, Major Henry Douglass of the 11th Infantry, then in command, bestirred himself by writing to the Adjutant General at San Antonio to say that the flag ought to float high over the fort.

While stationed at Concho in 1871 [he wrote] I heard General Sherman remark, not in flattering terms, concerning the absence of a flagstaff at Fort Concho. The same is noted and commented upon by almost every stranger visiting the Post. . . . I desire to destroy the possibility of further comment.

Since carpenters were hard to find he wanted to hire "a mechanic near this Post who, formerly being a ship's carpenter, is familiar with the fashioning of masts and spars," and hence could conceivably shape a flagpole. Douglass pointed out that the matter was really pressing as "the stems of two (2) trees intended for a flag staff at this Post (after lying for a year or more at Fredericksburg, Texas) arrived here about eight or nine months ago." [30]

Thus Fort Concho stumbled toward completion. Considering the lack of plan, the frequent change of commands, and the obvious fumbling throughout the year, it is remarkable to record that a neat and well-ordered post finally took form. Then at last the flag was flown high above it to symbolize the efficient, the proud and mighty jurisdiction of the United States.

A decade later Fort Concho was deserted. Through the intervening years the substantial rock buildings, so painfully erected long ago, have served civilian needs. Its site had always been in private hands.

[30] Charles Nauwald to N. S. Constable, October 27, 1872, *Letters Received; Letter Book*, Fort Concho, 1874, p. 201.

[148]

CHAPTER IX

Futile Scouting After Indians

FORT CONCHO became the focal point of a broad design for the protection of the frontiers of Texas. Unlike most posts it was conceived with a double-barreled objective. At the apex of that restless, westward wedge of people pushing through the center of the state, it was calculated to protect the borders from hostile Indians still dominating half of Texas. Other forts to the south along the Rio Grande, with Fort Griffin and related outposts on the north, were intended to protect the extremities of the frontiers. But Fort Concho was thrown up as a shield across the very heart of Texas. The first objective was protection.

The other objects in its founding lay in the fact that it was the place of venture, of jumping-off, of departure, for almost all the southern travel that worked its slow and painful, its always dangerous and often tragic way—whether by horse, pack, herd, or rumbling wagon—toward the West Coast and the Northwestern Territories. Obviously, Fort Concho was designed as a way station on important trails.

The explanation of both factors was geographic. The Staked Plains blocked travel to the north for nearly three hundred miles. To the south, the ridges and canyons of the Edwards Plateau retarded the flow of travelers, while offering a retreat to Indians intent upon waylaying them. To the southwest, that rocky segment of Texas sliced off by the Rio Grande and the Pecos, with refuge in Mexico in case of hot pursuit, made the Lower Trail easy prey to the Apache and many other renegade Indians.

Thus the twin forces of hostile land and savage men stretched barriers across the two extremes of western Texas to funnel the straggling traffic of a vast world through this pleasant break in the bosom of Texas that is the valley of the Conchos.

Through this region moved trains of emigrants, anxious to escape the indignities heaped upon the South by carpet-baggers and the army of occupation, hopeful of something better on the California Coast. Across the Staked Plains to the west, by an eighty-mile drive without water, grim-faced cowmen were easing herds that died of thirst in bunches to follow the Goodnight Trail to markets in New Mexico, Colorado, and Wyoming. The El Paso Mail again came to life with Mexican mules scurrying like jackrabbits across gravel ridge and alkali flat, ahead of the heavy stages. The San Antonio-Chihuahua Trail bent in a vast loop to guide the ox-drawn *carretas* of Mexico up through Presidio del Norte, by way of Fort Davis and by a rutted course through the Concho country, with cargoes of corn, wheat and silver for San Antonio.

With the founding of the post came the army traffic: the weary march of infantry, the spirited canter of cavalry, the guarded payrolls of the posts, and the long wagon trains of forage and supply moving up the line of defense from San Antonio. In spite of the waste and sloth in construction, Fort Concho was bound to be an important place. It stuck right out as the point of advancing settlement that was gouging its unwelcome way into the heart of the red man's country. The Indians hated this invasion, for the Conchos were favorite range. The bounty of nature made it so. Plenty of water and grass, game, wood and protection, made this land a fine place in which to live or camp.

Naturally the Indians resented this brash intrusion that took and destroyed the life of their land, that hindered their easy invasion of Texas for the stealing of horses and cattle, and that stood in the way of their illicit traffic in captives and herds from Mexico. And being tough and warlike people, they fought with a savage tenacity to hold it.

Just as Fort Concho was being established, ill-advised federal policy was adding to the border troubles of Texas. When General Grant became president he was persuaded into letting the Quakers take over the administration of the Indian affairs of the country. It was not the first nor was it to be the last time in this country that maudlin sentiment was substituted for common sense. With the honest but no less mistaken zeal of some other messiahs, the Quakers applied themselves to the conversion of the Indians. But neither they nor the Lord cooperated. Federal indulgence was taken for weakness, as indeed it was. The Indians drew their rations, listened to the preachments with ill-concealed contempt, slipped out of the reservations, and continued to terrorize the Texas frontier.[1]

This policy ran slap-dab into the honest efforts of the leaders of the army in the reconstituted Department of Texas, where able officers were trying to hammer some semblance of respect for lives and property into the heads of the federal wards. The reluctance of the reformer to see through the aura that surrounds the ideal and recognize the stark realities of life stood in the way of a solution of the problem. The policy-makers forgot that love is lost on the field of battle. Savage conflict is met with force. Tolerance and sympathy cultivate mutual understanding and affection after the fight is won. For Texas and the frontier, this was war. In many respects the army was stymied. Hard-headed officers could fight and swear but could not convince the Quakers that the Indians were savages, nor dent the eternal self-righteousness of the reformer in power. Meanwhile the border wars went on.

[1] Dr. Richardson, in *The Comanche Barrier*, and Colonel W. S. Nye, in *Carbine and Lance*, Norman, 1937, give sound and vivid accounts of the results of the so-called Quaker Policy.

Actually, the Indians were few in numbers and were then more or less located in three widely scattered regions far from the Conchos. To the north, along the foot of the Plains and in Indian Territory, were the Comanches and Kiowas. Far to the west, in the mountains of New Mexico, were the Mescalero Apaches. To the southwest, in Mexico, were the scattered Seminoles and Lipans, and the once-friendly but now embittered Kickapoos. From these three sections in the light of the moon raiding parties passed in and out through the Concho country.

The work of the new post was well defined. For months the chief function of Fort Chadbourne and its outpost called Permanent Camp had been to patrol the cattle trail to Horsehead Crossing, and furnish guards for parties along the military road from Fort McKavett to Fort Griffin, and thence to newly-founded Fort Richardson at Jacksboro. During the summer of 1867, herds continued to drift across the open ridges from the east to welcome water, grass and shade near the Permanent Camp, while their dusty, weary and dangerously-armed owners rode over to the outpost to seek soldier escorts for the demoralizing drive across to the Pecos.

The first work of Lieutenant Peter M. Boehm, the New Yorker who founded the Permanent Camp, was to escort three herds to the Pecos in July, 1867. He found plenty of Indian sign and though he flushed no warriors, he returned to the Concho with the loss of three mules and two men—strayed and deserted. Other herds followed at intervals throughout the summer.[2]

Colonel E. B. Beaumont came from Chadbourne to relieve the detail on August 5, and scouted up and down the Middle Concho in hope of intercepting passing Indians, while an

[2] Boehm entered the service from New York in 1858, served throughout the Civil War, was cited for gallantry in taking up the colors and rallying Custer's retreating men in action at Dinwiddie during that conflict, and was later breveted captain for distinguished service on the Texas frontier. Heitman, *Historical Register and Dictionary of the United States Army*, I, 227. P. M. Boehm to Chas. A. Vernon, August 19, 1867.

escort under Sergeant John Rooney went west with a small herd. By long drives of from eighteen to twenty-three miles a day, the herd crossed the Plains from the head of the Middle Concho to the water on the Pecos in four days, along a trail already marked with dead cattle.

On August 25, 1867, while he was gone, two soldiers carrying the mail from Beaumont's camp ran into a party of Indians. When half a mile off they mistook the savages for Mexicans. One of the men, Private Carney, warned of possible danger, but the other, Hugh Collins, "rode persistently and deliberately toward the Indians . . . although he could have escaped with ease."

When at last within thirty yards of them, the soldiers opened fire with their carbines, their saddle-guns, and whirled their horses to run. Collins was shot in the back and killed, but Carney, on a good fast horse, rode into the Permanent Camp six miles away and reported the incident. Beaumont ordered eighteen men to stick some crackers in their pockets and led them toward the north to cut the Indian trail ten miles from camp. The badly cut up ground showed that the savages were riding hard.

Beaumont took the trail, sometimes riding at a lope, and again slowly, to trace the sign across the rocky ridges. His lookouts topped the hills to scan the country ahead for telltale specks on the horizon or streamers of dust in the air. He

pushed on across the North Concho. At last, upon "finding myself in the midst of a prairie covered with *Cat Claws and Mesquite*, with a view of fifteen miles and no sign of the Indians, I gave up the chase as hopeless . . ." he reported on his return.

Private Collins, the first army man to fall to the Indians on the Concho after the Civil War, was buried at the Saw Mill Camp, sixteen miles above the site of San Angelo on the North Concho.[3]

When the news reached Fort Chadbourne, Lieutenant Boehm hurried out on the 26th with orders for Beaumont to back-track to the Saw Mill Camp and there entrench. His detachment crossed the ridge between the rivers next day and found that the workmen at the sawmills had already built a strong corral for their horses. Beaumont had them clear the mesquite for two hundred yards about and throw up a small breastworks, where, he figured, forty men "well armed in the works, could bid defiance to a thousand Indians."

When he was relieved by Lieutenant George A. Thurston on September 1, he started at once for Chadbourne to report upon his various scouts. His men had searched without success for a reported spring on the Plains. They had seen two small dog towns upon the wide plateau — which were hopefully taken for signs of water, under the mistaken supposition that the dogs dug down to a supply. They speculated upon the digging of wells, and they reported on Indian rumors and signs.[4]

Permanent Camp was left at the sawmill location on the North Concho just west of present Carlsbad, forty-one miles from Chadbourne, until it was abandoned after the founding of Fort Concho. Meanwhile, in spite of the proximity of the soldiers, herds were being stampeded and drivers killed on

3 E. B. Beaumont to Charles A. Vernon, September 10, 1867. His grave was just west of Carlsbad on the Henry Hollman ranch. The floods have washed the stone away from the original site.

4 Beaumont, as cited; John H. Rooney to E. B. Beaumont, September 7, 1867; Benjamin Fabre to E. B. Beaumont, August 31, 1867, Fort Concho Files.

the Goodnight Trail in the relentless exposure of the open plains. J. D. Hoy from the San Saba country lost two herds to the Indians that year, while wagons were plundered and burned, men killed, and other herds stampeded and stolen.[5]

In December, 1867, word came to Camp Hatch that several men of the James Ketchum party had been massacred at the head of the river. Lieutenant Thurston rode to investigate. With twenty-two men he left the post near noon on the 19th, and reached the old Overland Station at the head of the river "at sunrise on the morning of December 21st," after a march of fifty-five miles. A half-mile southwest at the base of a hill, he found the bodies of four men in the bend of a gully where they had taken refuge in the fight. "A fifth body was found lying in the chaparral, some fifty paces out."

James Ketchum had driven a herd from the San Saba and sold it in New Mexico. He and his party had reached this point upon their return when the Indians jumped them. Thurston suspected from the sign—the moccasin tracks, an Indian stirrup and the many arrows about the place—that the attackers were Kickapoos. Ketchum's body "bore evident signs of torture, being charred and blackened with smoke." And yet strangely the men had not been scalped. Fragments of twenty-dollar bills from the sale of the herd were scattered over the battleground.

The soldiers dug a grave ten feet long and six wide. From left to right, they buried the Ketchum brothers, James and John, and their companion cowboys, William Truman and Thomas Darnell, in the order named, and placed a small stone at their heads. They turned over the fragments of money to a cowboy from San Saba. Then noticing the southwest course taken by the large attacking band, with its numerous horses, the soldiers swung northwest six miles to a bold spring which Thurston suspected to be the extreme head of the Middle Concho. They turned northeast to the head of the Kiowa, down it to the old Mail Road, and thence down the river to

5 Haley, *Charles Goodnight*, as cited, 148 ff.

Camp Hatch to report.[6] While 1866 had been relatively peaceful for those who were driving the trails west, there was blood on the moon in 1867 and plenty of violence along the Conchos. It was a portent of things to come. For several years war would be waged to the knife with the Indians from both the northern and southern borders of Texas.

The following March, horses were stolen from the post herd as it was grazing adjacent to the fort. A sergeant and five men were put on the trail which circled the post and crossed the North Concho between there and the "lower saw mill." Some miles to the north the troops came upon the raiders—two Indians who had stopped and were skinning a buffalo. They charged at once and succeeded in killing one Indian and capturing ten horses, which were brought back to the post.[7]

For some time Fort Chadbourne was maintained as an outpost for picket details from Fort Concho while a number of other picket posts were established. One company left Concho April 27, 1868, for a three months' station at the head of the Middle River "to guard the Overland Mail route . . ." and apparently the same month Camp Charlotte was located adjacent to the Mail road on the same stream, just below the mouth of Kiowa Creek, forty-two miles west of the fort and ten miles from the old mail station called Head of the Concho.

This camp was a genuine stockade fort with outside dimensions approximately 190 by 115 feet. Inside, with a twenty-foot run-around, was the company stable, 75 by 150 feet. Stockades for defense stuck out at the four corners. Entrance was by a large gate opening to the east toward Fort Concho. Directly in front and outside the stockade was the guardhouse, and still in front of it were the officers' quarters. Tents for the soldiers were pitched at regular intervals inside and against the stockade walls, with special tents for the waggoner, the blacksmith, the stable police and the forage man at the front

6 George A. Thurston to Captain G. G. Huntt, December 27, 1867, Fort Concho Files.

7 Charles Gale to G. A. Thurston, March 12, 1868, Fort Concho File.

[156]

end of the stable, with others for the cook, the tailor and the saddler at the back, adjacent to the mess hall. Major Rendelbrock was soon in charge.[8]

On June 24 he wrote that he was ready to push on west and "establish the picket post at the 'Central Station,' on the Staked Plain." Ben Ficklin, contractor of the new mail line that followed the old Upper Road by way of Concho, had furnished him water barrels. A little over a month later Rendelbrock wrote that the first garrison had been sent to what he then called Middle Station, which was to be maintained as "a picket dependency of Camp Charlotte." By mid-summer of 1869, picket posts were being kept there, at the Head of the Concho, the old stage stand of Johnson's Station near present Arden, and at Chadbourne and Lone Tree.

That fall, orders were issued for permanent guards at three of these — the Head of the Concho, Johnson's Station, and Chadbourne. Captain George H. Gamble, then commandant at Fort Concho, was ordered to erect a fortification, a stone building thirty feet long by ten wide, at the Head of the River. It was to consist of two rooms—one for the guard of an officer and four men, the other to serve as a stable for their horses.

The building at Johnson's station was to be on the same plan, "roofed with poles, covered with mud and should be so placed that the sentinel watching the stable could also watch that of the Mail Comp'y...." Two men of each regular picket should be Cavalry, and "the rest either Infantry soldiers or dismounted Cavalry." In addition to this slender garrison Captain Gamble was ordered at his discretion to keep a detachment of as many as twenty-five "well mounted men at the Head of the Concho," who should, except for a small detail, scout after Indians at least four days each week.[9]

By the following year, 1869, Camp Colorado, to the east—the old army post established on Jim Ned Creek in the fifties,

[8] *Post Returns*, Fort Concho, May 1868; see diagram received at Fort Concho, May 7, 1868.

[9] Edward Donovan to Geo. H. Gamble, October 13, 1868.

in Coleman County—was garrisoned with details from Concho. It was shared with the Reconstruction state police, or rangers, who operated under orders of the army in that peculiar and often unhappy mixture of military and civil authority that comes with occupation of a conquered country after war. Thus the defenses around Fort Concho were drawn.[10]

In spite of these outposts and the pursuit of vagrant bands, the Indian problem grew worse. But just at this juncture there marched upon the scene a real military man, Ranald S. Mackenzie, who more than anyone else was to assume the responsibility for settling the Indian problem of the Southwest.

He was of distinguished and rugged stock. His father, Alexander Slidell, had added the name Mackenzie out of high regard for his Scottish mother's brother. Another uncle, John Slidell, was the Confederate diplomatic agent. Alexander Slidell Mackenzie was the author of many popular books of travel and biography and a famous man of the sea. In 1841 he was in command of the steamer *Missouri* of the home squadron. In 1842 he was placed in charge of the brig *Somers* and sent on a long voyage with dispatches to the African squadron of the American fleet.

While on this mission he discovered plans for mutiny upon his own boat. With stern and courageous discipline he executed two of his men at sea, one of whom was Philip Spencer, son of the Secretary of War. Upon his return Mackenzie was bitterly assailed, but all attempts at court-martial and civil prosecution failed and "the verdict of posterity" sustained him. He died at forty-five years of age, September 13, 1848. One of his sons died gallantly in battle on the island of Formosa in 1867 and the other came to Texas.[11]

This young man, Ranald S. Mackenzie, was born in New York, July 27, 1840. He was a student at Williams College at

[10] *Post Returns,* Fort Concho, April, May and July, 1868; *Medical History,* as cited, 2-3; *Letters Received,* July 25, 1869; Joseph Rendelbrock to Wirt Davis, June 24, 1868, in *Letters Received;* and James M. Swisher to Alvan C. Gillem, September 26, 1870.

[11] *Dictionary of American Biography,* XII, 90-91.

[158]

fifteen, was appointed to the Military Academy, and notwith-standing some misgivings as to his ability came out of West Point with first honors in the class of 1862. He marched off to war at once and that summer received the first of his many wounds at Manassas. After recovery he was shifted to the Engineer Battalion, where he served with conspicuous bravery for two years before being appointed Colonel of the Second Connecticut Heavy Artillery.

From then on his star really began to shine. He helped defend the Capitol against Early's raiders, took part in the Shenandoah Campaign, and finally, as commander of a cavalry division, fought under General Sheridan until Lee surrendered at Appomatox. He was wounded several times, received seven brevets in less than three years, was a Brigadier General at twenty-six years of age, and, Grant said, was "the most prom-ising young officer in the Army." Upon the reorganization of the Regulars at the end of the Civil War he was given the Colonelcy of the 41st Infantry, a colored regiment, and came to the Texas frontier. He was transferred to the 24th Infantry and eventually to the command of the 4th Cavalry,[12] where he really felt at home.

When he reached Fort Concho he was a handsome, smooth-shaven man of thirty years, with strong but sensitive features and determined, mirthless eyes and mouth. There was no monkey-business whatever in his makeup. He was a rigid disciplinarian who took the Negroes of the 41st Infantry and whipped them into the semblance of soldiers.

. He properly conceived that he was in Texas to do a job and solve a problem. Duty called and comfort be damned! Within the grueling limits of his exceptional ability and his tenacious strength, he would not falter nor would he quit. He was imperious and impetuous in manner and design, irritable and irascible on the march, and gallant and invincible on the field. Except for his lack of humor, he seemed completely his father's son.

[12] Cullum, *Biographical Register of the Officers and Graduates of the United States Military Academy*, 842.

And yet as with others of like mould "he was modest, diffident and simple," and beneath his brusque mask, "chivalrous, warm, loyal, and . . . without reproach. . . ." He was the tough combination that Texas needed in the sixties and the seventies.

He came to Fort Concho in September, 1869, as Commander of the Sub-District of the Pecos, and made a formal inspection of the post. But formal inspections were no satisfaction to him. When Indians hit the borders of Texas, he believed in running them down and killing them, and fortunately, with Sheridan and Sherman immediately above him, he had the backing he needed.

On September 6, 1869, he sent an expedition of a hundred men from Fort Concho "in a generally northwest direction" to hunt Indians. They marched through the Colorado country to the Salt Fork of the Brazos, where they ran into "a large force of Indians . . . whom they fought for two days." By restrained reports received at Concho just a month later "the belief" was "that they were unable to make any impression on the savages." Therefore Mackenzie at once ordered out a larger expedition of 150 men under Captain John M. Bacon. a Kentuckian brought up from Fort Clark.

His expedition was made up of cavalry and infantry. It marched up the military road to Fort Griffin and was joined near there by twenty-five more troopers and a detail of Tonkawa scouts—a remnant of a friendly Texas tribe kept at Griffin for use in trailing. The combined force took the trail of a large band of Indians, and in a long fight on the 28th and 29th of October soundly trounced and demoralized them.

Bacon's men took most of the Indian horses early in the fight. The warriors afoot, encumbered with their families, fought at a disadvantage. Bacon burned their camp and supplies, captured eight squaws and children and a herd of horses, and estimated "75 to 100 Indians . . . killed and wounded." Lieutenant Albee brought one of the squaws back to Concho optimistically "with a view to her civilization and education." But Dr. Notson found her suffering with an old organic disease and was put to much bother as to how to get her back to the reservation.[13]

James Trainer, the post trader, carried the "cheering news" of the Indian defeat to the settlements. The *San Antonio Star* exulted over the battle, the "most effective chastisement that has been inflicted on these incurable robbers," and passed the usual Texas judgment upon the mistaken Quaker policy that was running head-on into the efforts of the army. Noting that an estimated four hundred warriors had taken part in the fight, and that the captured squaws said that "as many more had, a few days before, left for Fort Cobb [in Indian Territory] to draw their annuities and presents from the National Government," the *Star* ironically concluded:

Today our Indian system is a pleasant thing to contemplate; the Administration fights the savages with one hand, and supplies them with food, guns and quakers *ad libitum*, with the other. Above all things commend us to philanthropy of the philandering, full blown, chuckle headed sort.[14]

Colonel William R. Shafter, another man of considerable note on the borders of Texas, took command at Concho in January, 1870. Mackenzie, with his first successful venture against the Comanches chalked up to his credit, passed on a hurried inspection of the frontier soon afterward. Shafter took a vigorous hand in the building of the post. He too was distinguished in the Civil War, and while never spectacular is noted for his determined marches after Indians throughout west Texas.

Heavy of build, walrus-mustached, usually mild of manner and disposition and deliberate in maneuver and design, he was in many ways the antithesis of the flashing Mackenzie. Years later, in sound command of the American forces taking Cuba in the Spanish-American War, his careful, humane and successful conduct of that campaign brought him bitter and unjust appraisal by the American public—an injustice fostered

[13] *Post Return*, Fort Concho, November, 1869; *Medical History*, as cited, vol. 401, pp. 138, 141, 145.

[14] Reprinted in the *Dallas Herald*, December 4, 1869.

by Richard Harding Davis and the yellow press of that period, to which Shafter never bowed nor pandered. He was an old-fashioned fellow of proper dignity who thought his first duty was to win a war instead of catering to the public.

He was a sturdy and able native of Michigan. Without benefit of West Point training, he entered the Northern army at twenty-six years of age. He fought with distinction from Yorktown to Fair Oaks, where he was wounded but refused to leave the field of battle—a service for which he was eventually awarded the Congressional Medal of Honor. He steadily rose in the ranks until in 1865 he too was breveted Brigadier General. Shortly after the War he was sent to Texas and assigned to the 41st and then the 24th Infantry. While upon a scout in this section he won the nickname of Pecos Bill.[15]

He settled down seriously to the job of building the post at Concho and made considerable progress at this unhappy task, though his period of command was marked with discord among the officers.[16] When he took over, it was noted that in spite of Mackenzie's successful campaign of the fall before, the Indians had been "more than usually troublesome during the last two months and unusually daring." In January, 1870, they had, with contempt and impunity, stolen and escaped with eighteen mules from the Quartermaster's Corral in the heart of the post.

In February Dr. Notson wrote that "Signs of small parties of two to five are daily reported in various directions around the Post. On the 18th a citizen was killed and scalped within a quarter of a mile of the old Post Limits. Five arrow heads were found in his body, and one impaled in a vertebrae was preserved for the Army Medical Museum." [17] Thus science could be served when life could not. But the system, rather than Shafter, was primarily to blame. The Indians fought a

15 Heitman, as cited, I, 876; *Post Return*, Fort Concho, January, 1870; and, for a sketch and the defamation of his character at the hands of the press, Stewart H. Holbrook's *Lost Men of American History*, New York, 1946, pp. 283 ff.

16 *Post Return*, Fort Concho, January, 1870; *Medical History*, as cited, 169, 173.

17 *Medical History*, as cited, 157.

swift guerilla warfare at which soldiers in permanent camp were no ready match. And yet in the field and on the trail, Shafter personified that dogged nature associated with the Saxon race.

In the perpetual rotation of command, he was shifted to nearby McKavett in June, 1870, and Major John P. Hatch took over at Concho. Two days later Company F of the 24th Infantry left for station at Fort Davis, where, during the heat of the following summer, Shafter, then in command there, made his long and determined scout into the White Sand Hills to let the Indians know that this hitherto inviolable refuge could be penetrated by the army.

While at that mile-high post in the Davis Mountains, on the Sunday morning of June 18, 1871, Shafter got word that the Indians had stolen fifty-one mules and three horses and stranded Captain Crandel's detail at Barella Springs, on the trail to Fort Stockton. Shafter at once sent mules to replace the teams, and taking a lieutenant, a doctor and "all the Cavalry that could be mounted," just twenty-four "in all," set out for Barella.

On the 20th his force was swelled to six officers, seventy-five enlisted men, and two guides by the arrival of a detail from Fort Stockton. He followed the trail due north twenty-three miles to Toyah Creek and twenty-six more northeast to make a dry camp on the night of June 22nd. Five miles farther he reached and forded the Pecos and camped at an Indian crossing. Next day he marched north for thirty miles into the Monahans country and late in the evening came to permanent water in the White Sands, where the Indians had camped three days before. From here on his trail was a crooked and devious one. It shifted and turned and wove in and out of the Sand Hills in a puzzling maze of criss-crossed tracks, but Shafter kept after the elusive enemy day after day.

At first he marched northwest and made a dry camp. On the 26th he continued three miles farther to strike a large

trail running east and west through the Sands, with fresh
tracks going in both directions. Those of shod mules indicated
his Indians were headed east and Shafter took after them. As
he left the Sands he became convinced, as the trail still pointed
east, that there was no water to be had nearer than the Mustang Springs far out on the Staked Plains. So he turned back
southwest and after a day's march of an estimated seventy
miles reached the first holes close to his original camp, near
the southern edge of the heavy Monahans Sands. He spent
next day grazing and resting his horses.

To mitigate the effects of heat on men and mounts, he did
not leave until sundown the following day. All night they
rode to the north and west, and until noon on the 29th when
again they came to the large trail running east and west.
Here Shafter found that the mules had again just passed over
it, but this time headed west. At this point on the trail he was
apparently northwest of where Kermit stands, in present
Winkler County, Texas.

With dogged tenacity he turned his drawn horses upon it
and skirting the heavy sands to his left, followed the trail as
it turned back south toward the site of Kermit. On the west
side of the White Sands he found another large camp that
had been deserted, apparently by some 200 Indians just two
days before. Water was to be had in the Sand Hills a short
way east just below the corner of New Mexico. Though his
men had already covered thirty-five miles on horses almost
pulled to death by the heavy going, he took the saddle again
at eleven that night and followed what was a plain and much
used trail to the northwest, toward the Pecos. At daylight he
discovered that the elusive mule tracks were gone.

Still he was on a fresh trail and if he could not catch his
own Indians he would take any he could find. He rested awhile
and pushed on, generally a little north of west, until he spied
an Indian camp about four in the afternoon. No impetuous
Custer-like charge for Shafter! He stopped and looked the
situation over.

[164]

After a careful survey of the ground [he reported] I observed a few small Huts near the herd of horses and after starting Lieut Morgan with fifteen men for the herd I took the balance of the command and charged the Huts As we had come out in plain sight before going fifty yards we were of course at once discovered, and the Indians only three in number each mounted on a pony and escaped.

After chasing them about four miles through the scattered brush, the soldiers were so far outdistanced that they reined in their panting horses and slowly jogged back to the Indian camp. There they found that the other troops had rounded up the Indians' ponies, and had jumped a number of Indians at a camp about a mile to the left. These had scattered into the sand dunes, afoot, shooting as they went.

After following them for a short distance all the men but two privates and the Guide returned to the Indian Camp. The result was that no one was hurt as there ought to have been [Shafter observed]. The captures were ten horses and five mules five lodges about a six months supply of Dried Beef for the number of Indians seen, 25 or 30 Buffalo robes all their saddles about 75 bars of lead several flasks of powder and etc. I selected a few of the best robes and burned the balance including Lodges and poles.

Shafter turned back on the old Indian trail, which continued a little south of west toward the Pecos. On July 1, 1871, he again took up the chase, and while he and an orderly were about two miles in advance of the column they suddenly came upon a very old squaw on a fine mule, trying to herd a couple of broken-down horses along. As soon as the column arrived they turned her over to the soldiers. Shafter took a lieutenant and twenty men and struck a high trot down the fresh trail in hope of at least catching the raiders. Night came and they stopped at a small stream of remarkably clear but exceptionally bitter, gyppy water, which some of the horses refused to drink in spite of the long hot ride. At nine o'clock the weary command came up and made a thirsty, miserable camp.

Shafter's scouts had reported that they were now within four miles of the Pecos, and they marched before sunup to quench their thirst at that devious and brackish stream. Here

[165]

they found from the sign that the large party, probably two hundred in all, had been warned by those that had escaped the charge in the Sand Hills, and had turned up the Pecos the day before.

Shafter took stock of his own condition. For fourteen days he had been marching continuously on the same horses, some of which were already broken down. The Indians were fully posted as to his movements. He was almost out of rations. He decided to turn back to Fort Davis.

He crossed on the Indian trail by the best ford he had found on the Pecos. Instead of the sharp-cut banks characteristic of the stream, the approaches to the river here were gradual and easy, the bottom was of solid rock, and the water only eighteen inches deep. The command went into camp and rested that day. On the third of July he took up the march down the barren river, across the gray and shimmering alkali flats, up through the palisaded fastnesses of the Davis Mountains, and into the post at the head of the Limpia, which he reached on July ninth.

For the first time since the war the army had reached out its slow but long arm into a region where the Indians were hitherto completely unmolested—into the heart of the Sand Hills, to prove to the savages that at last they could find no settled refuge there. Shafter had found water from near present Monahans almost to the New Mexico line, filtering through the clean white sand to be caught and held in pools by the underlying hard-pan in the deepest depressions between the hills. Large willow trees grew at the edge of the northern holes and though the highest hills were completely barren and slowly shifting in the eternal winds, there was an abundance of grass in the "valleys" or flats a short way to the east and west on either side. Armed with this knowledge Shafter concluded that the Sands, instead of presenting an impassable barrier, could be crossed at any point.

His guide learned from the captured Apache squaw that the band of fifteen Comanches that had stolen the army mules

at Barella Spring had pulled out for Red River. He learned
that two tribes of Apaches and one of Lipans had just ended
a period of enmity with the Comanches by meeting at a peace
council in the Sands and burying the hatchet. The bar lead,
with a St. Louis smelter print, and the powder and calico
Shafter had captured at the camp, had, the squaw said, but
recently been acquired from New Mexican Indian traders,
the *Comancheros,* whom they had met on the head of the
Colorado a few weeks before.

The *Comancheros* had returned with their pack-mules to
New Mexico. The Apaches, after the Sand Hill council with
the Comanches, had gone back "to make peace with the
government at Fort Stanton," at the Agency, and the Comanches had quirted their mules toward Red River. For what
appeared to be the most barren, inhospitable desert region in
West Texas, the White Sand Hills had been a busy place.[18]

This extended but futile punitive expedition upon which no
one was hurt, though "there ought to have been," did yield
much information about a long-shunned region. Likewise, it
gave Texas some knowledge of the nature of the short-legged
Shafter himself, who would again return to scour the South
Plains several years later in a clean-up action that was to
fasten his name upon one of its lakes, though who he was and
what he was doing there has, for the natives, long been lost
in history. It is an unfortunate, ironic fate that too often befalls
the modest man of honor.

While there is a physical appropriateness in calling one of
those useless bodies of water shimmering in the mirages of
the Staked Plains by the name of Shafter Lake, the man who
won the Spanish-American War in Cuba with a minimum loss
of life deserves a more striking monument in this land of his
seasoning than an alkali hole in the ground. Immortality still
remains a mysterious thing.

[18] W. R. Shafter to H. Clay Wood, July 15, 1871, Fort Davis Files.

CHAPTER X

Ⲙⲁⲥⲕⲉⲛⲍⲓⲉ ⲧⲟ ⲧⲏⲉ Ⲫⲓⲉⲗⲇ

THE BIRTH of "the seventies" promised much in danger and change for the frontier of Texas. The region was faced by hostile forces on three sides—renegade Mexicans and Indians to the south of the Rio Grande, the warlike Plains tribes to the north of Red River, and Apaches on the west. '

The muddleheaded Quaker policy instituted by President Grant, on one hand, and the injustice visited upon the Kickapoos, on the other, added fire to the troubles springing from the natural hatred of the Indians for the Texans. General W. B. Hazen, who had been attempting to settle the Indians on reservations in the Territory, had been succeeded by Quaker Lawrie Tatum, July 1, 1869. Tatum, by his own admission, "knew little of the duties and responsibilities devolving upon an Indian agent. But after considering the subject as best I could in the fear of God," he said, "and wishing to be obedient to Him, it seemed right to accept the appointment." [1]

Strange inequities sometimes flow from the zealot's honest but misguided conviction of his Christian duty. It would have been better for Texas had Tatum feared the Lord even less and his own ignorance and ineptitude considerably more. The Quaker policy of appeasement cost many lives and the

[1] Requoted from R. N. Richardson, *The Comanche Barrier*, 326.

destruction of much property. The Mexican border troubles were actually a continual guerilla warfare, and the Apaches were always a dangerous nuisance. Texans, bucolic at their best, but now seething under Reconstruction, raised an awful ruckus. Even the *San Antonio Express,* mouthpiece of the radical federal forces, joined in the clamor for frontier protection early in 1870.[2]

As a sort of an offset to the troubles caused by Federal policy was the rise of capable military men on the frontier of Texas. Standing head and shoulders above them was Mackenzie. There was nothing soft or sentimental in his makeup. His physical fiber was tough and his moral nature was stern. He simply knew that when depredations were committed upon the settlers he was charged with protecting, the guilty should be run down and made to pay the penalty. His expeditions to the upper reaches of the Brazos in 1869 were but a mild sample of his tactics and his wrath.

The year 1870 found the Indians, encouraged by the laxity of the Quakers, on the warpath worse than before. They drew their rations and raided out of Fort Sill while Colonel Benjamin H. Grierson, commander there, was doing little to punish or restrain them.[3] Among his insolent and unwilling wards were leaders tough in their own right, and now well remembered in Indian history: The Kiowa chieftains Big Tree, White Horse, Kicking Bird, Satank, Lone Wolf and Satanta.

As Grierson concentrated on building Fort Sill, Big Tree conceived the idea and almost succeeded in a plan to steal all his horses. White Horse left the reservation to kill and scalp, and take some captives in Texas, while Kicking Bird, smarting under an accusation of cowardice, crossed Red River with a hundred warriors. Near the site of Seymour he roundly whipped Captain C. B. McClellan's command, scouting out

[2] For a calendar of some of the depredations for that year, see West Texas Historical Association *Year Book,* II, pp. 18-30, as well as the *Express,* 1870.

[3] Richardson, as cited, 336-338; W. S. Nye, *Carbine and Lance,* notes that Grierson "was an enthusiastic supporter of the Peace Policy" of the Quakers, and, as commander at Fort Sill, "paid little attention" to the Indians, pp. 99 ff.

of Fort Richardson. Old Satank returned to Texas to recover the bones of his son who had been killed on a raid the year before and to carry them with him as he wandered about brooding vengeance. These red men were real warriors whose trails were marked with blood.

The frontier was seething with resentment while Grierson deployed his men in ineffectual patrol along Red River and ranted in rebuttal against the Texans who were accusing his Indians of the raids. Meanwhile he was being outsmarted by Lone Wolf and the insolent Satanta in council at the agency.[4] With the backing of his superiors, Mackenzie was pushed to the front to cope with the problem in Texas. He grimly set himself to the task.

During his years in Texas he had whipped the Fourth Cavalry into an efficient force. Despite the fact that he kept his own counsel to the point of secretiveness and was often irritable and unapproachable in the field, he had capable officers who usually served him loyally. Captain R. G. Carter, who had just brought his young wife to Fort Concho, appreciated and understood him well. Carter pointed out that under Mackenzie there was no insubordination: no mess-hall strikes for "thicker soup," and no mutiny at post or in the field. On the other hand, he said, there were no retaliatory or cruel measures to impress the troops with the meaning of authority.

"The discipline in the Fourth Cavalry was perfect," he continued, "because it was *constant* and *unremitting* and based upon absolute fairness and justice. The men were marvelously obedient to *such* discipline and training, punishments were generally administered in the Company under the strictest supervision and control of the most experienced officers and non-commissioned officers of the Civil and Indian Wars. Under these conditions, the regiment was always ready for a 'fight or frolic'."[5]

Mackenzie again reached Fort Concho from service to the

4 Nye, as cited, 108-116.

5 R. G. Carter, *On the Border with Mackenzie*, Washington, D. C., 1935, p. 468.

south, February 25, 1871, and business picked up at once. A month later to a day, the headquarters and five companies of the Fourth Cavalry were ordered to Fort Richardson to be nearer the Indian country. Two days later they were ready to march. Obviously this was to be no routine scout, but a major expedition moving with dispatch.

For days there had been a bustle about the post. On the morning of March 27, 1871, the air of nervous expectancy culminated with orders for the column to mount. Excited children ran about the galleries of the officers' quarters and anxious wives were on hand to wave their husbands goodby. Then the usual precision and decorum of the army on the parade ground was completely disrupted by the pack animals.

Mexican mules, as well as their more sedate cousins from Missouri, when fresh and full of vinegar seem to be compounded principally of contrary notions. As the move to start was made, some broke loose and bucked all over the reservation. Nervousness with mules, as panic with people, spreads as if by instantaneous contagion. The handy *aparejos* or pack bags were not then in use, and supplies of coffee, flour, bacon and salt were pitched and kicked loose from the old saw-buck pack saddles in every direction. It was enough to make a trooper swear.

The air was heavy with dust and blue with profanity as hostlers and packers herded the outlaws back to the corrals, caught them again, led them back to the parade ground and recovered and repacked the loads. Here and there a soldier, wobbly from the previous night's spirits that would have been shunned by saints as well as angels, though acquired across the river at the new village of Saint Angela, was boosted to an unsteady seat on a docile horse, while elsewhere steadier soldiers joined forces and severely disciplined some fractious mount.

But at last [as Captain Robert G. Carter recorded], the hearty cheers of the assembled garrison were given and the column splashed through the clear waters of the sparkling stream and stretched out on its long

[171]

march. 'Mt. Margaret,' named after the most accomplished, loving and devoted wife of one of our favorite Captains, E. B. Beaumont, was passed—the Colorado was reached and forded in the midst of a cold, driving rain storm, which made our fires of drift cottonwood at that night's camp more acceptable than usual, and the glowing embers of the mesquite, heaped up in the mess kettles, which we used as stoves, more necessary for those *better halves* who—notwithstanding the many frowns and incredulous smiles of our gallant, yet *unconverted,* bachelor Colonel—had chosen to share the fortunes of their bold trooper husbands upon the Indian border.[6]

Some of the wives of the officers were going with the command to Fort Richardson to be nearer their husbands in the field. Fortunately it was early in the march, for the "bachelor Colonel" Mackenzie had little patience with sentiment, or excess baggage in any form, when it came to business. As his campaign took shape, and the grueling days in the saddle and his intense preoccupation with his design engaged all his physical and mental faculties, he became taciturn and irascible. There would be none of this in the field. But as there was little chance of action along the military road he could afford to mix an occasional incredulous smile with his many frowns.

The column pitched camp next at old Fort Chadbourne, where a prairie dog town was spreading across the abandoned parade ground. Buffalo had been seen in bunches along the line of march. They grazed in hundreds near the bivouac, and lumbered across the old parade ground. March 31st the troops cautiously made their way through Mountain Pass, scene of Indian surprise attacks, and in coming out into the prairie country to the north found its green expanse covered with buffalo. Cumulus clouds of a West Texas spring billowed about a dome of heavenly blue, mothering dark shadows that drifted lazily across the grass in keeping with their leisurely movements.

The leaders of the column looked over the pack train, back toward the pass, to see the canvas-covered wagons moving in sinuous tandem. It was an unforgettable sight. Down wind,

6 Carter, as cited, 59.

the scattered buffalo herds, catching scent of the column, "commenced to raise their heads in alarm. The old leaders of each herd seemed to give them a warning, and immediately the whole mass was set in motion."

Captain Carter claimed that buffalo, like antelope, "when alarmed, would always cross the trail of his supposed enemy and get to leeward, but they would *never pass to the rear of that enemy, or of a moving body....*" Their action now tended to substantiate this interesting observation.

Crowding with a reckless and resistless brute energy [Carter continued], each herd, therefore, with its chosen leader, gradually worked along towards the head of our leading company, until at length it brought them in front of the entire command. Our march was blocked, and we were compelled to halt to bide the time of our beast companions.

And so the cavalry sat in their saddles; the pack mules, now quite conservative after several days beneath their loads, merely lifted inquisitive ears in the direction of the moving mass; and the heavy iron-tired wagons ground to a halt. The camping place selected for the night was still far away and Mackenzie, impatient with even nature's enforced delays, grabbed a carbine from an enlisted man, stepped off his horse and blazed away in an attempt to break the strange blockade.

The lumbering rhythm of the vast herd was broken as it swerved from its course and stampeded alongside, crowding dangerously near the column. Terrified horses lost their heads and became unmanageable, while in the general excitement of having such monstrous game so close, the cavalry, forgetful of orders, opened a fusillade at the animals. Several buffalo were killed and others were wounded.

Every frontier fort had its generous assortment of stray dogs. Some were adopted by soldiers for company and others rustled their living from the post refuse. When a column took the field, some were always along. In their ever-loyal way, they paid little attention to the military order that such pets be left behind. These now added to the din by baying the passing herd and charging a wounded bull.

[173]

Among the dogs was "a large, white English bull-dog, weighing about seventy-five pounds, belonging to the regimental band." This powerful dog had been trained in the slaughter corral at Fort Concho to pull down beeves by seizing them in the nose. He was known as King, and when the buffalo loped by, King decided it was time for him to take hold. He caught the bull in the nose and held on with all the tenacity for which his breed is famous. The buffalo tossed his head in mad gyrations while the dog, still swinging on, cut figures in the air.

The struggle dragged on until the white dog was covered with blood—until, at last, Mackenzie ordered the buffalo shot. Only then did the dog let go. He had achieved such unusual renown that when orders were issued for dogs—"an accumulative nuisance at all frontier posts"—to be exterminated annually thereafter, King "was exempted by a *special paragraph* for his 'gallant conduct.'"

Past the buffalo, the command marched on by old Fort Phantom Hill on the Clear Fork of the Brazos, where "some twenty chimneys, outlined weird and ghost-like against the sky," suggested phantoms, though there was no hill. The column turned east. On April 4, 1871, it reached Griffin, where the friendly Tonkawa Indian scouts, camped on the Flat between the fort and the Clear Fork, were objects of interest. Thus the march continued by the regular military road for a total of 220 miles, past abandoned Belknap into Fort Richardson. There the bachelor officers gallantly vacated their flea-infested rooms for the ladies in the column, and from his new headquarters Mackenzie began to map his first great campaign against the Plains Indians. It was high time for action.[7]

Less than two days' march out of Fort Richardson the cavalry had passed some fresh mounds, above which the crosses bore the simple legend: "Three negroes killed by Indians Jan. 3, 1871." This was evidently the burial place of Brit Johnson,

7 Carter, as cited, 62-68; for the itinerary, see A.G.O. file, No. 2,236,858, *War Records*, National Archives.

one of the bravest and most noted Negroes in the history of Texas, whose family had been captured in the Elm Creek raid of 1864. For years, single-handedly he had followed the vagrant bands that held his wife and children captive and eventually recovered them all. While he and other Negroes were freighting from Weatherford to Fort Griffin, a band of Kiowas fell upon them. Brit killed his horses for breastworks and fought like a cornered bear. But the odds were too great. A detail sent from Richardson buried the bodies and took after the Indians, but its commander was wounded and the men retreated to the post[8]

This was merely a sample of what was coming. Early that year the Indians were leaving the reservation at Fort Sill and striking south through the frontier settlements. The Quakers were not yet disillusioned, and Colonel Grierson, as is often the case with failures, was laying the blame on the other fellow— this time the fighting Texan across Red River. Resentment was seething there. Mass meetings were being held in border towns, protests were being fired into Austin, and vitriolic petitions aimed at Washington, where the question was being asked: "Who is to be believed? Grierson and the Quakers or the hell-raising Texas rebels?" Washington naturally discounted the Texans.

General W. T. Sherman, four-star commander of the army, decided he would tour the frontier and find out for himself. In company with a member of his staff and the Inspector General, veteran R. B. Marcy, he made his way to Texas. After sumptuous entertainment by General J. J. Reynolds at San Antonio, they headed north by way of Forts Mason and McKavett, and reached Concho in May. They pitched camp in the post limits near the fork of the rivers, visited casually with the officers at Hatch's headquarters, and perfunctorily looked over the hospital, the completion of which was giving Dr. Notson so much concern. Then, as Notson recorded with

[8] For Brit Johnson, see Haley, *Charles Goodnight,* as cited, 117; Nye, *Carbine and Lance,* 123, says there were four Negroes killed.

[175]

acid judgment in the *Fort Concho Medical History*, they called on all the ladies of the garrison—"a politic if not a sanitary action."⁹

From here they followed the military road taken by Mackenzie's column. As they passed through the Belknap country Marcy noted in his journal that many ranches were devastated, and made the astonishing observation that "this rich and beautiful section does not contain today so many white people as it did when I visited it eighteen years ago, and if the Indian marauders are not punished, the whole country seems to be in a fair way of becoming totally depopulated."¹⁰

General Sherman, however, was still skeptical of the Texas reports and far from convinced. As the party made its way across Salt Creek Prairie in Young County it precariously escaped annihilation at the hands of a hundred Kiowa warriors who watched from a nearby hill and were held in check only by their medicine man. After making medicine and invoking his incantations the night before, he had told the Indians that two parties would pass along the Richardson-Griffin Trail on the morrow, but that the first should go unmolested as the second would be the richer prize. And so Sherman probably owed his life, not to his own military genius, but to the uncanny suggestion of an Indian medicine man.

Later that day, May 18, 1871, the ten-wagon train of Henry Warren, a government freighter, did appear and crawl into the open flat to the credit of Indian medicine. Satanta, chief of the waiting party, tooted a bugle he carried to announce the charge. As the warriors raced their ponies into the open, the teamsters hurriedly corralled their wagons, but not in time to be set for the sweeping attack. Seven of them were killed. One was chained to a wagon wheel and burned. The wagons were looted, forty-one mules stolen and the balance killed, while three drivers raced for the shelter of the timber on foot.

9 *Medical History*, as cited, vol. 401, p. 217.

10 Requoted from Carl Coke Rister, *Border Command, General Phil Sheridan in the West*, Norman, 1944, p. 174.

Late that night a wounded teamster limped into Fort Richardson and next morning told Sherman the wild story of the massacre. The General at once dashed off his orders. Mackenzie should take the available cavalry, investigate the report and, if found true, spare neither horses nor men in running down the raiders. The Fourth Cavalry hit their saddles and left in a blinding rain.[11]

When they got to the site they found the bloated, ripped, gutted and horribly mutilated bodies of the seven teamsters. All had been scalped. Some of them had been beheaded; some had their brains scooped out and others had their privates cut off and stuck in their mouths. The body of the chained and burned victim was drawn up in the final contortions of his terrible agony. There could be little improvement on the finished nature of Indian torture.

Mackenzie took what little of their trail was left by the heavy rains, which pointed in the general direction of the Wichitas to the north. For days he hunted the raiders in the broken country, and then turned north across Red River and marched toward Sill.[12]

Meanwhile Sherman had made a hurried and good-humored inspection of Fort Richardson and headed for the same place. Dispatches announced his coming, and on May 23, watchers from Signal Hill heliographed his approach upon sighting his dust. Grierson and a guard of honor met him, made him comfortable in the Colonel's quarters, and then trailed him as he hurried away to see Lawrie Tatum, the Quaker agent. Sherman wanted to know if any party of Indians was missing from the reservation. Here was his personal chance to investigate the truth of the Texan charges that they—Uncle Sam's peaceful wards—were guilty of the raids.

He tersely told the story of the Salt Creek Massacre to

11 Rister, in *Border Command*, 172-180, traces Sherman's movements excellently, while Nye, in *Carbine and Lance*, 124-132, gives a splendid and vivid account of the Indian attack.

12 Carter, as cited, 81-82, 90: J. J. Reynolds, "Annual Report," September 30, 1871, A.G.O., *Letters Sent*, Dept. of Texas, National Archives.

[177]

Tatum. That horrified Quaker thought Satanta and others had been away, but said he would find out for sure when rations were issued a few days hence. By that time the war party had returned and, when inquiry was made, Satanta boastfully and contemptuously told the whole story. Tatum, an honest idealist now thoroughly disillusioned, advised Sherman of their guilt and asked for their arrest. This was effected at the fort after a stirring council between them and Sherman. Sherman left Satanta, Satank and Big Tree in chains for Colonel Mackenzie to take to Jacksboro for civil trial, while he hurried on to Fort Gibson.[13] Mackenzie, irritated because he had failed to catch the warriors, got into Sill on June 4.

He placed the manacled chiefs in wagons and started down the trail toward Richardson, while Satank—of the highest order of the Kiowa tribe—chanted his death song from his perch on a sack of grain as the train pulled out. On the way he slipped his manacles by tearing flesh and hide from his hands and drew a hidden knife and attacked his guards, who shot him down. Mackenzie delivered the other two leaders to the sheriff at Jacksboro, where, in a highly dramatic and significant departure from past treatment of Indian renegades, they

[13] Rister and Nye have covered this subject thoroughly; the latter in colorful detail both from the Indian and white points of view in his story of Fort Sill, *Carbine and Lance.*

[178]

were brought to trial for their violent murder of the Texans.

They were at once sentenced to death. As usual, the maudlin and sentimental side of American life, far removed from the seat of trouble, raised its strident voice in protest. But Sherman was adamant. The Governor of Texas, however, commuted the sentences to life imprisonment, and the two proud warriors were thrown into the penitentiary at Huntsville to the consternation of their tribe.

Then Mackenzie, after brooding over the Indian problem, wrote Sherman that the garrisons of the Texas posts should be organized at once for a campaign against the marauders. He had definitely determined that they were coming from two points: from the reservations and from the Staked Plains of Texas, mainly from the headwaters of the Brazos. The only way that Tatum could "elevate these people, the Kiowas and Commanches," he wrote, was by their being "dismounted, disarmed and made to raise corn. . . ." Perhaps in implied disdain for Grierson and his slack policy at Fort Sill, he continued:

The Kiowas and Commanches are entirely beyond our control and have been for a long time. Mr. Tatum understands the matter. He is anxious that the Kiowas and Comanches now out of control be brought under. This can be accomplished only by the Army. The matter is now within a very small compass. Either these Indians must be punished or they must be allowed to murder and rob at their own discretion.[14]

Obviously action was necessary, for after the arrest of their chiefs the Kiowas had pulled away from the reservation. Mackenzie's plan was approved by Sherman. Grierson set up a supply camp on Otter Creek, in the Territory, while Mackenzie turned his commissary problem over to one of the great men in that indispensable field—Henry W. Lawton. In view of the long distances at which they were to operate, the difficult terrain, and the problems of sustaining men and horses, this was a fortunate choice.

Lawton, a man of action, was six-feet-four in height. His wiry hair was brushed stiffly and sharply back from above his

[14] Requoted from Nye, as cited, 148.

dark brown eyes, while his face was adorned with long, droop-
ing whiskers and mustache. Quick of speech, restless, tireless
and full of fire, he had no patience with theoretical palaver in
the field and little with red tape anywhere. The more proper
West Pointers considered him a "roughneck wagon master,"
but while others were debating the possible and best ways to
proceed, he impatiently brushed them aside and shouted:

"Take hold here men, *with me*, and we'll soon have this
d——d thing straightened out." [15]

All troops of the Fourth Cavalry were ordered up to Richardson from the border. On July 16-17, 1871, two troops came
in from Concho, another from McKavett, and two more from
the Rio Grande. The Cross Timber post at Jacksboro was
already overcrowded with officers and men preparing for the
campaign, and these new arrivals camped out on the road
toward Weatherford.

Late in July two companies were put on the move for the
Little Wichita, and a few days later another was ordered to
pitch camp on the West Fork of the Trinity and await the
arrival of Mackenzie and the headquarters. That night the
Colonel and his staff rode away from the post to join them.
"The low fires of his bivouac glowed in the shadows of the
pecans and post-oaks surrounding and skirting his camp" as
Mackenzie, Captain Carter, Lieutenant Boehm and his Tonkawa Indian scouts from Griffin rode slowly through the
sleeping soldiers without disturbing them. They too rolled up
in their blankets and "with feet to the blaze, and without tents,
were soon fast asleep with the tired troopers," the Colonel
right among them. The campaign was peacefully underway. [16]

Mackenzie marched to join the balance of the command at
Gilbert's Creek, continued across Red River, and to Grierson's
supply camp on Otter Creek early in August, 1871. Here the
two commanders briefly conferred, agreed as to their respective courses in the campaign, and set out in pursuit of Kicking

[15] Carter, as cited, 106-107.
[16] The same, 114.

[180]

Bird's Kiowas. Mackenzie turned to the west and crossed the North Fork of Red River, just a few miles from the camp.

As the column moved up the North Fork on August 17, with its guides scouring the country ahead for Indian sign, a courier reached Mackenzie with dispatches. The Colonel read the messages in silence, but his officers observed that he was greatly disturbed and agitated. He set his lips and said nothing but at once the expedition seemed to lose its drive and purpose. Captain Carter recalled that "all our movements from then on seemed strange in view of the real object of our expedition."

At length Mackenzie's officers suspected that he had been ordered to locate Kicking Bird "but make no offensive attack on him. . . ." And so more or less aimlessly they moved into the gypsum breaks of the eastern Panhandle. As their horses wore out in the roughs and the men were sickened from diarrhea brought on by the gyppy water, they simply floundered about.

The puzzled staff could not fathom the mystery, but years later Captain Carter got the story direct from General S. M. Woodward, who was then Grierson's adjutant. Grierson was in accord with the "peace policy" and had the confidence of the "Indian ring"—those promoting the unfortunate Quaker views in Washington. This group bitterly opposed any punitive measure against the tribes, and knowing Mackenzie they feared that he would attack the Kiowas wherever he found them, and thus precipitate an Indian War. According to Woodward, the ring circumvented General Sherman by getting a direct order that so long as the campaign went forward in Indian Territory, Colonel Grierson, commander at Fort Sill and senior in rank, should "assume command of both columns . . . in order to hold Mackenzie in check and avoid such a calamity." [17]

Meanwhile Grierson took things leisurely until he got word from Tatum that Kicking Bird had turned in forty-one mules at the agency in compliance with Sherman's demand that the

[17] The same, 124.

[181]

Indians make restitution of the Warren teams. Grierson then sent his interpreter to warn the Kiowas against Mackenzie, and to suggest that they move clear over to the "east of the reservation line" to be sure that they would not be attacked. Grierson then returned to his post and optimistically reported direct to General Sherman himself but with implied criticism of Mackenzie.[18]

Mackenzie led his men out of the gypsum breaks and turned back toward his supply camp. On the way his scouts crossed the trail of a small party of Indians, with whom the Colonel held a parley under a flag of truce. And though his Tonkawa scouts were thirsting for blood and the bewildered troopers were ready for a fight, Mackenzie made no effort to capture or kill them, but let them pass.

His befuddled officers shook their heads as they rode toward the supply camp on Otter Creek. They were unaware of course, as Carter later recalled, of the "double cross our partner in this game of 'hide and go seek' (Grierson) had played" upon their command.

When the expedition reached camp they discovered that Grierson had already gone into Sill. They found Captain Lewis H. Carpenter in charge and dining in courses from a sumptuous board off *"a table-cloth."* In disgust Mackenzie turned south toward Richardson, where Captain Carter sat down to write his reports.

Yet on September 19, 1871, the command was ordered west to Griffin to prepare for another campaign. But their fighting commander seemed chagrined beyond measure, obsessed with mortification. His officers felt that from the time the courier had caught him on the North Fork there "was the beginning of a bitter disappointment which seemed to possess his soul and disturb his peace of mind." It could have been the inception of the tragic fate which eventually overtook this brave and zealous soldier whom Grant had called "the most promising young officer of the Army."

18 Nye, as cited, 149; Carter, as cited, 124-143.

[182]

CHAPTER XI

War on the Plains Indians

For months prior to MacKenzie's departure the Indians had given little trouble around Fort Concho. After he left, "Dobe" Hatch got busy with mud bricks as the proper indigenous building material for the post. While he worried with them, Dr. Notson recorded the lack of progress with characteristically critical eye in his *Medical History of Fort Concho*.

In February, 1871, Notson posted the first mention of Indians in many months. Scouting parties were sent out to run them down, but returned, the surgeon dryly added, "with the usual negative results." In March the marauders were worse. They attacked the mail stages and extended their depredations to a branch of business new in that vicinity—namely cattle stealing from the ranges of the cowmen.[1]

As the season progressed, the raids steadily grew worse until the Indians were stealing stock from the army. The Fort Concho command surmised that their increased activity was due to the arrests of their chiefs at Fort Sill and their removal to Jacksboro for trial.[2]

[1] *Medical History*, vol. 401, pp. 205, 212.

[2] The same, 221-222. The usual impression, however, was to the contrary. See Carl Coke Rister, *The Southwestern Frontier*, Cleveland, 1928, pp. 142-143.

[183]

Whatever the unrecorded politics and chicanery of the "Indian ring" in Washington, it apparently had succeeded in keeping Mackenzie from intercepting and whipping the reservation Indians still raiding in Texas with comparative impunity.[3] As the Colonel had indicated in his letter to Sherman, however, there was still another source of trouble along the eastern edge of the Plains of Texas. Tribes there, especially a branch of the Comanches called the Quahadas, scorned the reservation and lived on wild game and wilder raids on the Texas settlements. Mackenzie assured Sherman that their arbitrary conversion to civilization was behind schedule.[4]

Late in September, as he still brooded over his frustrated plans against the reservation outlaws, Mackenzie was ordered west to Fort Griffin, in present Shackelford County, to organize a campaign against the Plains tribes. His command left Richardson, September 19, 1871, and concentrated at old Camp Cooper about five miles from Griffin. By the 25th a force of officers and men and thirty Tonkawa scouts, making up eight companies of the Fourth Cavalry and two of the Eleventh Infantry—the latter from Fort Concho—were encamped there.[5]

On the 30th, Captain R. G. Carter was sent with a detail of cavalry and Tonkawas to scout out a road and choose a new camp farther west along the Clear Fork. He returned on the third and the column broke camp. The Tonkawas fanned out in the lead to cover the country ahead and Carter took the troops over the chosen route.

The mules were in good shape but the horses were weak. Again the men were in fine spirits and sang their old regimental song, *Come Home, John, Don't Stay Long*, as they rode away from the rendezvous. They pushed west to set up a supply camp on Duck Creek near some dugouts that had been

3 Nye, in *Carbine and Lance*, touches upon this problem, 160-161.

4 R. N. Richardson, in his scholarly work, *The Comanche Barrier*, spells it *Kwahadi;* Nye, *Quohada,* while the more common spelling of the period is followed here.

5 Carter, as cited, 157-158; "Tabular Statement of Expeditions and Scouts, 1871," 4099 A.G.O., from Rister files; Carl Coke Rister, *The Southwestern Frontier*, 150.

[184]

made by the *comancheros*—the New Mexican Indian traders who had been crossing the *Llano Estacado* to barter with the wild tribes. Here Lawton was left in charge with the infantry as guards.

Mackenzie then ordered the cavalry to saddle and struck out on a night's march to the northwest, across to the Fresh Water Fork of the Brazos, toward where it broke out of the Plains through Blanco Canyon. He expected to find the Co-manches under Quanah, the half-breed son of Nocona and Cynthia Ann Parker, a white captive, camped there. The Indian scouts discovered their approach, and all Mackenzie found was their abandoned camp. After a day spent in scout-ing he went into bivouac with his command near the mouth of Blanco Canyon.

As added precaution against the loss of his horses by stampede, Mackenzie had his men "cross side-line" them by hobbling one hind foot to the opposite front foot. In the middle of the side-lines was a ring and a swivel which kept the horse from twisting himself up. Ropes were tied in the rings and fastened to picket pens driven into the ground. It was impossible for a horse to run when side-lined, but he could flounder around and get some distance away where the Indians might catch him, cut the hobbles and steal him. When a horse thus side-lined and staked attempted to run, he would be violently thrown to the ground.

With everything apparently doubly secure, the command posted guards and went into camp at the foot of the Plains west of the site of the village of Dickens. Sharp-eyed Indian scouts were watching them. In the middle of the night a band raced through the camp ringing cow bells, dragging rawhides and, in the old Texas phrase, really "squalling like Coman-ches." The aroused cavalry cut loose at the elusive forms in the darkness to add to the pandemonium, while the terrified horses snorted, floundered and struggled at the ends of their stake ropes in such wild abandon that many of them jerked loose. The order rang out to look to the horses, and shouting

[185]

and excited cavalrymen rushed about in the darkness in search of their mounts through a tangle of ropes and a barrage of flying picket pins that were more dangerous than the shots of the Indians.

It was all over in a few minutes. The shots went wild in the confusion and obscurity of the night, and the Indians were soon gone—sixty-six of the horses with them. Next morning the mounted cavalry and a lot of disgruntled others on foot took the trail. A small detachment under Captain Carter jumped a few Indians in the breaks. In hot pursuit they rode over a ridge and almost upon a large party of mounted braves. The soldiers quickly turned to retreat toward the command, conserving their fire and fighting a rear-guard action to keep from being cut down. Lieutenant Boehm and his Tonkawas arrived in time to prevent their annihilation, but not before Quanah himself had killed one of their men at point-blank range. When Quanah saw the Tonkawa reenforcements, he whipped back into the hills as Mackenzie, who had also heard the firing, came charging up from camp.[6]

The Tonkawas reported a big trail directly up Blanco Canyon which they thought must lead to the main Indian camp. Mackenzie sent the footmen back to the supply camp on Duck Creek and fell upon the trail through the lovely grass-grown valley of the Blanco. He found the camp-site, but the Indians were gone. The Tonkawas kept right up the canyon, stopping at last in some confusion. Finally they figured the Comanches had doubled back on their own trail. The column back-tracked as the scouts worked their way almost to the site of the camp again before finding where the wily Comanches had turned out over the caprock to the west and had taken to the High Plains.

Mackenzie and his men wearily worked their way to the rim and on October 12, 1871, followed the scouts "out ... upon what appeared to be a vast, almost illimitable expanse of

6 Carter, as cited, 160-181; Richardson, *The Comanche Barrier,* 347; Nye, *Carbine and Lance,* 150-152.

prairie. As far as the eye could reach, not a bush or tree, a twig or stone, not an object of any kind or a living thing, was in sight." Before them was nothing but a sea of grass. Pointing into the unfathomable distance, west by northwest, was the fresh trail of a great drove of horses—perhaps a thousand in all. The parallel tell-tale marks of many lodge poles, packed and dragged on either side of the squaws' horses, proved that this was the main band fleeing from the troopers who at last had invaded their camping grounds.

The command sighted the Indians far in advance. As it gained in the chase, the warriors deployed to the sides of the caravan and dropped back in an effort to lure the troops into a fight, and thus give the women and children time to escape. Meanwhile the Tonkawas caught up their war horses and painted for battle. But Mackenzie spurned the diversionary tactics of the Indians and kept straight on after the main body. At this juncture the favorable weather of the High Plains did what it can always be expected to do in Texas. It changed, and as usual it changed for the worse.

Though fall was at hand the troops were still in light uniform. Extra ammunition had been stored in every blouse pocket, the pack mules had been gathered under close herd, and orders for the fight, except for the final word to charge, had been given, when a howling blizzard out of the north cut the command like a knife. Cold rain and sleet chilled the men to the marrow. Had Mackenzie charged at once he would have demoralized the fleeing camp and probably have taken it. But this time he leaned to caution against breaking up his men in the storm, which soon became so severe that he had to call a halt.

The mules were herded close in the center, as it would have been fatal for the men to have lost their supplies in this wilderness. The men gathered as close as they could around the mules as their clothes froze into sheets of ice and their horses humped up, tails to the wind. Tarpaulins were dragged from the packs, and blankets and coats pulled off their saddles by

[187]

the shivering troopers. Thus without anything to eat, they wore out the night beneath their scant protection. Possibly Mackenzie suffered most, for his Civil War wounds were still bothering him and he could hardly stand the exposure. He had no overcoat but a sympathetic officer wrapped him in a buffalo robe, and the command spent a miserable night.

Next morning broke clear. The soldiers took up the march again, but the animals were suffering for water and about played out. From his maps Mackenzie found that the Pecos and Fort Sumner, the nearest settlement, were still far away. As rations were getting low, he wisely decided to turn back. That night they made a dry camp. Next day they reached a lake and stopped to rest and cook some food over fires made from the abandoned cedar lodge poles they had picked up on the return march.

Again they dropped down into the Blanco and discovered two Comanche scouts examining the command's cold trail. Tonkawas and troopers took after them with a hue and cry, while the surprised scouts sought refuge in brush along the ravines. As Boehm and his Tonks were attempting to smoke them out, Mackenzie, impatient with the delay, joined the search and got shot in the leg. He hurried back to the rear to get the arrow cut out while the Tonkawas finished the Comanches, but not before they had shot another soldier through the bowels.

The Tonkawas were a friendly Texas tribe, once virtually wiped out by the Comanches and now their mortal enemies. Captain Carter reported that after the two Comanches were killed the Tonks shot a few more bullets into them, "as was their custom, scalped them, ears and all, and then cut a small piece of skin from each breast, for good luck, or rather 'good medicine'." The command went into camp nearby while the surgeon, Dr. Rufus Choate, Lieutenant Kentz C. Miller, and two Negro field cooks cut off the Comanches' heads, put them in a tow sack, and carried them into camp to be "boiled out for future scientific knowledge."

[188]

That night the wolves cleaned up the carcasses, while Miller, with gruesome humor, called Carter and Major C. Mauck from their own mess to share "something good" for supper. They took their cups and were ushered over to a pot of "soup." When they went to help themselves, Carter said, "we saw the two Comanche scalped heads, with the stripes of paint still on their faces, and with eyes partly opened, bobbing up and down in . . . the mess kettles, mingled with the bubbling, bloody broth." [7] Carter grabbed his stomach and ran.

The return march continued by way of Blanco Canyon. Mackenzie was all but incapacitated, as a less rugged warrior would have been. Dr. Choate gave his best care to the wounded soldier, though no hope was held for his recovery. His punctured intestines protruded from the bullet hole in his back, and the fecal matter oozed out with them. He was placed on a litter of blankets and poles and packed down the Blanco between two horses, as miraculously he continued to live. He could retain no food, but Dr. Choate kept making a broth by boiling buffalo meat and pouring it down him. Some little substance was absorbed in its passage, and eventually the man completely recovered.

The trip into camp was an ordeal. Several horses died of exposure and use and others were completely broken down before Lawton met them with fresh supplies. Mackenzie, convinced that Quanah would turn east into the breaks instead of crossing to the Pecos, divided his command, and in spite of his wound turned north toward the Pease River breaks to hunt

7 Carter, as cited, 186-200; *Tabular Statement of Expeditions,* as cited.

him. But Mackenzie's leg became so bad that he left Major Mauck in command and rejoined the others at the supply camp on Duck Creek. He stuck to his tasks with increased irritability until Dr. Gregory, his surgeon there, hit upon a ruse for keeping him in his tent.

Gregory let everybody in on the joke and then went to dress the wound. After examining it carefully he told the commander that his condition was much worse and, that if he did not control his temper and maintain absolute quiet, amputation must follow. Mackenzie flew into a rage and attempted to brain the doctor with his crutch as that chagrined individual flew through the flap, much to the amusement of the camp.

Carter was ordered back along the old trail to Cottonwood Springs to set up a camp where the disabled men and worn out mounts could recruit, while Lawton was sent to Griffin to load and hurry back with corn. As for meat they were in the heart of the buffalo range.

While they were at this new camp, Major Mauck got in from the Pease River country in the middle of a snowstorm, November 8, 1871. He had not found Quanah, but he had lost a lot of his own horses that died at the end of their picket lines from fatigue and exposure. Lawton's wagontrain came in with badly needed corn, and slowly and painfully the command eased back to Griffin, which they reached on November 12th, singing: "Come home John, don't stay long; come home soon to your own Mary Ann."

Through continuing severe weather they reached Richardson on the 19th. They had marched 509 miles, and lost one man and many horses, but had barely damaged the Indians.[8]

Meanwhile, Indian troubles had really grown serious around Fort Concho. The raids had increased in size and intensity, until a large band struck into Coleman and Concho Counties in what old-timers claimed "for audacity and magnitude surpassed anything" in the history of the American frontier. They

8 The same, 204-206; Robert G. Carter, *The Old Sergeant's Story,* 70.

meant by this the reckoned loss in cattle, since they estimated 12,000 head were driven away in this foray alone.

Among the largest cowmen of the country to the east of Fort Concho were Coggin and Parks. From their headquarters on Home Creek in Coleman County, they claimed to be running 31,000 head of cattle in that and the adjoining counties of McCulloch, Concho, and Tom Green. But whatever their exact number, their herds were sufficiently obvious to attract the Indians, and later the owners filed a claim against the government for 1300 head of beef steers and 2600 head of stock cattle lost in July, 1871.[9]

To the dismay of the entire frontier, the depredations continued. On November 22 the large train of a government contractor was attacked on the Kickapoo, just twenty-nine miles from Fort Concho, and 118 mules and two horses were taken from it. It was one of the worst nearby raids since Concho had been established, and though much shooting took place nobody was hurt. Numerous scouting details from the post were sent to the field but returned with "the usual negative results."

Company G of the Fourth Cavalry under Lieutenant W. C. Hemphill, who had just come in from the expedition to the Staked Plains with Mackenzie, followed their trail back toward the same wild terrain until beyond the head of the Colorado, but returned without catching them.

Lieutenant John L. Bullis was sent out of Fort McKavett for the same purpose. He pursued them until his supplies were exhausted and subsisted for several days on buffalo. He broke down his mounts and straggled back to Concho to say that he had discovered some springs where the Indians camped and had "brought in three Indian letters or despatches found near their camp fires." These letters, Dr. Notson reported, "are symbols roughly painted on bone, usually the scapulas of the buffalo. . . . One of the bones was evidently descriptive of the last raid on Kickapoo."

9 Case No. 5008, in Court of Indian Claims, Washington, D.C.

If the soldiers could not catch the culprits, it was something, it would seem, for them to take the record they had left of the raid—an interesting bit of history which, unfortunately, never found its way into the National Archives.

One incident of these fall campaigns, illustrative of the nobility of animal nature, should not go unrecorded. In the Double Mountain country Hemphill's command lost some of their horses—stampeded by Indians. When the bugler sounded his stable call at Fort Concho one evening, weeks later, reminding the hostlers that it was time to feed and care for their horses, its sound fell on the alert ears of a tired and long-missing horse that had made his way southward through lonely and hostile land for 150 miles. As the reverberating notes died away, he gallantly "trotted into the post and took his usual place in the company corral"—voluntarily home for service and for duty at last.[10]

At Christmas time the Indians were making merry in the Concho country again, striking the principal ranchmen and levying heavily upon their herds. Coggin and Parks claimed a round figure loss of 4000 cattle on December 26th, while old Rich Coffey, most noted of the early ranchmen at the junction of the Concho and the Colorado, lost forty cattle, eight oxen and a few colts and mules at the same time.[11]

The old-timers themselves often joined in the attempt to run the raiders down, but the soldiers were so slow in getting off that the Indians were usually clear out of the country by the time the pursuers got started. When the commander of Concho tried to get a detachment of Tonkawa scouts and trailers from Fort Griffin, the request fell through principally

[10] *Medical History*, vol. 401, pp. 242-243.

[11] Cases Nos. 5008 and 5003, Court of Indian Claims. M. J. and S. R. Coggin moved from Bell to Brown County with a herd of cattle in 1857, and established their ranch on Home Creek in 1860. W. C. Parks came in with 4000 head, and in 1868, the partnership was formed. They drove 5000 on the Goodnight Trail. They quit the business in 1872 because they claimed the Indians presented an impossible problem.

James Cox, *Historical and Biographical Record of the Cattle Industry and the Cattlemen of Texas and Adjacent Territory*, Saint Louis, 1895, p. 364.

because these Indians, now threatened with extinction, did not wish to leave their kinsmen. Their tribe numbered but 127 in all, of which twenty-four were enlisted as scouts for one year, and the balance were made up "principally of old men, women, and children." [12]

With his horses and pack animals back in condition in the spring, Mackenzie was again ready to tackle the job of wiping out the source of the troubles. While the Quaker agent, Lawrie Tatum, was completely disillusioned and demanding punishment for the renegades, the maudlin policy of appeasement still possessed the political mind at Washington. Grierson at Fort Sill was still in accord, and hence the reservation was a handy sanctuary for bold warriors who wished to continue raiding south of Red River. Fortunately, however, this group held no jurisdiction over the wilderness at the foot of the Staked Plains where the Quahadas liked to camp, and General Sherman favored cleaning them out. That still sounded like proper business to Mackenzie.

A change in command of the Department of Texas came in time to strengthen this sensible policy. General J. J. Reynolds, whose chief concern had been the reconstruction of the rebels and the protection of the Negroes instead of the frontier, was replaced by General C. C. Augur, January 29, 1872. As a veteran of the Mexican and Civil Wars, Augur suffered no illusions as to the guilt of the reservation Indians, and also favored action. [13]

During the spring a simple incident brought the eyes of the army into focus upon the Plains Indians. In Texas the usual impatience of American civilians with the army had been sharpened into disdain and even contempt by the Civil War and Reconstruction. It may be hardly Christian but it is entirely human to reciprocate, and hence the army was slow to see the rebellious frontiersman's point of view. It was not then the policy of the federal government to help everybody

[12] *Letters Received*, December 9, 1871, January 5, 1872, Department of Texas.
[13] Rister, *The Southwestern Frontier*, 147.

who demanded to be heard, and so when, in view of their antipathies, the cowmen reported losses of herds to the Indians and asked for help, the officers of the army of occupation could well ask:

"What in the name of creation would the Indians want with cattle?"

It was a logical question. The Indian range was alive with buffalo and other wild meat. And besides, cattle required work, and Indian men, like many later whites, were notoriously out of harmony with labor. For years this situation militated against a mutual understanding, and hence against cooperation in frontier defense, even though such men of outstanding integrity and experience as Charles Goodnight had repeatedly pointed out one persistent cause of trouble. It is hardly human, however, to learn from history, and the army had to "discover" the cause for itself.

For many decades the *comancheros*, or Comanche traders, of New Mexico had been carrying on a profitable if illicit barter with the Plains Indians in cattle and horses. The stock was stolen from the fringes of Texas. The trading grounds were reached by at least two great *comanchero* trails across the unexplored, and for the white man the forbidding *Llano Estacado* of Texas. All of which was as ABC to the seasoned Texas frontiermen, but nothing short of Sanskrit to the army.[14]

This trade, which had been going on for a century and a half, boomed into the "cow business" during the Civil War as the Yankees encouraged the Indians to depredate in Texas. When Goodnight swung up the trail from the Concho country into Fort Sumner to supply beef to the army in 1866, he became acquainted with the *comancheros* themselves and found that army officers at Fort Bascom, where the trade had been common knowledge for years, were taking part in it. Even

[14] For a treatment of the history of this, see the author's "The *Comanchero* Trade," *Southwestern Historical Quarterly*, XXXVIII, January, 1935, pp. 157-176; *The XIT Ranch of Texas and Early Days on the Llano Estacado*, Chicago, 1929, pp. 24-29; *Charles Goodnight, Cowman and Plainsman*, 185-197.

the Governor of New Mexico issued a proclamation against the traffic in August, 1870, and abjured the judges in the border counties to "arrest and bring to justice the guilty parties." [15] Still the army in Texas was skeptical until the spring of 1872.

In March, Sergeant W. Wilson was sent out of Concho "in pursuit of a (supposed) body of Indian marauders," as General Augur reported to the Secretary of War. When near Mucha Que, the country near the head of the Colorado river,

he overtook them and had a brisk little fight, killing 2, wounding 3, capturing 1. This prisoner proved to be a New Mexican, and his account of himself, in brief [Augur continued], was that he was one of about fifty men from New Mexico, who were regularly employed to come to Texas to steal cattle. He gave the name of his employer and the wages he was to receive, mentioned the camps of Indians on the road who were working in concert with them, and related his operations generally to the day of his capture. He stated what was hardly credited—that there was a good wagon-road across the Staked Plains with plenty of permanent water and grass, and that all the stolen cattle were driven over it to New Mexico. [16]

The wild but true story of this vagrant Mexican did what all responsible sources had failed to do: It convinced the army in Texas that "the nigger in the woodpile" behind this atro-

15 Haley, "The *Comanchero* Trade," as cited, 170.

16 *Report of the Secretary of War*, 1872, pp. 55-56, and *Post Return*, March, 1872. For a discussion of the trade, see C. C. Rister, "Harmful Practices of Indian Traders of the Southwest, 1865-1876," *New Mexico Historical Review*, July, 1931.

cious raiding was the *comanchero* of New Mexico. General Augur relayed the "discovery" to Washington, which began to suspect that the militant Mackenzie, in his desire to civilize the Plains Comanches with powder and lead, might be right. It was easy enough to turn a deaf ear to the complaints of the Texans, but a confessed culprit in hand could hardly be denied.

Major John P. Hatch, commander of Concho, organized "a large exploring scout" under Captain N. B. McLaughlin of the Fourth Cavalry[17] and sent him back with the captive to find the Mexican traders and investigate the strange report more fully. On May 11, 1872, McLaughlin returned to say that the Indians were gone, but that the signs of the traders' trails and camps were there to verify the Mexican's story. When Augur summoned Hatch and Mackenzie to San Antonio for a "council of war," the general impression prevailed at Concho that the information on the Indian traders around Mucha Que would "form the basis of the summer's work."

On April 20, 1872, another "incident" had occurred to stir the frontier afresh to its vital problem. A wagon train on the Lower San Antonio-El Paso road had gotten as far out as Howard's Wells, in present Crockett County, when it was attacked by a band of Comanches and Kiowas under Big Bow. A few hours later two companies of the Ninth Colored Cavalry under Captain N. Cooney, on their way to Fort Clark, found the train in flames. Inside the wagons were the sixteen charred bodies of the teamsters. Cooney's men engaged the Indians who were still about, and who took refuge in the rocks and ravines, but Cooney quit the fight after a lieutenant was mortally wounded.[18]

These and other outrages prompted Post Chaplain Norman Badger to write from Fort Concho to the Secretary of Interior in tart inquiry:

[17] C. C. Augur to John P. Hatch, May 17, 1872; *Medical History*, vol. 401, pp. 261, 265, 269. See Heitman, as cited, vol. I, 674.

[18] Richardson, as cited, 348; Rister, as cited, 148-149.

[196]

"Can you wonder that there are hundreds of desolate and vacant ranches in the region and that the hardy pioneers are retiring to the interior and severely blaming the government for risking and protecting untamed savages on our borders?" [19]

Hatch hurried back from San Antonio on June 1 to prepare the Fort Concho garrison for its part in a joint movement against the Plains tribes.

By an order from headquarters on May 31, Mackenzie took command. He was to draw three companies of the Fourth Cavalry from Richardson, one of the Fourth and one of the 11th Infantry from Fort Concho to make up his command.

General Augur summarized their plan:

"With a view of breaking up this cattle stealing, and stopping incursions of hostile Indians along the northern frontier, I directed . . . Colonel Mackenzie . . . to establish a camp of cavalry and infantry on the Fresh Fork of the Brazos, from which his cavalry should operate in pursuit of hostile Indians." [20] He thus stated a basic change of policy in harmony both with Mackenzie's bold and insistent demands and the long and tragic experience of the frontiersmen of Texas.

The efficient Lawton was again placed in charge of transportation and supplies. Heavily loaded wagons rolled out from Concho and McKavett. Six wagons, one with each company from these posts, were filled with twenty days' rations for the men. Ten days' supply on three other wagons was sent directly to Lawton. The balance of the train, consisting of eighteen wagons concentrated at Concho, was each loaded with 3000 pounds of forage for the horses. Lawton calculated this would last until the train had time to make a return trip. [21]

Augur ordered additional wagons up from San Antonio to

[19] Requoted from Richardson, as cited, 348.

[20] *Report of the Secretary of War*, 1872, as cited.

[21] H. W. Lawton to General Mackenzie, June 4, 1872. Mackenzie had been brevetted a brigadier general during the Civil War. He came to Fort Concho a colonel after the reorganization of the regular army following the war. Though serving in his actual rank, it was common for an officer to be addressed, particularly socially and by his subordinates, by a former honorary title.

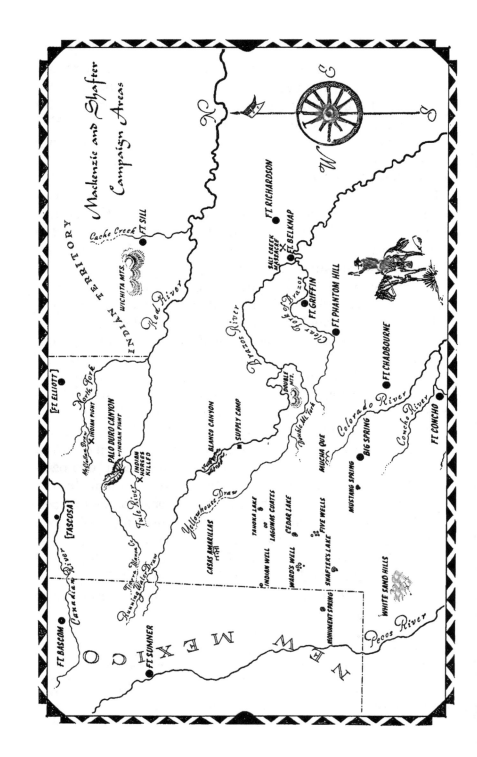

Mackenzie and Shafter Campaign Areas

meet the demands, while Mackenzie urged the General to impress on Shafter the necessity of plenty of corn for the horses in the rough country they would be scouting. Repairs were provided for wagons broken down on the march and forges and other equipment were brought along for the black-smiths. On June 12 the depot quartermaster at San Antonio, at Augur's urging, sent out eleven teams under Train-Master Crevenstine, each with a lead- and trail-wagon and a supply of *aparejos* or pack bags, as well as rope and other gear for Concho, while additional wagons were ordered from Fort Brown at the southern extremity of Texas.[22]

Mackenzie left Richardson on June 14 and marched to his old camp on the Clear Fork. While Shafter was making plans to leave he got the discouraging report that MacKenzie and three soldiers had been killed by Indians on the Little Wichita, in Clay County. Anxious inquiry proved it false. Shafter reached Concho with two companies of colored infantry on the 22nd and marched off three days later to join Mackenzie "at the rendezvous."[23]

Mackenzie, in camp near Fort Griffin, wrote Augur on the 20th outlining his immediate plan of action. Within ten days he would start for the Indian country, traveling slowly so that Shafter would have plenty of time to catch him. He would set up his permanent camp and "arrange to start down the Fresh Fork from its head," near present Plainview, on the first of July. Shafter was to follow him into the mouth of Blanco Canyon, through which flowed the Fresh Fork, Catfish, Running Water, or White River—as it has variously been called. The plan was well laid, but he took note of the contingencies which might break their schedule.

Of course in such a distance [Mackenzie continued], in a country without travelled roads and [with] the possible interference of rains

22 R. S. Mackenzie to General Augur, June 5, 1872; C. C. Augur to Commanding Officer Fort Concho, June 12, 1872; Benjamin C. Card to John P. Hatch, June 12, 1872.

23 W. R. Shafter to Augur, June 19, 1872; *Medical History*, as cited, vol. 401, p. 270; Carter, *The Old Sergeant's Story*, 82.

and Indians, it will be very hard to arrange to meet in the cañon.

I have one very hard march to get to the head of the Fresh Fork. If by any chance we could catch the Indians between us in that cañon, we ought to get their horses at least, and probably some of the Indians.[24]

He knew he was dealing with a wily and elusive foe, and his careful remarks are those of a sober realist instead of a political general.

In keeping with this design Mackenzie moved out by Fort Griffin and followed his old course west—from now on to be known as the Mackenzie Trail—across the Clear Fork at the Big Bend, across Paint and California Creeks, and over the Double Mountain Fork to Cottonwood Springs. From there he marched to the Fresh Fork of the Brazos and established his supply camp near the mouth of Blanco Canyon. His four companies of cavalry averaged over fifty men, but the company of 11th Infantry was "very weak." He moved deliberately while urging Shafter to make "the best time" possible and not to be drawn aside by any diversionary Indian movement.[25]

Mackenzie took the captive *comanchero* and scouted up the Blanco without finding the hostile Indians. But he did discover the cart road that the Mexican had said was there, and by easy stages and sufficient waterings followed it across the Plains north of Fort Sumner to Alamogordo Creek, tributary to the Pecos. He tried to locate the traders themselves, but these wary individuals scattered to their homes among the friendly natives and were not to be found.

From Fort Sumner he crossed the divide to the Canadian and proceeded down to Fort Bascom. From there his return trip seemed to have approximated another prominent *comanchero* trail which pointed south of east into the Texas Panhandle, across by the head of the Trujillo, to the Palo Duro, the Tule, and thence into the Quitaque country. On September 2, 1872, Mackenzie was back at his camp on the Blanco and reporting to General Augur upon his trip across the Plains.

[24] R. S. Mackenzie to General Augur, June 20, 1872.

[25] The same; Carter, *The Old Sergeant's Story*, 82.

He had covered much of the Plains country, but he had not yet found the Indians.[26]

Thus it was that the army dispelled for itself the bugaboo of what Marcy had once called "the dreaded *Llano Estacado*— the great Zahara of North America." Mackenzie's report delighted Augur, who relayed the news to Washington, saying:

This is the first instance, in my knowledge, where troops have been successfully taken across the Staked Plains. This fact, that troops can be so moved, and the general knowledge of the country, and the specific knowledge of the routes and *modus operandi* of the cattle-thieves, obtained by Colonel Mackenzie, I regard as very important and well worth the summer's labor.[27]

In a letter to Hatch, at Fort Concho, Mackenzie indicated that he was puzzled over the whereabouts of the Indians. Hatch had thought they would be found in the breaks of the South Plains. Then fortunately Mackenzie figured they might be on the upper tributaries of Red River and even as Augur wrote his report, Mackenzie and men were marching north through the breaks in search of the Quahadas.[28] On September 29, 1872, he discovered the Comanche Mow-Way's large camp on the North Fork seven miles above the mouth of McClellan Creek. With five cavalry companies consisting of seven officers, 215 enlisted men and about twenty Tonkawas, he quickly made his plans and attacked, taking the camp virtually by surprise. The troops swept through it, killing twenty-three Indians whose bodies were found, and capturing 127 women and children as the warriors scattered from the battlefield like a bunch of blue quail. Mackenzie burned their lodges—262 in all—and took their horse herds which he estimated at 3000 head.

The Tonkawas stood guard over them that night. But the Comanches returned and stampeded not only their own but some Tonkawa and cavalry horses besides, thus recovering the whole herd. Next morning the Tonks sheepishly walked in leading a lone burro loaded down with their saddles. Thus

[26] *Report of the Secretary of War*, 1872, p. 56.   [27] The same, 56.
[28] Ranald S. Mackenzie to John P. Hatch, September 7, 1872.

Mackenzie learned another lesson. Thereafter he never tried to keep Indian horses that he captured, but rounded them up and had them shot.

The command pulled out for their camp on the Fresh Fork of the Brazos. It was a hard march, a warrior and a few women and children dying on the way, "some of them from injuries received during the fight." Mackenzie reported that "all such [casualties] were accidental." His own loss was four men killed and several wounded.

Among the mules held in the Indian horse herd were teams belonging to the wagon train taken at Howard's Wells, which proved that the camp was a rendezvous for many of the renegades from Fort Sill as well as for the wild Quahadas. Mackenzie carried his prisoners south to Blanco Canyon, and sent them under guard to Concho.[29]

Two companies of the Fourth Cavalry reached the post with 115 Indian captives on October 21, where they were held as prisoners of war while negotiations were carried on with the tribes at Fort Sill.

The Indians there still held many captives and slaves, and Mackenzie's holding of their own women and children brought this tragic matter to a focus. A number of Texans including Clinton Smith, who had been captured near Boerne, March 3, 1869, were released. A flaxen-haired boy of thirteen years named Adolph Korn, stolen while herding goats on the Llano near Castell, was also brought in on January 1, 1870. He had been the object of a long and frantic search by his father, who, protesting his unwavering devotion to the Union, humbly importuned everybody from the commander of the Department of Texas to Governor E. J. Davis to "grant such aid" as they deemed "fit and proper."[30]

29 Carter, *The Old Sergeant's Story*, 83 ff.; Richardson, as cited, 362-364; Nye, as cited, 160-163; A. A. A. G. to John P. Hatch, October 29, 1872.

30 Louis Korn to E. J. Davis, March 22, 1870, date of filing; Louis Korn to James H. Carlton, January 10, 1870; Richardson, as cited, 364; *Medical History*, vol. 401, pp. 285, 298-299; Carter, *On the Border with Mackenzie*, 389; J. Marvin Hunter, *The Boy Captives*, Bandera, Texas, 1927, pp. 28 ff.

One of the Comanche chiefs named Horse's Back "constituted himself special agent for the recovery of the captives,
and soon brought in a dozen or more Mexican children." Kicking Bird also did his part, as "this severe drubbing had a
salutary effect on the Comanches and the Kiowas, as well." [31]
Early in December, General Augur wrote Hatch that "Horseback . . . has been very active in returning white captives,"
and hence he was ordering the release of five prisoners, all of
whom were relatives of the chief. They were relayed from post
to post, up through Richardson to Sill under proper guard.
One died on the way but the others reached there safely and
well-fed, to the delight of the reservation Indians. [32]

The balance of the captives were kept under guard at Fort
Concho, while the tired troopers marched back to their respective posts for winter quarters, satisfied at last with a job well
done. Other straggling bands of Indians drifted from the
Plains into the agency to protest their good intentions if not
to make amends, at least so long as this tough, tight-lipped
commander who fought alongside his men held their women
and children as hostages. Thus all signs augured a milder
winter on the frontiers of Texas.

[31] Richardson, as cited, 364.
[32] C. C. Augur to John P. Hatch, December 5, 1872; Nye, as cited, 163.

Mackenzie's Cleanup Campaigns

Spring came in comparative quiet to the Concho country as the Indians stayed close to the agency. Many of the older chiefs were convinced of the futility of further resistance, and the punitive policy against the renegades, now approved thoroughly, even by the Quaker Agent Tatum, was having its effect. The fact that Satanta and Big Tree were still in the penitentiary at Huntsville and over a hundred women and children were held captive at Fort Concho put an effective damper on the wild spirits of the tribe.

Yet the peace group was still in power at Washington, and Tatum resigned in the spring as Governor Davis inclined to yield, but slowly, to pressure for the release of the convicts. With the captive Indian women and children the problem was different. On April 14, 1873, General Augur ordered them sent from Fort Concho back to the reservation.[1] Captain Robert McClermont carried them to Sill where they were delivered in general rejoicing. The braves, upon finding how well their women had been treated, were warm in their appreciation and even promised to take the path of peace. Some of them so seriously considered settling down that they even sent their women into the fields to see what work was like.

[1] J. A. Augur to Commanding Officer, Fort Concho, April 14, 1873.

The Indian ring believed that the release of the Kiowa chieftains from Huntsville would mollify the cantankerous segment of that tribe, and after long negotiation Satanta and Big Tree were taken to Fort Sill and turned loose. But appeasement of the demands of a strong and bold people as a means to peace usually works in reverse, and so it was with the Indians. Few moons grew full before the young and restless of the tribes were again raiding beyond Red River.[2]

As was to be suspected Texas boiled with resentment, and General Sherman wrote Governor Davis in unrestrained anger, reminding him that he, the General, had once, "in making a tour of your frontier," run the risk of his life but that he would not so hazard it again. He believed, he continued, that "Satanta and Big Tree will have their revenge . . . and . . . if they are to have scalps, that yours is the first that should be taken." Considering what the majority of the Texans thought of the Reconstruction Governor, they for once agreed with Sherman —a name anathema to the South.[3]

The suspense was short. The favorite horses of the young braves were fat and the lure of the great Comanche Trail was strong. In November, 1873, shortly after the release of the chiefs, a party of twenty-one Comanches and nine Kiowas— the latter the aristocracy of the tribe—struck south through Texas. At times they covered sixty to eighty miles a day before they finally drew rein near the headwaters of the Nueces River, away to the south of Fort Concho. Here they set up a sort of camp, left their spare horses hobbled, but unguarded, and continued south across the *Rio Bravo* between Eagle Pass and Laredo into Mexico. In the Olmos country they killed fourteen Mexicans and took one captive, rounded up 150 horses and mules and struck towards Guerrero, continuing their pillage. They crossed back into Texas on the Laredo and San Antonio road, where they killed two Americans. The news

2 Richardson, as cited, 366-370; Rister, *The Southwestern Frontier*, 141-144; Nye, as cited, gives the details of the negotiations and the release of the prisoners in dramatic detail, 168-175.

3 Requoted from Rister, as last cited, p. 142.

went out along the line of forts while they rode hard for their old camp in Edwards County.

Lieutenant Charles L. Hudson, scouting with forty-one men of the Fourth Cavalry from Fort Clark, discovered their hiding place, took charge of their horses and waited their return. He got fresh word of their movements on December 9 and intercepted them. In a hot fight he put them to flight, captured fifty of their horses, and killed at least nine of the braves. The party suffered further loss at the hands of John R. Buell, on the Double Mountain Fork, and when the news reached the Kiowas in January, 1874, at their camps in the Territory, the whole tribe wailed in grief.[4]

For decades the Mexican border had been a sore spot. The Civil War on this side and revolution on the other had accentuated the usual lawlessness incident to the wild regions of the *Rio Bravo*. One of the worst sources of trouble was the once-friendly but now thoroughly alienated Kickapoos, aided and abetted by Lipans, Pottawatomies, and savage Mescalero Apaches, who lived sixty miles beyond Eagle Pass at the edge of the Santa Rosa Mountains. These could raid in Texas almost at free will and be back across the river before the news got out and forces could be organized to catch them. In 1872, General Augur took notice of them, too.[5]

Colonel Mackenzie returned from the Staked Plains to Fort Richardson with the Fourth Cavalry in the late fall. In spite of the preachments of the peace advocates, his sound thrashing of the Comanches on the North Fork had temporarily quieted the troubles there. The problems of the Mexican border were laid before President Grant by General Sherman and they determined to concentrate next on them. Mackenzie was ordered back to Fort Concho, and he and the towering Lawton came into the post on January 1, 1873, which again became regimental headquarters for the Fourth Cavalry.[6]

4 Nye, as cited, 182-183; Richardson, as cited, 371.

5 *Report of The Secretary of War*, 1872, p. 57.

6 *Medical History*, vol. 404, p. 81; *Post Return*, January, 1873.

After conferring with Grant, Sherman wrote General Augur, still in command of the Department of Texas at San Antonio, that "the President wishes you to give every attention to affairs on the Rio Grande frontier, especially to prevent the raids of Indians and Mexicans upon the people and property of Southern and Western Texas." In view of Mackenzie's success in the Panhandle and Grant's high estimate of him, he was the logical man to lead the campaign.

Sherman ordered the Seventh Cavalry to Richardson, while directing that the Fourth, "as soon as it is safe to move, should march to the Rio Grande. In naming the 4th for the Rio Grande," Sherman concluded, "the President is doubtless influenced by the fact that Col Mackenzie is young and enterprising, and that he will impart to his Regiment his own active character." 7

Mackenzie kept his headquarters at Concho until early spring, when he ordered the five troops at Richardson to march to the same post. They started on March 4, 1873, complete from equipment down through wives and laundresses to domestic help, the latter seated uncomfortably on top of the loaded wagons. They followed the usual route out by Griffin to Phantom Hill, and southwest toward Chadbourne. Captain R. G. Carter worried himself to a frazzle with rickety and broken-down wagons on the rough road, and dispatched a courier asking that supplemental forage be sent to meet them on Oak Creek. At the crossing of the Colorado, between there and Fort Concho, the imposing and confident figure of Henry Lawton, the great wagon-master, loomed up to meet them, much to Carter's relief. Behind him was the crack water team of the Fourth Cavalry, made up of "eight magnificent gray mules."

A cloudburst barely beat them to the North Concho on March 18, and the river was booming when they approached. Mackenzie himself was down to see them ford it. Carter doubled the teams, and with the skinners cracking their black-

7 This letter, February 5, 1873, is reproduced in full in Carter, as last cited, 418a.

snakes and plying their profanity, the column crossed, climbed the slippery banks, and was corralled at the post by dark.

There was a flurry of visiting and gossip among the women in the officers' quarters as those long absent at Richardson were brought up to date. For further diversion the women went down to the captive corral to see the Comanche squaws that their husbands had taken on the North Fork—now growing fat on the enforced leisure and bounty of the federal government. In the affectionate fashion of people everywhere, the Indians fondled the white papooses of indulgent mothers, much to the later discomfiture of the women when they found themselves and infants infested with lice. But the unsuspecting incubation stage had yet to run, and that night Chaplain Norman Badger arranged a dance. Everybody among the married group made merry as the rhythm of graceful waltzes drifted across the dark Concho, there to be lost in the raucous racket that attracted the single enlisted men to diversion in the dives of Saint Angela.

On March 20, 1873, the veteran campaigners left on the road to Fort Clark by way of McKavett, at which point Mackenzie, coming up from San Antonio, rejoined them. Colonel A. McD. McCook, a genial veteran of the Civil War, was in charge at McKavett and insisted on giving them a fine dinner and another big *bailé*. From here they marched south to Fort Clark, at present Bracketville.

There the Secretary of War, General P. H. Sheridan, Mackenzie, and Colonel Wesley Merritt held a long conference on April 12 and reviewed the Fourth Cavalry. It was tough and seasoned, but a little disgruntled over having to give up relatively new quarters in the delightful live oaks at Richardson for old and dilapidated ones at Fort Clark, since that post had not been rebuilt. But the marvelous springs of Las Moras, with their water cress for salads, were always welcome to men grown stale to the point of scurvy on heavy diets of meat and bread. A short distance away, the Rio Grande marked the bounds of trouble and adventure for two republics. At the moment, directly south at Eagle Pass, the Joint Commission of the United States and Mexican governments was then in session working on the Indian problem.

Obviously, with such an array of officialdom at the rather sordid post at Bracketville, serious business was afoot. Nothing leaked out at the time, but Mackenzie was being told by Sheridan to plan his own strategy to cope with the situation in his own way, and to see that the raiding was stopped. As for his authority, it was apparently direct from President Grant himself.[8]

Even as the Indians along Red River had found refuge under the protective wing of the peace party on the reservations, those raiding upon the Rio Grande border found sanctuary across the river in Mexico. For obvious reasons, in view of the medicine the military minds were brewing, Mackenzie's orders were oral—delivered direct and in person. And in view of the gravity of the decision, they were broad enough to permit him to cope with any contingency.

The man whom Grant had personally directed to the border was a true son of his father—the sturdy and determined officer who did not hesitate to hang the mutinous son of the Secretary of War to his own yard-arm on the high seas. Mackenzie, brooding in the privacy of his quarters at Fort Clark, mapped his plan to wipe out the trouble. He looked to his pack outfits, freshly shod his horses and mules, whipped his men into condition, severely drilled them in gunfire and, strangely it seemed to them, for they had never been used in their campaigns, ordered them to grind their sabers to razor-like edges.

Then suddenly in the dark hours of May 17, 1873, men at the post and others out in the brush on patrol were rudely awakened and ordered to pack and saddle. Forces were brought together and Mackenzie, without divulging their destination, led 400 men and some twenty Seminole scouts south to the river, across, and into Mexico. When the pack mules could not keep up the pace, Mackenzie dropped them

8 The same, 422.

and pushed on without supplies. Sixty miles below the border he furiously fell upon the Lipan and Kickapoo villages near Remolino in the edge of the Santa Rosa Mountains. With him it was war to the knife.

In a sweeping action he burned three of their villages, killed nineteen of their braves, captured forty of their women and children, as well as Castillitos, chief of the Lipans, took fifty-six head of their horses, and drove their demoralized defenders into the hills. Thus far he had marched without stopping. He herded his captives together, kept his men in the saddle and headed back. And though he was threatened with mutiny among his officers when they discovered he had invaded Mexico without orders, and though his men cursed and slept and reeled in their saddles, he would not quit, but spurred them on toward Texas.

After four nights and days without sleep, and after 160 miles of continuous marching, they whipped their "ga'nt and give-out" horses across the Rio Grande, and literally fell off on rough but friendly soil to rest. Mackenzie had lost only one man killed and three wounded, and was back in Texas before the aroused Mexican officials could get into action against him. He sent his captives into San Antonio, from where they were forwarded to Fort Gibson in Indian Territory.[9]

A great furor arose at once in official quarters. Naturally the Mexicans were outraged, and just as naturally the Texans were delighted. As the storm of protest rose Mackenzie assumed complete responsibility. He had confided to his faithful captain, R. G. Carter, that he anticipated court-martial if the expedition proved a failure. The protest of the Mexicans against his invasion of their soil was voluble and vigorous.

Official Washington could not fail to take notice. Notwithstanding his political ineptitude, President Grant would not leave a loyal officer holding the sack. In spite of the howl in less lustful regions than Texas, the administration supported

9 "Report of General Augur, Commanding Department of Texas, 1873," Carter, as cited, 422-470; *San Antonio Express*, May 17, 1901.

[210]

Mackenzie. The racket died down, as it always does, but so did much of the devilment below the Rio Grande, since the raiders there were apparently no longer immune to reprisal.

Eventually the action was accepted as a wise one by the better Mexicans.[10]

For years, effort had been under way to bring the Kickapoos back to their reservations. Understandably, in view of the Dove Creek fight, they had been giving the Texans a lot of trouble. At San Antonio, in April, 1868, Federal Judge G. H. Noonan tried to enlist the United States and Mexico in their removal, and "the Kickapoo Committee" of twenty citizens considered the problem. A meeting resulted in the appointment of a group made up of George W. Brackenridge, Ben F. Ficklin, Henry C. Logan and A. Siemering to draft a letter to the Secretary of Interior urging their removal from the Santa Rosa region of Mexico by proper treaty.[11]

In time, commissioners were appointed by the Secretary of Interior, and in March, 1871, General J. J. Reynolds issued a general order to the commanders of the posts in Texas advising them that a delegation of "four to six" Kickapoo chiefs was on its way to Mexico "for the purpose of holding a conference" with the tribe there, and, he continued, a little prematurely, "to accompany them back to their old home north of Red River." The commanding officers were ordered to give the chiefs food, transportation and escorts "to the next post in their route to Fort Duncan. . . ."

Then, following a raid by the Lipans on the border of Texas, the commissioners were horrified to hear of Mackenzie's march into Mexico and his devastation of their villages. Yet this had a salutary effect, even for the commissioners, and on September 1st of that same year, military headquarters at San Antonio ordered the commander of Concho to watch for the coming of "all the Pottawattomies, and about 250 Kickapoos with their

10 C. C. Augur to A. A. G., Military Division of the Missouri, September 30, 1873; Rister, as cited, 153-154.

11 *San Antonio Express*, April 11 and 16, 1868.

families" who were scheduled to leave on the 28th, without escort, and proceed to the Territory by a route "outside the line of posts." "Strict orders" were issued to the command and sent "out by courier to all scouting parties not to molest these Indians. . . ." In this ticklish business nobody wanted a tragic recurrence of Dove Creek.

The balance of the Kickapoos at that time sent word that they would stay where they were until they heard how the first had fared, while the Lipans and Mescaleros were so scornful of the whole business that they refused to make any talk about it and headed for the hills. Nearly a year later, the commissioners were able to report that about 400 had been moved. Their success might have been complete, they continued, except for the smoldering recollections of the Dove Creek fight and the "strong influence" that Mexico had put in their way. Mexico felt that these Indians were an effective barrier against the raiding Comanches from our side, "and were also good hands at stealing Texas stock." Undoubtedly Mexico was right.

Mexico eventually became amenable and Governor Cepeda, of Coahuila, was especially cooperative. On April 15, 1875, U. S. Indian Commissioner H. M. Atkinson wrote out a recommendation and a sort of passport at his camp in Mexico, asking safe passage for the Kickapoo chief, Mosquito, and about 130 of his tribe. The tribe made its way north and safely, if apprehensively, came into the sub-post at the head of the Middle Concho early in June. Charles H. Merriam, in charge of the detachment there, reported their destitute condition.

They are entirely out of Rations and no Game to be had Horses played out! I have gave them what rations I could spare and send this in by one of my Men in company of two of the Indians themselves they want rations enough to bring them into Concho where they will make arrangements for going on to Sill.

They at last reached the reservation. A distrustful fragment stayed where it was, eventually to merge with the lower classes of northern Mexico. Thus the savage problem compounded by the indiscretion and passions of the Texans at Dove Creek simmered out as the descendants of this once-great tribe were scattered and gradually amalgamated.[12]

General Augur reported upon the new state of affairs along the border with optimism. He was pleased that even the commissioners, who felt at first that their efforts at peaceful settlement of the problem had been thwarted, soon admitted that their success was largely due to Mackenzie's campaign. At the same time Augur noted that cattle stealing along the lower Rio Grande had virtually come to a halt.[13] Hope was at last being felt for the entire frontier of Texas.

As already noted, however, appeasement, as a poor substitute for high policy, was still seeping out of Washington. Satanta and Big Tree were turned loose, and some of the boldest and the best of the Kiowa braves took to the warpath. Augur's premature optimism gave way to concern. The Comanches were falling under the spell of a new medicine man who warned them against the enervating way of life of the whites, and with powerful appeal was making headway toward consolidating the always independent branches of that great federation of tribes. As if to help, the buffalo hide hunt that had started in western Kansas was pushing south, cutting away their supply of wild meat, and unfortunate administration of their rations at the reservation was adding to their unrest. They too began looking to their best horses, their weapons and their war paint.[14]

Fort Concho was somewhat preoccupied with its usual worries of construction, first under Major Henry Douglass, after Mackenzie's departure, and then under Lieutenant Colonel Wesley Merritt, of the 9th Infantry. In the early spring

[12] A. A. G. to Commanding Officers of Military Posts in Texas, March 13, 1871; Chauncey McKeever to C. O. Fort Concho, September 1, 1873; Herman Schreiner to C. O., Fort Concho, April 9, 1875; H. M. Atkinson, to whom it may concern, April 15, 1875; Charles H. Merriam to Post Adjutant, Fort Concho, June 8, 1875; *San Antonio Express*, August 2, 1874; C. C. Augur, "Report," etc., 1873, as cited.

[13] Augur, as cited.

[14] Richardson, as cited, 371-376; Nye, as cited, 181, 187-190.

of 1874, Indians fired into the camp of soldiers on Home Creek, attacked the mail station at Kickapoo Springs, and even stole twenty-three horses from Captain Dodge's troops near Johnson Station. They were discovered within three miles of the post, and a party was "seen at San Angelo," [15] while in the Territory the leaven of social revolution, preached by the Comanche medicine man, Isatai, was stirring them up.

After a medicine dance a large force of warriors concentrated and moved on the newly founded buffalo hunters' trading post of Adobe Walls in the Panhandle of Texas with the idea of wiping the hunters out. The young Quanah distinguished himself above the older chieftains while the hunters fortified themselves in the Adobe Walls, and after the first savage onslaught kept the Indians at a distance with their long-range Sharp's rifles. The warriors lifted the siege. But a number of hunters were killed there and at scattered points on the buffalo range, and the others retreated in a hurry to Dodge City. Meanwhile it became obvious that the troubles with the reservation Indians were far from settled, and General Augur, with Sherman's backing, moved to put a stop to this intermittent warfare once and for all.

Lieutenant Colonel J. W. Davidson, then in command at Fort Sill, ordered the friendly Indians in the Territory to the east of Cache Creek so that they would not be attacked by mistake. But owing to unfortunate policy and poor administration, "probably one half of the Comanche, Kiowa, and Cheyenne tribes were openly hostile during the early autumn of 1874." [16] Only a handful registered at the agency by the deadline early in August, and thereafter the military considered all the others hostile and wild. The situation was so serious that at last even the Interior Department was convinced that punishment was essential and agreed that the army could attack the hostiles wherever they found them—on

15 *Medical History*, vol. 404, pp. 143, 146, 147; *Post Return*, February, 1874; *Letter Book*, I, 108, 169,, 172.

16 Richardson, as cited, 386.

the reservation if necessary. The army then definitely went into action.

Colonel Nelson A. Miles was ordered out of Camp Supply, in the northwest corner of Indian Territory; Davidson was to move west out of Sill; Major W. R. Price was to come down the Canadian against them out of Fort Union, New Mexico, from the west; Lieutenant Colonel G. P. Buell was to work his way up Red River from Griffin; and most importantly Mackenzie was ordered up from Clark and back to his familiar territory on the Fresh Water Fork of the Brazos. Summer was well along when the orders were issued.

Mackenzie at once sent Sergeant John B. Charlton with messages to Fort Sill. Charlton was ordered to travel only at night because of the risk, but was told that the matter was urgent, and to push on the bridle reins. He changed mounts at each post on the way and made a remarkable ride of 580 miles into Sill in six nights. Upon his return to Concho, he found that the command had moved back to that post. Mackenzie and General Augur soon showed up from Fort Clark with the regiment and several troops of the Tenth Infantry. Their column reached Kickapoo Springs on the 18th of March and found that the Indians had attacked a citizen's wagon train there the night before.

Again Fort Concho was a-bustle with preparations for the campaign when the column moved in on the 21st and camped near the post. All companies there were detached to Mackenzie's command. Two days later eight companies of cavalry and three of infantry were ordered to march. A mile from the post they passed in review before General Augur and Mackenzie and then broke into columns of four to proceed less formally on the long march.

Captain Boehm had been sent from Fort Davis to join them; a company was sent to Richardson from the outpost at Camp Colorado to the east; and a trailing commissary of sixty-five head of beeves, with herders and butchers from San Antonio, was drifted along to supplement their other supplies.

[215]

The command moved off, up the North Concho and across the divide to Rendlebrock Springs, to the Colorado, the Double Mountain Fork, and finally to Blanco Canyon. A scouting detail made up of six white men, thirteen Seminoles and twelve Tonkawas was brought together under Lieutenant William A. Thompson to scour the country for sign of the hostile Indians.[17]

Mackenzie and Augur went on to Griffin, from where Mackenzie turned west to rejoin his command. On August 28, 1874, Augur wrote that Buell was being sent from there with six companies of cavalry and two of infantry to join him. And to impress upon all the fact that monkey-business was out, and the army was in the saddle, Augur continued:

> As you are aware, the object of the proposed Campaign against the hostile Cheyennes, Comanches, Kiowas, and others from the Fort Sill Reservation, is to punish them for recent depredations along the Kansas and Texas frontiers, and you are expected to take such measures against them as will, in your judgment, the soonest accomplish this purpose.
>
> The Country accessible to these hostile bands is very large, and affords innumerable hiding places for themselves and their families and herds, and it is not expected that the object of the Campaign is to be accomplished in a day, unless by great and unexpected good fortune; but it is not proposed, however, to release efforts in the least, until the Indians are eventually found and punished, and made to subject themselves to such terms as the Government may impose upon them.[18]

Furthermore, Augur continued, should the Indians leave their hiding places in the canyons along the eastern edge of the Staked Plains and seek refuge at the reservations, he, Mackenzie, was to follow them in, assume command of all troops, and "take such measures as will insure entire Control of the Indians there. . . ." The tough logic of war at last was having its way. The Quaker agents were not to interfere, and the sympathetic Grierson was out of the picture.

Davidson, operating from a camp on Otter Creek, was so

[17] Carter, as cited, 473-475; W. E. Kingsbery to N. S. Constable, July 8, 1874; C. Mauck to Major Norman, August 6, 1874; C. C. Augur to C. O., Fort Concho, August 5, 1874; *Medical History*, vol. 404, pp. 154-155.

[18] C. C. Augur to R. S. Mackenzie, August 28, 1874, Letters Sent, U. S. Army Commands.

far from Mackenzie as to be forced on his own. But should Mackenzie wish to coordinate their campaigns, Augur made clear, Davidson was to be under him. At last too the sturdy metal of courage, resolve and ability had been felt. The hard, taciturn and irascible Mackenzie, still suffering with three wounds from the Civil War, was in full charge of the campaign. He now had an army in the field and he knew what to do.

From his own camp near the mouth of the Blanco, he sent a memorandum of his movements to Augur, who had gone in to Sill to keep in touch from there. He noted that the troops, in three columns, were about to go into that wide, rough and broken country between there and the head of Red River. His command would search out the ravines and canyons through the Quitaque to the upper Red, and perhaps to the Salt Fork, in the present Clarendon country. Davidson, with eight companies, was working west from Fort Sill, while, in between, Buell was to march north from Griffin, across Pease River to the Red, and up the main branch of that stream until he came to the trail Mackenzie had cut in his campaign of 1872.

Mackenzie had seasoned much since then. He had learned how to cope with those gyppy badlands around the head of the Pease and Red Rivers. He had learned that the choppy country wore good horses out, and that the alkaline waters of such creeks still known as Bitter, Gyp, and Croton, could literally tear a command of the toughest men to pieces. And so he travelled light, with six weeks' rations and only thirty days of *half forage* for mules and mounts. Wagon trains could not keep up with any command operating swiftly enough to catch the Indians, and the only way to get the job done, he emphasized, was to take good care of their horses and keep a-moving. The campaign was to start about the middle of September, 1874.[19]

And so the columns were put in motion. Miles and Price, working in cooperation, began giving the scattered bands

[19] A.G.O., Department of Texas, Letters Sent, September 6, 1874; Carter, as cited, 475-476; Richardson, as cited, 388-389; Nye, as cited, 211-214.

trouble in the northern Panhandle and kept them on the move in the McClellan Creek and North Fork regions. Miles' advance scouts and guides under Lieutenant Frank D. Baldwin came into Adobe Walls just in time to discourage a second attack by the Indians upon that tiny, beleaguered place. From there he crossed the Canadian and routed a small band near the mouth of Chicken Creek. He then turned back and rejoined the main command coming from Camp Supply, to the northeast, at a point twelve miles west of Antelope Hills in Hemphill County.

From there they pushed southwest toward the Sweetwater, in the beginning of the squeeze from four sides which was designed to force the scattered tribes into their roughest retreat along the headwaters of Red River, where Mackenzie was advancing to meet them.[20] On the Sweetwater, in Wheeler County, Miles' force struck the trail of a considerable body of Indians, engaged in a spirited fight, and put them to flight with great loss of equipment. The Indians passed over the North Fork and headed southwest, across the *Llano Estacado.*[21]

At the same time, Davidson was working through the Indian country west of Fort Sill, picking up segments of the tribes that realized the futility of further rebellion against "the white man's road."[22] Miles camped on McClellan Creek in the eastern Panhandle while his men continued to harass the scattered bands. Those wily warriors turned the tables, however, by corralling his wagon train on the Washita as it returned from Camp Supply, where, except for the fortunate escape of a volunteer through its lines after help, it would probably have

[20] Nelson A. Miles, *Personal Recollections and Observations of*, Chicago, 1896, pp. 163-167; Alice Blackwood Baldwin, *Memoirs of the Late Frank D. Baldwin*, Los Angeles, 1929, pp. 70 ff.; and Annual Report of C. C. Augur to A.A.G., Military Division of the Missouri, September 28, 1874. In his memoirs Miles notes that all the columns were "moving toward the same locality and for the same general purpose, but without any definite concert of action." p. 163.

[21] Miles, as cited, 168; William Harding Carter, *The Life of Lieutenant General Chaffee*, Chicago, 1917, pp. 70-72.

[22] Nye, in a splendid investigation of the Indian side of all these troubles, gives the dramatic details. See also Augur's Annual Report, September 28, 1874, *U. S. Army Commands.*

been wiped out,[23] though Price, apparently badly scared of the whole business, wandered by with his command within hearing of the shooting.

Miles continued his operations to the north of the main fork of Red River until fall. On November 8, one of his captains, Frank Baldwin, tore into an encampment of Cheyennes on McClellan Creek in a considerable engagement and recaptured two little girls, Adelaide and Julia German, who had been taken captive when the Indians killed their parents on the trail in western Kansas.[24]

Back to the south Mackenzie was on the move. He left his supply camp on Catfish Creek and worked his way northward

past the head of the Wichita into the valley of the Quitaque. The weather grew worse as rain storms broke upon them and howling winds turned to cutting northers. A few worn-out horses had to be dropped, and as there was little room for sentiment in the stark business, Mackenzie had them shot to keep them out of the hands of the Indians. The storms continued, and as rain poured on them in the Quitaque the faithful and indefatigable Lawton was forced to drop his wagon train behind, but that night he showed up with twelve mules snaking a load of welcome beef through the mud.

From the Quitaque they turned west between a gap in the

[23] Nye, as cited, 215-218; Miles, as cited, 172 ff.

[24] Baldwin, as cited, 70-75; Nye, as cited, 226; Miles, as cited, 176; Grace E. Meredith, *Girl Captives of the Cheyennes*, Los Angeles, 1927, pp. 15 ff.

caprock and toiled up the caprock of the Staked Plains, Lawton's fighting his way through the mud and up on top with the supply train to rejoin them after they had marched but four miles. Here another wet norther continued to buffet them. Farther west a detachment reached Tule Canyon, and on the 25th of September the column marched to the head-springs of that gorge while the wagons were left behind, bogged down in mud.

Mackenzie detached Lieutenant Thompson with his Tonkawa scouts and guides in pursuit of a party of Indians he had discovered. On the night of the 25th the braves attacked Mackenzie's main camp in force but did not succeed in stampeding the horses. There were light skirmishes with scouting parties that day, while Lawton again managed to catch them with supplies. That night they marched north toward the Palo Duro, and before day the column was met by scouts who reported a fresh, large trail.

Just as day was breaking, September 27, 1874, the column came up to where the Palo Duro cuts its colorful and sheltered way through the great plateau, near where it describes the big bend to the east of the village of Happy. The scouts peered over the rim of the canyon to see hundreds of Indian teepees stretching along its bed far below, to the north, past the mouth of Cañoncito Blanco. Not an Indian was stirring.[25]

In single file the soldiers worked their way down the precipitous canyon wall toward the teepees. Three companies were at the bottom before the Indians, sleeping late in perfect confidence of their security, discovered them. Scattered firing

[25] Mackenzie captured a noted Indian trader, Jose Piedad Tafoya, during this campaign. According to Charles Goodnight, Tafoya knew the Plains like a book. Mackenzie ordered him to lead the command to the Indian camp. He refused until the determined General had hanged him three times to a propped-up wagon tongue, and then, after he came to, he was willing to talk and showed the scouts to the Indians in the wild and fancied security of the Palo Duro. In his resentment over what he considered their betrayal, Quanah, the Comanche chieftain, told Goodnight he was going to broil the *comanchero* alive if he ever caught him. See *Charles Goodnight, Cowman and Plainsman*, 196; Carter, as cited, 498-500; and the account of his hanging, Frank Lloyd to J.E.H., June 12, 1935.

began while the troops still on top scrambled down, quickly fell into battle formation, and joined in the fight. The braves broke and scurried up the sides of the canyon, finding shelter behind the boulders and the cedars, while all about were snorting and running horses, screaming women and children, and wild confusion.

Beaumont's company made a circle and rounded up the Indians' horses and mules, bringing them back down the canyon in a great herd. Then the braves opened fire from their vantage above and wounded a bugler. Mackenzie, aware of his danger from this source, sent troops to cover the rear of his command while he concentrated on the destruction of the villages. By mid-afternoon he had devastated the camps, and realizing that the scattered warriors could not be run out of the rocks without undue sacrifice on his part, he ordered his men out of the canyon and went into camp with 1424 captive *"ponies, mules,* and *colts"* held in close herd, completely surrounded by the command.

Next day he turned some of them over to the Tonkawas and ordered the balance, 1048 head, shot. "The Bone Pile," marking the site of the worst horse slaughter on the Plains of Texas, was a gruesome landmark along the Tule Canyon for many years—until hauled away to be sold for fertilizer by the early hard-pressed farming settlers of the region.

From his camp on the Tule, October 1, 1874, Colonel Mackenzie, in keeping with his usual brevity, sent a fourteen-line report by runner through Fort Sill to General Augur. The expedition thus far, he noted, had killed only four Indians whose bodies "fell into our hands"—one in the fight just before they had dropped into the Palo Duro, and three in the Canyon proper. He could not know, of course, what other casualties the elusive Comanches, Kiowas and Cheyennes had incurred but they were quite light.[26]

26 R. S. Mackenzie to C. C. Augur, October 1, 1874, *U. S. Army Commands.* J. H. Taylor to C. C. Augur, October 12, 1874, A.G.O., Department of Texas, Letters Sent, 622-623; Nye, as cited in *Carbine and Lance,* erroneously reports that

After further scouting on the Plains between Blanco Canyon
and the Palo Duro, the command again turned south, evidently with the intention of marching to McClellan Creek.
Their course more or less paralleled the canyon. On October
6 the troops came upon six Mexican wagons drawn by oxen,
the owner of which claimed to be hunting buffalo for his
winter's meat. Next day Mackenzie caught two more New
Mexicans with a *carreta* who admitted that they had been
trading with the Indians. He put them under arrest and con-
fiscated their oxen and a bunch of burros. The command then
obviously struck the Tierra Blanca and turned down it to camp
within sight of its junction with the Palo Duro Creek, near the
western end of the gorge, about where the town of Canyon
stands. That night their Tonkawa scouts came in, and next
morning Mackenzie ordered the command upon the back-
trail.[27]

On the way toward the Tule they met three of their wagons
with badly needed corn and learned from the drivers that the
Mexicans, the alleged buffalo hunters, had joined about a
hundred Indians that were headed east and north into the
breaks along Red River. On October 12, Mackenzie started
his infantry on their way south to the supply camp. They were
engaged in guarding the wagon train, a detail of cavalry with
some sixty broken-down horses, and all the sick and disabled.

He took a pack outfit with fifteen days' rations and turned
east, passing through what is now the Silverton country, and
down a long ridge, probably that which is now known as
Schott Hill, into the breaks. After marching north about two
miles he reached Red River, crossed it, and emerged on a
large prairie, in the present JA Ranch, now known as Mulberry

---

the Indians suffered no loss. Mackenzie noted that the troops were in excellent
spirits and did not even mention his wounded man. Sergeant John B. Carlton, who
was with the scouts, recalled that upon their return ride through the canyon they
"passed over dead Indians everywhere," and that the troops suffered two dead and
one wounded." Carter, *The Old Sergeant's Story,* 109.

27 Carter, *On the Border With Mackenzie,* 482-499.

Flat. He followed the Indian trail until dark caught him, and then pitched camp on Mulberry Creek. Next day his scouts jumped a party of Indians and captured thirteen of their ponies without succeeding in engaging the braves in battle.

After a big circle to the north and east, the column turned south again to cross Red River near the mouth of the Salt Fork. They replenished their meat with buffalo killed on the march, passed Quitaque Peak at noon on the 18th, and thence rode south by the head of the Big Wichita to their old camping site at Cottonwood Springs, where they laid up to rest men and horses and await the arrival of Lawton's train from Griffin. When he got there, on schedule as usual, the rations and forage were quickly packed on mules, and the command struck out for the supply camp in the present Spur country, thirty-five miles away, while Lawton turned back down the Mackenzie Trail to Griffin in his steady struggle to keep them going.[28]

Buell had moved up Red River as planned, and on October 9 struck some Indian camps on the Salt Fork, destroying three: one of seven, another of seventy-five, and "finally one of about four hundred" lodges. He killed only one Indian, but chased the main band out on the Plains, from where they turned north toward McClellan Creek and the North Fork, and from where some of them headed for Sill to beg for peace.[29]

All columns kept up a continual call for more corn for the mounts and mules and supplies for the men, for the fall and winter of 1874 were long to be remembered, even on the Plains of Texas, for relentless severity. While he was in the Red River country, Mackenzie had sent his wagons northeast to load out again at Camp Supply, Indian Territory. The wagons reached there with teams badly broken down. Meanwhile, he ordered that corn be sent the expeditions in the Panhandle by way of Fort Bascom, in New Mexico, and Camp Supply, in the Territory.[30] At the same time, the news was relayed to General

28 Carter, as cited, 500-503.

29 J. H. Taylor to C. C. Augur, October 24, 1874, A.G.O., Department of Texas, *Letters Sent.*

30 J. H. Taylor, to C. C. Augur, October 29, 1874, *U. S. Army Commands.*

Augur, October 29, 1874, that the savages generally were so harassed by the converging columns that "the Indian war in this section is rapidly collapsing" as various tribes hot-footed it for the reservations.

Nevertheless, plans were being made to establish a new post in the Panhandle, and on the thirteenth of November Mackenzie was ordered to proceed to McClellan's Creek as soon as he could assemble enough supplies to maintain him, and select a site for a new camp with an eye to "its fitness as a base of supplies . . . for winter operations." The exact location of the new post, the forerunner of Fort Elliott, would "be determined hereafter when more accurate knowledge of the country and its resources in that vicinity has been obtained."[31]

Upon his return to his old camp, Mackenzie had found that the wagon train to Camp Supply had crossed a big Indian trail to the north, which apparently pointed to the headwaters of the Blanco. Again he sent out a column to investigate. It found that the trail turned and headed south across the Double Mountain Fork of the Brazos, down by Lagunas Cuates or Double Lakes, and by Tahoka.[32] The troops camped one night at Tahoka Lake and next morning marched sixteen miles, east by south, discovered a small Indian camp, and in the hot fight that followed killed four braves, captured twelve squaws and seven papooses, and a horse herd of 156 head. Next day they bore to the north and dropped off the plains to water out on Yellowhouse Creek, and from there swung back to the Blanco to report again at camp November 9th. They were badly in need of rest, for rains and northers kept beating the mounts to death in spite of the churning of the wagon trains back and forth to Griffin, fetching corn over the Mackenzie Trail.

Mackenzie knew that discipline and condition of men had to be maintained. Drilling went on despite a storm that froze the tents into solid sheets of ice on November 19th. Mackenzie struck out with the command a few days later toward Mc-

31 A.A.G. to R. S. Mackenzie, November 13, 1874, *U. S. Army Commands*.

32 For log of expedition, see Carter, *On the Border With Mackenzie*, 514-519.

Clellan Creek but was forced to stop and camp at the head of the Running Water. From there, November 27th, he wrote Augur that he had been lying in camp for three days because his teams "were entirely unable to get through" the mud on the Plains.

He had sent Lawton back down the canyon to the supply camp thirty miles away to bring up a fresh train and additional forage and rations, while his spies again combed the Quitaque country and the Palo Duro around the mouth of the Canoncito in search of Indian sign. As he wrote, they suffered another sleet and snow. Nevertheless, he reported that upon leaving he expected to be able to make the march to McClellan Creek in five days or less—a most ambitious schedule.[33]

His scouts returned to report no fresh sign in any direction except at the Yellowhouses, far to the southwest. Further exchange of dispatches with Augur confirmed Mackenzie in his growing conviction that it would be better to take his column back to post, recruit men and horses, and set out for McClellan with a fresh command. On December 3rd, he sent his wagon train back from the vicinity of Plainview, and marched himself, with a "view of breaking up the expedition."

On the way he could not resist another lick at the Indians. He headed south by the Yellowhouse and Tahoka Lake, off the plains again near the head of the Colorado, and down by Mucha Que, the singular peak near the village of Gail in present Borden County. After a few minor skirmishes with small and scattered bands, the column pushed east over heavy ground in absolutely devastating weather, through snow, ice and mud, at last into Fort Griffin on December 28, 1874. Mackenzie had left it at Duck Creek upon getting word that the Commander of the Department of Texas wished to see him in San Antonio on Christmas Day—hardly for the purpose of celebration, though Mackenzie had earned one.[34]

33 R. S. Mackenzie to C. C. Augur, November 27, 1874, as quoted by Carter, 509-511.

34 Carter, as cited, 514-517.

The campaign was over. In effect the Indian Wars of Texas were done, though in the years before the frontier was gone there would be other expeditions, bloodshed and serious fighting. They would be nothing to compare with the devastation that had been wrought by the reservation tribes against Texas in the period just past, and Mackenzie's determined movements against them.

Other notable men were to come to Fort Concho. But not again would this post fall under the command of such a resourceful campaigner, determined disciplinarian, and stern driver of men and self as this battered warrior, Ranald Slidell Mackenzie—the sort that the country has fortunately produced and placed in the lead when needed most.

In the taciturnity induced by his suffering, reserve, and innate dignity, his men at times resented him. With just but undeviating discipline, he broke his officers for showing less tempered steel than his. But their resentment never led to loss of respect. For somehow they knew that the ruthless nature of the implacable Plains of Texas, coupled with the rugged fiber of the red-men they faced, would tolerate no other kind.

Mackenzie saw additional frontier duty at Forts Clark and Sill. He served in the Black Hills and against the Utes in Colorado and the Apaches in Arizona. For awhile he commanded the District of New Mexico and finally the Department of Texas, after which, still suffering from his wounds, he was retired March 24, 1884, "for disability in line of Duty."

He was a gallant though diffident figure before the ladies and was never married. No time could be found for love or gracious living in the rigorous work he set for himself. With his lonely, introspective nature accentuated by bodily suffering, he died a tragic death at the youthful age of forty-nine. He had sacrificed his mind as well as his body in the service of his country. Today a prosperous but heedless people scurry across a forgotten trace upon the Texas Plains that he originally blazed with toil and suffering—a trace once known as The Mackenzie Trail.

[226]

CHAPTER XIII

Shafter and the South Plains

WHEN THE ARMY called off its winter operations late in 1874 and the weather-beaten columns limped back to their respective posts, they carried with them rather intimate knowledge of the geography of the Panhandle of Texas. Two years before, General Augur had commented enthusiastically upon the fact that Mackenzie, in his march to the Fort Sumner country and his return by way of the Canadian to the Palo Duro, had proved that herds could be driven directly across the Plains. By the time four different expeditions and their many divergent details got back from the Indian war in 1874, they had covered the country that had once held travelers in fear and awe.

For several years, scouting parties and major expeditions from Fort Concho had explored the country north to Big Springs, to Mucha Que or the head of the Colorado, and on through Cañon Rescate or the Yellowhouses to the head-springs of Running Water Draw near present Plainview. In repeated "sash-shays" and forays, small details and great columns by foot, horseback and wagontrain had covered thousands of miles. Men who move thus slowly, alert to the dangers about them as essential to survival, and keyed to nature for food, fuel and drink, learn the land more intimately than in any other way.

Thus the Panhandle proper had lost something of its repellent nature, though in the happy absence of a chamber of commerce it was yet hardly considered a health resort. There still remained, however, a great portion of West Texas that almost every prospective traveler looked upon with trepidation. It included that broad sweep of Plains from south of the Yellowhouses to the old Butterfield Trail, and from the eastern caprock to the Pecos.

Except for the course that Marcy, Pope, and a few others had followed through the Midland country, and Shafter's floundering trails in pursuit of Indians in the White Sands—except for these this vast region was unknown. From the Staked Plains along the Running Water, with their surface as placid as Walden Pond, to where, farther west, their gentle, grassy undulations broke into choppy seas of dunes of sand and finally gave way to the alkali flats, it was still virtually an unknown land. The Texans who had by now taken the ranges of the Pecos in New Mexico kept within easy watering distance of that sinuous and gyppy stream, while those bound farther west usually followed the old Butterfield Trail from Fort Concho.

Straggling Indians drifted across the Plains into which the head-draws of the North and Middle Concho fingered out in a vain hope of finding water. Where these vagrant redskins went and how they managed to live when they got there were among the mysteries of that illimitable land of sunshine and space.

Upon these Plains the seasons were often unusually severe. A grasshopper plague that drifted south from Kansas in glistening waves in the bright summer sun of 1874 had been followed by a frigid season that began in early fall. Blizzards cut shivering troops to the bone wherever they went and left emaciated, drawn and dead horses on the trails behind them. Early in January, 1875, the report reached Concho that

Buell's column had to abandon everything and get into Griffin on foot. Captain Parke, 9th Cavalry was lost 7 days in the snowstorm. In

[228]

short, nature appears to have been opposed to the expedition, as owing to snow, rain, high streams, muddy roads, and cold weather and consequently lack of forage, there appears to be considerable distress everywhere.[1]

From Fort Concho additional supplies were sent to Captain J. B. Parke, who, in charge of the Supply Camp, was still on the Fresh Water Fork, but was trying to get back to the fort. He at last reached Concho with nineteen Indian women and children captives, who were kept corralled there for months.

At the same time, General Augur, relenting of his earlier decision of keeping the troops scouting throughout the winter, was watching the drift of scattered bands into Fort Sill and deliberating the possibility of further trouble from Mexico. While anticipating raids from that sector, he was trying to arrange a joint movement against the Indians there through General Fuero, "the Mexican Commandante of the frontier," whom he hoped to meet in February.[2]

At this time Fort Concho had eight sets of company quarters, and as the troops wearily worked their way south, Major Henry Douglass, post commander, was greatly put out over how to put them up. He complained that "there will be congregated at this Post ten companies of cavalry and 4 of Infantry" when the various commands got in. He simply planned to double them up, since it was essential that all be under shelter in view of the severity of the season. But the officers were already giving him trouble, as those temporarily at Concho were demanding the quarters of permanent officers whom they happened to outrank. Douglass favored his regular staff but called on the Adjutant General for help.[3]

Matters of larger import than the bickerings of officers in quarters were engaging the minds at headquarters. Plans for the first telegraph into West Texas were under way. The Secretary of War had approved the construction of the United

1 *Letter Book,* I, 366-368.

2 C. C. Augur to W. T. Sherman, January 11, 1875, Department of Texas, *Letters Sent,* 718-719; *Letter Book,* I, 459.

3 H. Douglass to A.A.G., January 13, 1875, *Letter Book,* I, 373.

States Military Telegraph Line which would shortly connect Concho with the outside world. Surveys for the extension of the Texas and Pacific Railroad, west from Dallas to El Paso, were being pushed, and escorts from Concho were detailed to see them safely across the *Llano Estacado*. Hundreds of hide hunters were killing off the buffalo, and with the rise of grass in the spring, cowmen began gathering herds on crowded ranges farther east to ease them west in that casual but artful way of finished hands with cattle.

Across the river from the post, San Angelo was spreading from its original picket *jacals* into a village of depravity and prominence, and was connected with the outside world through Benficklin, a village that had grown up around the stage station of the El Paso mail route a few miles away. Already, ambitious men had organized the county, that great political subdivision that the Legislature had generously cut out half across West Texas. It extended almost from the Painted Rocks to Horsehead and was named Tom Green, to keep verdant the memory of a notable patriot of early Texas.

In a very real sense, that broad and open world of wind and sod was being taken by enterprising men who moved without fear or inhibition. Mostly they came of the fair-skinned stock that originally poured out of northern Europe. For generations they had moved in migratory waves, successively overlapping those that had rolled out before. They were always eagerly looking for fresh fields of interest, endeavor and adventure beyond the setting sun.

But no matter their origin, they quickly fell in love with the ways of the West and came to believe, implicitly, that the Lord was a close and partial partner in the place they had chosen to live. The enthusiasm of these zestful and joyous spirits was something to behold. Some would stay, but in their optimism others suspected that farther west the land was better. What, they were beginning to ask, was the nature of the country that seemed to stretch into an infinity of grass beyond them?

[230]

The Military Department of Texas decided to find out. With Mackenzie now watching over the Indian warriors at Fort Sill, there still remained another officer of sturdy metal to whom the Department could turn. Lieutenant Colonel William R. Shafter was ordered to take a column out of Fort Concho to penetrate and explore the South Plains sea of grass.

Meanwhile the late commander of Sill, the ambitious but petty military apostle of the Indian peace policy, Colonel Benjamin H. Grierson, took over at Fort Concho, April 30, 1875. Two months later Shafter was ordered to move the headquarters of the 24th Infantry from Fort Duncan on the Mexican border and prepare for the new expedition. He set up camp near Concho and entered upon that considerable task, for which, by nature and long experience, he was qualified. Grierson was directed to furnish from his post five companies of the 10th Cavalry, of fifty men each, and the command began to take shape.

Shafter brought together the largest expedition ever to march away from Concho. With nine troops of the 10th Cavalry, two companies of the 24th and one of the 25th Infantry, he left in the heat of mid-summer, July 14, 1875. Lieutenant John L. Bullis commanded a party of Seminole scouts, while the Tonkawas, armed with Spencer rifles, and faithful in the chase though sometimes suspected of cannibalism in victory, were in charge of Lieutenant C. R. Ward.

This striking cavalcade of nine troops of cavalry, sixty-five wagons drawn by six-mule teams, a pack train of nearly 700 mules, and a trailing beef herd crawled up the North Concho and out of sight. It too was headed for Blanco Canyon. Seventeen days later and 180 miles farther north, Shafter stopped and set up his supply camp on the good water of the Blanco.[4]

4 M. L. Crimmins, "General Mackenzie and Fort Concho," West Texas Historical Association *Year Book*, X, 1934, p. 29; W. R. Shafter to A.A.G., January 4, 1876, U. S. Army Commands, p. 1; W. R. Shafter to Grierson, June 23, 1875. Shafter's report is published in the West Texas Historical Association *Year Book*, as cited, IX, 1933, pp. 82 ff.; J. H. Taylor to Commanding Officer, Fort Concho, July 17, 1875.

By this time the Quahada tribe, led by Quanah, had gone into the reservation, and knowing this, Shafter broke his command into units of two or three companies. Each planned "to scout as much country as possible and to scout mainly into the Plains lying west and south of Supply Camp, a country almost unknown, except to Indians."

It takes lots of water to supply such a large command. But Shafter anticipated no trouble since good rains had fallen. He knew many of the wet-weather lakes would be full, though so far as known, the country he faced had little or no living supply. In line with his plan of operation he had, on the way north, dropped Captain Nicholas Nolan and two companies of cavalry at Rendlebrock Springs, between the North Concho and the site of Colorado City. Nolan scouted west and rejoined the command on the Blanco after destroying a large Indian camp "with all their dried meat, lodges, skins, cooking utensils, clothing, etc."

Shafter sent a detachment under Captain C. D. Viele by way of Mackenzie's Trail to Portales Spring in eastern New Mexico and thence to the Palo Duro in the Panhandle to prove his suspicion that there were no Indians on the North Plains.[5]

Shafter took four companies with Seminole scouts and struck out upon what was perhaps the most remarkable march in the history of West Texas, "for the purpose of intercepting the band of Indians, found by Captain Nolan. . . ." These Indians had headed into the unknown region that reached for 150 miles west from the colorful breaks of the Colorado into that confusion of shinnery and sand that borders on the Pecos.

With characteristic self-effacement, Shafter devoted only one paragraph in his extensive report to this exceptional march of 840 miles through a region which was supposed to be devoid

5 In April, prior to Shafter's campaign, General Mackenzie had sent Dr. J. J. Sturms and one of his old sergeants, J. B. Charlton, to the Plains to find the Quahadas and tell them that if they did not come in he would follow them until he wiped them out. The young chief Quanah was in charge when they found them on the Blanco, and agreed to return. This troublesome group was therefore gone when Shafter arrived. See Nye, as cited, 235.

of water. He left his supply camp in present Crosby County on August 5, touched at the site of Lubbock, marched west to the lake called *Casas Amarillas,* forty-two miles to the west, and then headed southwest through an absolutely unknown waste. "During this scout I crossed the Plains to the Pecos," he said simply, "thence down to Horsehead Crossing, returning to Supply Camp Sept. 25th" principally through country, he concluded, heretofore "unknown to troops."

He did not say a word about the suffering of his men on that long and gruelling march from Indian Well near the site of the village of Bronco on the Texas-New Mexico line, to where they at last came out of the inhospitable region bordering the Pecos to save their horses and themselves with welcome water from the river. He did not even suggest the horrible agonies of thirst and apprehension of death endured by his command in the last stages of his march. His men felt sure that some would perish, and exchanged final words to be sent by possible survivors to their dear ones in the settlements.

But with the unpretentious Shafter all that dramatic detail that others would have played up in personal aggrandizement was but a part of the price a patriot must endure in line of honor and duty. As for the Indians, the only damage he did to them was to burn some abandoned lodge poles at an old camp.

His accomplishment, however, was a notable one and more in line with peaceful settlement than pursuit of war. He backtracked from Horsehead Crossing up the river to the Falls, and turned northeast around the lower end of the heavy White Sands. From the familiar waterings there, he kept northeast to ascend the caprock over the future oil fields of the Permian Basin, and once again on the Staked Plains turned due north. When he began to suffer for water he headed due west for a long march to the willow-marked holes he had discovered four years before, near the corner of New Mexico.

He found signs of an old Indian trail that bore north by west. Characteristically, he determined to find where it had gone. He followed it to where the Indians had gotten water by digging in a sandy draw, which he named Dug Springs. Farther north he came to a prominent spring. He stopped there long enough to build a rock monument on a hill a mile and a quarter southwest. It was of white stone, eight feet at the base, four at the top and seven and a half feet high—a marker that could be seen for several miles in every direction. It immediately gave the name to the important watering, Monument Spring.

He continued almost due north to strike his outward trail near Indian Well, and turned northwest to the lake called Quemas, or Quemada, now known as Silver Lake, in the northwest corner of Cochran County. From here the command trailed back by way of the Yellowhouses to Punta del Agua, and thence to the supply camp at the mouth of Blanco Canyon.[6] There Shafter spent some time "recruiting his animals and reclothing his men," and then really turned in to cover the South Plains.

On October 12, 1875, he moved out with six companies of cavalry and two of infantry, again to the headwaters of Yellowhouse Canyon. Here he detached Captain Baldwin to march south by way of Tahoka Lake and the Mucha Que— or as he called it the Moo-cha-Ko-way country—to Sulphur Springs and to Big Spring, where Baldwin was to set up camp. From there he was to prowl the country south and west.

Shafter himself proceeded south, by a course a little farther west, by Lagunas Cuates or Double Lakes, seven miles northwest of the site of Tahoka, and thence to the largest lake on the South Plains, Laguna Sabinas or Cedar Lake, some twenty-five miles northeast of the site of Seminole. He described it as being six miles long and four wide.[7]

6 W. R. Shafter to A.A.G., January 4, 1875. Frank P. Hill, who has studied the South Plains history, topography and landmarks for years, has helped establish these old names in relation to the present ones.

7 The Plains landmarks had been named by the *comancheros* of New Mexico,

Like most of the Plains lakes it was too salty to use, but as Shafter reported, they "had plenty of good water in numerous wells or rather *dug* springs, in a ravine at the North end and several large wells at the south end, of slightly brackish water, but fit for use for men and animals. Water can be found by digging anywhere near the edge of the lake. Grass in vicinity excellent and plenty of wood (roots)."

Lieutenant John L. Bullis, detached from the command, reached Sabinas on October 18th and at this most prominent, as well as one of the most isolated, of the South Plains waterings, discovered an Indian encampment. He charged upon it but the Indians escaped. He did capture twenty-five of their horses and mules and "destroyed . . . all their supplies, consisting of 50 sacks of mesquite beans, 3 or 4 thousand pounds of buffalo meat, about 100 undressed buffalo hides, 100 good lodge poles, cooking utensils, etc."

From here Shafter, who followed him in, turned due south on the Indian trail for thirty miles "to five large wells," which were to become the site of a famous South Plains ranch. The Indian trail led on. Here he detached Lieutenant Andrew Geddes with two companies of cavalry and Seminole scouts, ordering him "to follow the trail as long as possible." Shafter took the two remaining companies and struck west toward Monument Spring.

---

though there was much corruption of the Spanish by Anglo-Saxons unversed in the language. Properly this should be *Laguna Sabina*, but I have followed Shafter's use, in keeping with his report and maps.

Geddes was one of those remarkably determined individuals, badly out of the place in the world today, in that he took the English language literally and believed in following orders. He left Shafter at Five Wells and took the trail that led southeast, finding water in the depressions, or rainy-weather lakes, along the way. He watered at Mustang Springs, continued south and discovered another large salt lake southeast of Midland, now known as Peck's Springs. The lake was dry but the Indians were getting water at a spring on the south side.

Here Geddes found signs of a much-frequented Indian camp where some raiding party had been holding a herd of cattle. Apparently they had butchered the remnant and boned and packed the meat upon breaking camp, as the heads of fifteen freshly killed beeves were scattered about. Geddes again took the trail, still bearing east of south, until he reached the Centralia Stage stand on the old Butterfield Trail near present Stiles. Finding no water there, he turned east along the mail road to the Mustang Water Holes, refilled his kegs, packed up, and again pushed on. He followed the tracks of the Indian ponies across the lower portion of the Staked Plains and down Howard Canyon to where the Indians had watered out at Howard's Wells on the Lower San Antonio road.

Here Geddes told the drivers of his wagons to follow the road into Fort Clark, re-stock with provisions, and meet them on the "way back." Continuing with his pack outfit, he cut west across the divide to the Pecos, forded the river below the mouth of Independence Creek, and turned south-southwest through rough country toward the Rio Grande. On October 31st Lieutenant Hans J. Gasman, who kept a diary of the scout, noted that "the command passed an old Indian camp numbering about twenty five *Wicker ups*. This days march was a very hard one over very mountainous country, and completely covered with Bear and Dagger grass, causing the lameness of several horses and mules."

[236]

On November 2nd, within two and a half miles of the Rio Grande, Geddes sighted the Indians in camp and charged them, killing the only brave there and capturing four squaws and a little boy. The women told him that "the chief and the balance of their party . . . had gone somewhere in Texas."

Next day the troops turned back. They marched slowly, as their horses were playing out in the "rough and rolling country." Gasman observed that many had gotten lame, because the "ground [was] completely covered with small and large flint rocks and with Bear and Dagger grass as well as Mesquit and cat claw." They found plenty of good water, but the horses began going to pieces "on account of the poorness of the grass." On November 5th the troops complained of the "country . . . exceedingly rough and broken, and no game in this section . . . having been hunted so much by the Indians, the only game at all on the trip was now and then a stray buck or doe."

They reached the Rio Grande at the Eagle's Nest Crossing. Here they forded the Pecos, went into camp, and sent a courier to San Felipe, present Del Rio, for rations and forage. On November 7th they marched to the San Antonio Road, where a wagon loaded with flour and forage met them. When they got to the Devils River they found that the teams sent in from Howard's Well to Fort Clark had given out, "and one days supplies *only*" had been sent by the post commander. From San Felipe they marched into Fort Clark, rested three days, and then took the military road back toward their home post at Fort Concho, passing, for a welcome change, up the valley of the Nueces "with game of every description abounding in the hills."

On November 27th this stubborn Iowan, who had advanced from privacy to a lieutenant-colonelcy in the Civil War and who had been cited for gallantry at Vicksburg and elsewhere, led his detachment across the peaceful parade ground at Fort Concho and reported to the commandant for duty. He had, with meritorious fidelity, marched 650 miles over trying terrain following the trail as far "as possible" within the territorial bounds of the United States, and had wound up with only one scalp. Had less than an impartial providence watched over the affairs of warriors—both red and white—he would have got back with a tow sack full.[8]

Shafter himself continued his march sixty-three miles west to Monument Spring and picked up a large Indian trail. He followed it southeast to abandon it in the upper end of the White Sand Hills. He then turned north to a hitherto undiscovered watering northwest of the site of Andrews, a body of water—when water there is—that is still known as Shafter's Lake.[9] It had been used considerably as an Indian camp ground, as evidenced by "a large lot" of teepee poles. The Indians had "scattered in all directions." On November 1, 1875, Shafter and his command were back at Cedar Lake.

He hoped that Baldwin—out of Big Spring, and Geddes, working south, in between—might intercept the Indians that he had chased southeast down Monument Draw, and into the Sands. Others had scattered to the north, perhaps toward Casas Amarillas. He detached Lieutenant Thomas G. Lebo to prowl for them.

Lebo took roundance of the broad unwatered region that lay between by retracing the command's route to Double Lakes, thence north to the headwaters of the Yellowhouse Canyon, and again west to Casas Amarillas—future site of the southernmost headquarters of the XIT Ranch. Lebo returned to their supply camp, now moved out on the Plains to Double

8 Shafter, as cited; A. Geddes to Adjutant, Fort Concho, December 9, 1875, Hans J. Gassman, "Itinerary of Scout;" Heitman, *Historical Register,* as cited, 450-451.

Geddes' discovery of water holes and camping places south of present Big Lake and southwest of the head of the Middle Concho had much bearing on the operations out of Fort Concho in the late seventies and early eighties. Peck's Springs, a noted landmark and salt lake southeast of Midland, was a good camping place because of abundant chaparral in the draws, and a dug spring of brackish but not bad water in a ravine on the south side.

9 Frank P. Hill notes that Shafter's Lake is one of the few that retains its original name. Hill, mss. "Notes on the Shafter Expedition," files of author. See Shafter, as cited.

Lakes, to report that he had found no Indians. But he had discovered another hole of water to the north of Casas Amarillas, which the army called Lebo Lake in his honor, but which the Texas cowpunchers later changed to Bull Lake—to nobody's honor.

Shafter sent another detachment from Cedar Lake to Tobacco Creek on the headwaters of the Colorado to pick a spot for a new supply camp. He followed with the main command, and thence marched south to Big Spring where he found Captain Baldwin in camp. Then, in his indefatigable fashion, he at once started another detail back to Cedar Lake by way of Mustang Springs to chart the distance and the topography between, while he set out for Double Lakes in Lynn County to remove the supply camp to the new location on Tobacco Creek.

When this was done he again struck out for Cedar Lake, where he was concentrating his command with a view of a third expedition into New Mexico. On November 15th he ordered Lieutenant C. R. Ward to march "direct to Monument Spring," while he went to Five Wells, thirty-three miles farther south. Both were long marches for mounts and teams, through a region of heavy and obviously unwatered sand. From the upper end of Cedar Lake, Ward broke camp, and unsaddled and hobbled out his horses sixteen miles west-southwest on the night of November 18th, noting in his journal:

"Country sandy—wood scarce—no water. Water had been previously sent here in Kegs so that the animals suffered very little—Each animal was watered to the extent of 1½ gallons."

Next day, miles farther, he came to "an arroyo,"—sometimes called Seminole Draw—which obviously took its name from the Seminole scouts with Shafter's command. There the detail found a remarkable series of wells, evidently "a favorite resort of the Indians." These shallow wells, dug out in the sand and ranging from fifteen feet deep at the lower end of the draw to only four feet at the upper, were "of excellent quality, and [capable of] affording water for several thousand horses or cattle." There were about fifty of them within a distance of a mile and a half, and they were scooped out with sloping walls so that horses could walk down to drink. These henceforth became known as Ward's Wells, though the winds and shifting sands of West Texas soon filled the holes.

Three and a half miles west Ward came to another draw, in which were about twenty similar wells, and three miles south in another his scouts found several more. Grass was good and mesquite roots fairly abundant. The party was west of the buffalo range, but scattered beef heads and old trails, radiating out through the sandy grasslands and shinnery-covered dunes in every direction, pointed vividly to the fact that the spot was a favorite refuge for vagrant bands. Ward rejoined the command at Monument Spring, where Shafter, who had gotten there first, was "scouting the country in every direction."

On November 27th Shafter took the back trail by way of the wells discovered by Ward. While exploring that region he received a dispatch from the commanding general of the Department of Texas ordering him in at once. He marched at daylight next morning, down by Five Wells, southeast past Mustang Springs, and by a due course to the headwaters of the North Concho, which he reached December 9, 1875. Here he broke up the command by sending the companies to their respective posts. Nine days later he was again at Duncan, his own post on the Rio Grande, working upon the remarkable report of his very maze of scouting expeditions into and out, through and about, the South Plains of Texas and New Mexico.[10]

The nature of the man himself and the character of his campaign are likely to strike an age surfeited with drama as dull and colorless. But for the weathered native of this region who understands and appreciates the long search for water,

10 Shafter, report, as cited: Thomas C. Lebo, "Itinerary of Scout," etc., November 6-16, 1875; Thomas C. Lebo to W. R. Shafter, November 16, 1875; W. R. Shafter to A.A.G., December 6, 1875.

the eternal dread of drouth, and the stern limitations that a relentless nature imposes on those who live in keeping with its laws—he will know and understand that Shafter had proved himself a man. At last he had completely dispelled the dreary myth of "the *Llano Estacado*—the dreaded Zahara of North America."

He had thoroughly explored the Plains of Texas from the Big Spring and the Lubbock country on the east, through the White Sands to the Pecos on the west, and from the old mail line between Horsehead Crossing and Fort Concho on the south, to the Yellowhouse Canyon on the north. He had observed the extreme western range of the buffalo at the edge of the Sands. He had by wagon road connected the unknown waterings of the Staked Plains with the *comanchero* and Mackenzie Trails at Punta del Agua near the site of Lubbock, and with others at the head of the Colorado, the Big Spring, and the Conchos.

From the forks of these rivers his unbroken ruts cut their traces through the hitherto uncharted sod, from Fort Concho directly northwest by available water. Soon they would be followed by seasoned men, conditioned teams, and trailing herds, all the way to Monument Spring in the lower corner of New Mexico. From Blanco Canyon his wagon tongues had pointed west to the *comancheros'* camp grounds beneath their caves in the yellowish bluffs, which, when seen from afar in the fantastic distortions of a mirage, had resembled a great city and had given the place its name—Casas Amarillas, the Yellow Houses!

From there his wagon road led west by Silver Lake and Indian Well through undulating but apparently endless miles of red sage grass, shinnery and sand, to the Pecos at the mouth of the Blue. He had scouted down the Pecos along the course of the Goodnight Trail for more than 150 miles, and then had worked his way back through the Monahans Sand to discover what became Monument Spring. From there he had marched north through a waterless, brushless plain where bald-faced cattle now mow needle and grama grass in the shade of forests of derricks that plumb the depths of the earth for oil. What he failed to find is not worth mention, while much that he did is about the same.

Shafter had shown that the warriors of the Staked Plains, while still an allergic irritant, were no longer a serious problem. "Unless there should be an outbreak of the Indians in the Indian Territory," he advised, "but few troops will be necessary to keep the lower part of the Plains free from Indians." He saw correctly that the country he had covered was a choice land for cattle, and sagely prophesied that with protection "the frontier settlements in Western Texas would be advanced 150 miles within two years."

He regretted the fact that his command had killed only one Indian and captured but seventy-five ponies, "most of them of little value," though eleven good mules were caught. He had given the best of the mounts to his Seminole and Tonkawa scouts. The Indians that he had found, he added, "were driven from the Plains to Mexico, where they now are."

In his report there is not the least suggestion that anyone had suffered discomfort or hardship in exploring this arid land. His supplies had "been of the best quality and the full amount asked for." Yet he realized the significance of what he had seen as he "accurately mapped" that "magnificent grazing country." His simply written, conservative and interesting report, with his meticulously made manuscript maps, were for a long time the most comprehensive and accurate documents upon the geography of West Texas.

They were immediately seized upon by eager Texans and enterprising others intent upon finding fresh range and upon building rail lines and promoting towns. His report was published almost entire in a widely accepted historical work on Texas and generously quoted in statistical and boomer literature of the period. Besides this, he gave commercial cartographers the basis for showing the section upon their maps as something besides a perfect blank in pale pink or summer-sky blue. Now, except for the originals safely buried in the gray mausoleum that houses the National Archives at Washington, and an uninviting lake in West Texas that bears his name—but without significance, even to the natives—the modest Shafter is forgotten.

One feature of his operation forever remains. The land filled up as he had foreseen. But men ceaselessly pursue his search for water, and only with partial success. It is the everlasting problem. Above the rippling waves of grass throughout his expansive range, thousands of spinning mills, always facing the eternal wind, purr their geared force through baths of oil to lift a little of the essential water that Shafter stubbornly sought.

cNolan's Lost cNigger Expedition

On the hot afternoon of August 3, 1877, two colored troopers whipped their tired mounts down the hill from the north, splashed through the ford, and trotted across the parade ground to precipitate the most intense excitement that had yet stirred the pulse of Fort Concho. There was a frenzied use of the new telegraph line to flash the news to headquarters, and a resulting flood of urgent orders back along the wires to the commanding officers at Forts Griffin, Concho, and Davis. There was a scurrying of men to take the trail to the head of the Colorado. For the story the Negroes told was that Captain Nicholas Nolan and his colored cavalry, along with a volunteer company of buffalo hunters, some sixty-five men in all, were lost and starving for water on the Staked Plains.

In view of the expeditions of Mackenzie and Shafter, it hardly seemed possible that their wild and distraught accounts could be true. Yet their tales were so stark and vivid as to banish all doubt. Nolan's command had penetrated the Plains in search of Indians, had gotten lost, and had been wandering in confusion for days. At last its mad soldiers were fighting over the coagulated blood and heavy urine of dying horses and men, and staggering off in mutiny and confusion to perish in search of water. The two Negroes had deserted the command, found their way out, and traveled 200 miles by foot and horse in about five days to bring the harrowing news to Concho.

The uppermost question in everybody's mind from the commanding officer to the lowliest guard was how in the world could it happen? Could it be that Shafter and Mackenzie had minimized the risks, and had just been lucky themselves? Could it be that the earlier reports upon that desert land were simply the bald-faced truth, after all? Even granting as much, then what had happened to that experienced plainsman, the *comanchero*, Jose Tafoya, whom Mackenzie had impressed' into service and who was now guiding for Nolan? And what could have happened to that company of seasoned frontiersmen who volunteered to help kill Indians, the bloodthirsty buffalo hunters, who obviously knew the open country like a book? Or was Nolan himself simply to blame? These and similar questions were being bandied about as a searching party left post haste for the Plains to learn the truth about "Nolan's Lost Nigger Expedition."

Nicholas Nolan was an old-time Irish soldier. He had spent twenty-five years in the army, rising from private to captain by the end of the Civil War, and coming to Texas with the 10th Cavalry. He had been at Fort Concho for several years where he had served apparently faithfully but without distinction, though he had been cited for meritorious conduct during the Civil War. In the light of his later record, it seems reasonable to suppose that Nolan was rather careless by nature,[1] though at one time in the spring of 1875, during Grierson's period at the post, he was briefly in command at Concho. Carelessness could have been the cause of the trouble.

Since Shafter's noted expedition, the settlers he had anticipated had pushed west, following the buffalo hunters almost

---

[1] Heitman, as cited, 750; *Medical History*, vol. 404, pp. 136, 238; *Letter Book*, I, 422. The date of the arrival of the Negroes at Fort Concho is often given as August 4, 1877, but Davidson got the news at Jacksboro by wire from Concho on the 3rd.

to the foot of the Staked Plains. Yet once in a while a band of Indians either slipped away from the reservation in the Territory and went back to their old haunts, or, upon being granted permits to return for a buffalo hunt, did some devilment, such as killing a settler or stealing his horses in passing. They were giving quite a bit of trouble to the buffalo hunters in the Double Mountain country in the spring of 1877.[2]

Consequently, Colonel Grierson ordered Nolan and Company A of the 10th Colored Cavalry out of Fort Concho on July 4th for the purpose of "destroying any bands of marauding Indians" they could find. Nolan was ordered to march into the Big Spring country, and in case he did "not find a suitable camp in the vicinity" he was to select "some other" from which he could "successfully scout the country in all directions and render the desired protection to the settlers. . . ."[3]

Six days later Nolan and Lieutenant Charles L. Cooper, next in command, left the fort and marched twenty miles up the North Concho. The weather was terribly hot, and on the following day one of his men suffered sunstroke, "but soon recovered. . . ." They marched to the head of the river, in what is now the U Ranch, and thence thirty-five miles northwest to the Big Spring. From this point Nolan kept north to the Colorado, and set up a supply camp on Bull Creek seven miles northeast of Mucha Que peak, near where the village of Gail now stands. Here he found a party of buffalo hunters stubbornly scouring the South Plains for Indians that had depredated upon their camps in the Double Mountain country.

This party was guided by the noted Jose Tafoya, who had learned the Plains thoroughly as a *comanchero*. "The party requested me to accompany them in their search for Indians,"

[2] *Galveston Daily News*, January 6 and May 30, 1877; Frank P. Hill, "The South Plains and Our Indian Country," West Texas Historical Association *Year Book*, XII, 1936, pp. 34 ff.; Frank P. Hill, "Indian Raids on the South Plains," *Panhandle-Plains Historical Review*, VII, 1934, pp. 53 ff.; John R. Cook, *The Border and the Buffalo*, Topeka, 1907, pp. 180 ff.

[3] B. H. Grierson to Nicholas Nolan, *Letter Book*, July 4, 1877; *Army Commands*, Fort Concho, 1876-1883, pp. 63-64.

Nolan reported, "and having no guide with my command I was only too happy to accede to their request. . . ." Since the hunters had searched out the country from the Blanco west to Casas Amarillas without finding the Indians, Jose figured they might be located at Cedar Lake.

Nolan decided to march west in hope of finding them there. He had no pack mules, but he took the leaders from his four six-mule teams for that purpose. After establishing his supply camp, he sent his empty wagons with four mules each back down the trail to Concho for an "additional supply of Rations and forage." He left a sergeant and nineteen Negroes to guard the camp, and with Lieutenant Cooper, forty cavalrymen, and twenty-two hunters pulled out from Bull Creek. On the night of July 19, 1877, they camped fifteen miles away on Tobacco Creek.

Next day a party of Comanches under the vigorous Quanah Parker rode into his camp and produced a pass from the Indian agent at Fort Sill, countersigned by Colonel Mackenzie, authorizing Quanah's trip into Texas for the purpose of bringing "back Indians that had left the reservations." The hunters observed that Nolan swore mightily, but he was convinced that the pass was genuine. Furthermore, upon finding Quanah "liberally supplied with Government Horses, Equipment, Arms, and Ammunition and Rations," he said, "I did not feel authorized in detaining him." At 7:30 in the evening the command left Tobacco Creek and made a night march to Cedar Lake, fifty miles away. There it "went into camp on the ground where Lieutenant Colonel Shafter . . . had his supply camp in 1875."[4]

Instead of an abundance in the shallow holes which Shafter had used, Nolan found a scant supply of water indeed. The hot and dry summer of 1877 was having its effect on the seepage from the sand, and Nolan's men were forced to dip

[4] Nolan to the A.A.G., August 20, 1877. This document, consisting of 35 foolscap pages of script, which was Nolan's official report, has been edited and printed in the *Southwestern Historical Quarterly*, XLIV, 1940, pp. 62-74, by Dr. H. Bailey Carroll.

water up a cup at a time and pour it into their camp kettles. Thus slowly and tediously they watered their mounts and pack mules. The following day, Jose and some of the hunters scouted south to Five Wells in search of Indian sign, while Quanah again visited Nolan and then rode off in the direction of Monument Springs.

After being thirty hours without water, the scouting party returned to report that they had found an Indian trail twenty miles to the west. It pointed northeast toward Double Lakes. With this information to spur him on, Nolan packed up and pulled out that evening to make a dry camp twenty-five miles away. At Double Lakes again he experienced the same difficulty in getting water. As he had found no further fresh sign, he sent Jose and a detail of hunters seventeen miles west to what they called Dry Lake—the present Rich or Salt Lake of Terry County.

At about eleven o'clock the following morning, July 2nd, John R. Cook and another hunter rode back to report that Jose had discovered forty Indians moving northeast. Nolan ordered his men to mount and rode off at once to join Jose at a point on the trail west of Rich Lake. The hunters later reported, as an evidence of Nolan's carelessness, that some of his men left Double Lakes without filling their canteens, a grievous oversight that cannot be attributed to the excitement of leaving, as they did not march for several hours after the hunters had returned.

They had a hot dry ride of about twenty miles to where they found Jose waiting upon the trail. Before they had even got there, the Negro troops had drunk all their water, and the hunters began sharing their supply with them. This was Nolan's second tragic indulgence. The water should have been doled over twice as long. Night caught them and they made another dry camp.

Next day they followed the trail in a northeasterly direction for about twenty-five miles, despite the fact that the horses were "ga'nt and giving out," and two of the men suffered

[248]

sunstroke. Nolan detailed others to care for them and pushed on. This was his third major indiscretion. He should have headed for water while all were still able to travel and then returned to the trail. Meanwhile, the Indians, aware that they were being followed, had scattered like a bunch of blue quail, and the great plain trail frayed out in the edge of the sands. Here Nolan temporarily gave up the chase. While the command rested, Jose picked up the trail again, where the scattered Indians had converged, and Nolan's men pushed wearily along it, farther west—fifteen miles deeper into the sands.

They had then been without water for about thirty hours, the days had been oppressively hot, and, as Nolan reported, "the command now commenced to suffer exceedingly for water. Three of his men had tumbled from their horses in sunstroke, and others were straggling badly. A detail was sent "to goad" them on. Nolan asked the guide if he could get them to Laguna Plata—Silver Lake. Jose told them that he could, but that if they kept southwest on the trail he would have them on water within eight miles, though they might have to fight the Indians to get it.

As they parleyed over what course to pursue, Jim Harvey, leader of the hunters, rode up and slid off in the shade of his horse. He proposed to take the canteens and some of his strongest men and march with them to Silver Lake, which Jose estimated they could reach by midnight. Cook spoke up to tell Harvey that Jose had said they could get to water much nearer—within eight miles, probably at that pinpoint of moisture in that drifting sea of desiccated sand called Indian Well.[5]

According to Cook, Harvey urged Nolan to take the guide's advice, as he and the hunters placed implicit faith in Jose. But Nolan broke down in tears, called attention to his "twenty-five . . . prostrated" men, and insisted that they turn back and

5 Lester Wood, who has given long and thoughtful study to this expedition, is convinced that this was the point Jose had in mind, and that the command was bound to have been within easy marching distance. He differs with Dr. Carroll, who puts the party much farther north in the edge of New Mexico near Nigger Hills, where local legend always had them.

try to reach Silver Lake. The hunters, touched by the old campaigner's grief and concern, reluctantly agreed. Apparently this was another bad mistake. Nolan gave one of his private horses to Jose and told him to march ahead. The guide took a northeast course toward the Yellow Houses, and the desperate command followed as best as it could. Nolan detailed troops to stay with those who had suffered sunstroke and struggled on. With night they stopped, Nolan in panic and his troopers in near mutiny.

He selected eight of his most seasoned soldiers, loaded them with canteens, and told them to push on through the darkness in the direction taken by the guide, whom he hoped had at last found water.

These men disappeared in the darkness, while Nolan sent a man back to pilot Sergeant William Umbles, who had been left with one of the stricken men, into camp. In time, Umbles, his companion, and the troopers sent to get them approached through the darkness, leading a mule and disregarding Nolan's shouts, passed the camp and vanished into the illimitable space of the plains. With this, open mutiny had begun, and Nolan failed to take the severe but necessary steps to stop it.

Next morning he and Cooper scanned the empty landscape for sign of the guide and the eight missing men with the canteens. Not an object was in sight. Since their best packer had deserted with Umbles the evening before, Nolan fell in to help load the mules. When he looked up from this job, he said, "the buffalo hunters were scattered over the plains, their horses gone." In the suffering attendant upon the night's camp, the distracted men had failed to stake the horses, and they had wandered off to find water. Now the hunters, despairing of doing anything with Nolan's growling, inexperienced and rebellious command, had struck off in an effort to save themselves.

What precipitated the break was Nolan's own insistence upon changing their course again. As is usually the case with the inexperienced man in time of trouble, he was sure the guide was lost, and he insisted that they reverse their course and head back, southeast, to Double Lakes. The hunters estimated that these were at least fifty miles away, while they figured that they could reach Silver Lake even on their dying horses within a few hours. Cook claimed that the command simply broke up when Nolan insisted on this new and suicidal course. The hunters missed Silver Lake but some of them reached the Yellow Houses late that afternoon, and with water-filled canteens returned to save their straggling companions. Nolan and the portion of his command that was still intact pushed out on their own.

As they started off, Old Bill Benson, one of the most experienced buffalo hunters, quit his own party, simply saying that he was going back to the soldiers—evidently with the purpose of trying to save them. But Nolan's Irish obstinacy could not be shaken, and finally Benson shouldered his heavy Sharps in disgust, and marched off by himself toward Punta del Agua— the headwaters of Yellowhouse Canyon, near present Lubbock. Wright Mooar, noted hunter on the range at the same time, though not a member of the party, recalled that Benson's tongue was swollen out of his mouth by the time he got there.

But Benson was seasoned in the ruthless nature of the Staked Plains. He figured that if he lay down to drink, as an outdoor man usually does, he might faint when he touched the water. So he sat down, stuck his feet into the hole, scooped up a double handful, leaned back and threw it into his face. He did faint. But instead of falling forward into the pool and drowning, he fell on his back. In a few minutes he revived, feet still in the pool, soaking up water. After he had managed to drink, his swollen tongue subsided, and he became ravenously hungry, since he had not eaten for days.

He took his buffalo gun and shot the head off a duck he found on one of the water holes in the canyon, built a fire, and started to pick the bird, growing hungrier all the while.

The more he picked, he said, the smaller the duck got, until in his frenzy he threw it on the fire and roasted and ate it, feathers and all.

But according to his recollections published fifteen years later, he found "nothing to . . . eat except wild plums, upon which he subsisted four days longer. . . ." From the headwaters of the Yellow House, he walked into a hunters' camp on the Blanco and soon recovered from "five days and nights without food or water, and four more with wild plums only to eat. . . ." He completely recovered, but he never did believe that the noted Dr. Tanner lived for forty days without food.[6]

Meanwhile the colored Sergeant Umbles, his two deserters, Nolan and Gilmore, and their mule, were well on their way. They reached water at Double Lakes, and from there feverishly pushed on to the supply camp on the head-draws of the Colorado.[7] There Umbles and his fellow troopers reported to

[6] Cook, as cited, 271; "The Great Staked Plains," an account of Bill Benson's recollections, in the *Roswell Record*, June 10, 1892; Nolan's report, as cited; Cooper's account, *New York Tribune*, September 8, 1877.

[7] Nolan reported this party as being led by Corporal Gilmore, who also deserted, but the subsequent court-martial for the men found Umbles was the one who passed that night. *Records of the War Department*, vol. 546, G.C.M.O., 45, National Archives.

Sergeant T. H. Allsup, commanding the camp, that Nolan, while perishing for water, had told his men to save themselves as best they could. And there too they were joined by another trooper, George W. Fremont, who had been detailed by Nolan to care for a stricken man, but had deserted him to his death and had headed on his own for water.

Just how far they had traveled is a matter of conjecture. They were certainly a good day's march from Double Lakes when they deserted Nolan, and another weary day's travel from their supply camp. They could hardly have left the headwaters of the Colorado before August 1, 1877, no matter how anxious they were to get off the Plains. Thus their ride of 140 miles into Fort Concho in two days' time was noteworthy traveling. They reported to the post commander that they had left Nolan perishing on the Plains after he had ordered them to save themselves if they could. They claimed that they had gotten water and returned in search of Nolan, who could not be found.

Fort Concho wired the alarming news to General E. O. C. Ord, then in command of the Department of Texas, and the lines were shortly singing messages to the commanding officers from Fort Davis to Fort Richardson, and to the headquarters of the Division of the Missouri, in Chicago.

From the rather confused accounts of the survivors, Morrison, just then in command at Concho, suspected that Nolan was probably within twenty miles of Double Lakes. Colonel Davidson at Jacksboro sped his suggestion that Fort Stockton be called in to help, while Blunt, commander there, in confused conjecture hurriedly demanded to know how far Nolan might be from the Pecos, what was the possible strength of the fugitive Indians, where were the Yellow Houses, and since Nolan was lost in the "sand hills . . . what Sand Hill do you mean?"

With a measure of good judgment, Davidson came back with a wire to say that Captain P. L. Lee was scouting in the same section out of Fort Griffin and that he had ordered Lieutenant S. R. Colladay, in command at that fort, to send a detachment of Tonkawa scouts and a doctor "to help find and save life." He inquired if Grierson, in actual command at Concho, had not better do the same. Thus a party left Griffin at once to find Lee and rush him to Nolan's aid. Departmental headquarters at San Antonio urged Grierson to keep it "constantly informed," and Davidson, with an eye for discipline, was already wanting to know what the officers there were "going to do with the men who deserted Nolan." [8]

In the meantime, Nolan and his men were struggling against the tragic fate posed by hot sun and waterless sand. By the time Benson quit them, all semblance of discipline and order was gone, and the command scattered in keeping with its wild and frenzied will. Nolan and Lieutenant Cooper, sticking together, kept up their march toward Double Lakes until heat, exhaustion, and delirium had completely torn the command to pieces.

Cooper noted that "our men had dropped back, one by one," unable to keep up. "Their tongues and throats were swollen, and they were unable even to swallow their saliva— in fact they had no saliva to swallow. . . . My tongue and throat were so dry that when I put a few morsels of brown sugar, that I found in my coat pocket, into my mouth, I was unable to dissolve it. . . ."

At this juncture Cooper stopped and lay down. One of his own private horses staggered and fell to the ground, and Cooper in desperation had the Negroes cut the animal's throat. Officers and men eagerly swarmed around to quench their agonizing thirsts, and Cooper and Nolan too "drank heartily of the steaming blood."

For a short while it seemed to alleviate their "intense suffering." But evidently the horses had become diseased, as Cooper

8 All these messages are recorded in *Letters Received File*, Fort Concho, August 3-4, 1877, and Ord to A.A.G., Department of Texas, August 4, 1877.

thought, from their own deprivation, and "in a short time," he said, "we were in worse condition than before . . . we were soon attacked with 'blind staggers,' with the same symptoms as the horses." Thus the night wore on while they struggled, as they hoped, toward Double Lakes.

Next day, July 29th, and their fourth without water, all their horses were playing out. Nolan was catching and trying to drink their urine, and in utmost desperation at last committed himself to that bitter and killing resort of dehydrated and dying men. Cooper described their plight.

"Men gasping in death around us; horses falling dead to the right and left; the crazed survivors of our men fighting each his neighbor for the blood of the horses as the animals' throats were cut. Prayers, curses, and howls of anguish intermingled came to one's ears from every direction."

Their condition at this stage was described by Captain J. H. T. King, post surgeon at Fort Concho, in a detailed report, a few days later:

Vertigo and dimness of vision affected all; they had difficulty in speaking, voices weak and strange sounding, and they were troubled with deafness, appearing stupid to each other, questions having to be repeated several times before they could be understood; but they were also very feeble and had a tottering gait. Many were delirious. What little sleep they were able to get was disturbed with ever recurring dreams of banquets, feasts and similar scenes in which they were enjoying every kind of dainty food and delicious drink. At this stage they would in all likelihood have perished had they not resorted to the use of horse blood. As they gave out they cut them open and drank their blood. The horses had been so long deprived of every kind of fluid that their blood was thick and coagulated instantly on exposure; nevertheless, at the time it appeared more delicious than anything they had ever tasted. . . . The heart and other viscera were grasped and sucked as if to secure even the semblance of moisture. At first they could not swallow the clotted blood, but had to hold it in their mouths, moving it to and fro between the teeth until it became somewhat broken up, after which they were enabled to force it down their parched throats. The horse blood quickly developed diarrhoea . . .; their own urine, which was very scanty and deep colored, they drank thankfully, first sweetening it with sugar. A few drank the horses urine, although at times it was caught in cups and given to the animals themselves. They became oppressed with dyspnoea and a feeling of suffocation as though the sides of the trachea were adhering, to relieve which they closed the lips and breathed through the nose, prolonging the intervals between each inspiration as much as possible, gazing on each other, their lips thus closed were observed to be covered with a whitish, dry froth and had a ghostly, pale, lifeless appearance as though they would never be opened again.

Thus they compounded their misery, and in their distress grew suspicious of one another until the command flew to pieces in sullen and open mutiny.[9]

And then, as if in mockery of the puny efforts of man, that essentially ruthless land of scorching sand and sun hung its rain clouds on the horizon, and swung its gracious life-giving curtains of moisture from the heavens—but at a vast distance, and not for them. "Can you wonder that the minds of men gave way," Cooper continued, "and that instead of having with us the forty rational men who left camp with us, our party now consisted of eighteen men?"

As night again came on, Cooper tried to harangue those who were left, pointing out that they must push on in the welcome relief from the devastating heat of day, driving their horses as far as they could, and then "killing them for their blood when required. . . ." Those rational enough to understand him agreed. And here at last, with unbelievably long-deferred judgment, they abandoned all their rations and "every unnecessary article" except their guns—for protection and possibly for killing buffalo for their blood. Even at this temporary halt, as they girded themselves for their utmost

9 J. H. T. King, *A Brief Account of the Sufferings of a Detachment of United States Cavalry from Deprivation of Water During a Period of Eighty-six Hours While Scouting on the Staked Plains of Texas*, no date, 7 pp., Fort Davis, Texas, Chas. Krull, Post Printer, obviously contemporary. Lieutenant Charles S. Cooper sent a copy to the War Department for filing with his official record, December 1, 1882.

effort, all their remaining horses but two blindly staggered about, fell quivering to the ground, and with flailing hoofs cut those tandem, tell-tale semi-circles in the sod that marked the agony of those noble creatures as they struggled and died.

But the mules, less sensitive and more conservative, were still serviceable. Cooper and Nolan mounted them in the cool of early evening and pushed into the east. About three in the morning they rode into a plain trail, which Cooper soon recognized as the approach to Double Lakes. He shouted the happy discovery back to the few colored troopers who still straggled along behind. They answered with a wild hurrah. After about "five miles on that blessed trail," on the early morning of July 30th, the two officers rode up to the Double Lakes, to their scanty water, and to life. They had been eighty-six hours without a drop to drink.

There they found six troopers who had managed to make it in. Two of these were loaded with canteens and immediately started back to meet and relieve the stragglers. They returned to report that the lost men could not be found. Other searchers were sent out and returned with the same story, though two others who had "straggled from the command" found their way.

The survivors recruited their strength in camp at Double Lakes. Nolan sent a detail back after some of the abandoned provisions. Meanwhile Lieutenant P. L. Lee and his Tonkawas, scouting out of Fort Griffin, had decided to strike up the Yellow House fork of the Brazos to Casas Amarillas, "one of the favorite haunts of the Plains Indians," as he observed, with the hope of intercepting "any band which Captain Nolan might strike or pursue." While on the way he was overtaken on July 29th by a scout and guide named Spotted Jack, who had cut his trail along with two other men and followed him up to notify him of Nolan's plight.

Four days earlier, according to Spotted Jack, he and his friends had lost some horses to a band of prowling Indians on the head of the North Concho, where they had been herding cattle. The three had followed the Indian trail toward Five Wells, had caught up with the Indians, and had engaged them in an ineffectual running fight. He said they had started out with Nolan, but "had found a scarcity of water and in consequence would not venture on the Plains." He claimed that he had told Nolan that he would go for Lee's help in pursuit of the Indians, though just how he knew about Lee is a matter of conjecture.

Thereupon, Lee changed his course and turned west by Tahoka Lake. He reached Double Lakes about 11 a.m., July 31, 1877, and at once placed his men at Nolan's disposal. Though they had been on water for nearly thirty hours, their "inclination to drink was irresistible; it seemed impossible to refrain from pouring down water, notwithstanding that their stomachs could not retain it. As they kept filling themselves with water, it was vomited up...." Food affected them the same way. Only warm coffee could be retained, and it slowly revived them.

Still they continued to drink. Nothing would really "assuage their insatiable thirst," according to Surgeon King, "thus demonstrating that the sense of thirst is like the sense of hunger... located in the general system [so] that it could not be relieved until the remote tissues were supplied."

On August 4th, Sergeant Allsup and the fifteen men who had been left at the supply camp marched to Double Lakes in search of the command, following the report that Umbles had given prior to his leaving for Fort Concho that "the command had all perished." There Allsup notified Nolan of Umbles and the other deserters.

Greatly disturbed, Nolan sent two couriers to follow them up, to report to headquarters in brief on the condition of the command, and to say that "all statements made by Sergeant Umbles to the contrary would be false." Meanwhile Captain Lee sent a scouting detail to Cedar Lake, which found that

Indians had left there two days before with an estimated 250 horses—obviously a party picked up by Quanah. As Lee later learned, Quanah had by-passed them safely and easily and was on his way back toward the reservation, much to Lee's chagrin. A few days later Lee made his way back to Fort Griffin to report on Nolan's condition and to complain of a military and Indian policy that allowed a crafty young chieftain to come out under "a flag of truce" and pilot the guilty raiders in while army details were scouring the Plains in an attempt to punish them.[10]

On August 5, 1877, Nolan left Double Lakes and marched to his supply camp on Bull Creek by way of the headwaters of the Double Mountain Fork. On the 6th he met Surgeon King with men and ambulances from Fort Concho dispatched for his relief. Next day he broke up his supply camp and headed for Concho, where he arrived on the 14th to face an official accounting for the loss of four enlisted men, one civilian, twenty-three government horses and four mules, plus most of his supplies and equipment.[11]

Widespread legend among the frontiersmen held that Nolan was court-martialed, but actually it was his deserters instead. There was dispute as to actual losses: Cooper reported the loss of four Negroes, while Morrison, wiring the Texas headquarters from Concho before Nolan's arrival at post, referred to "the three missing men." Umbles and his fellow deserters were at once placed under arrest. But when Nolan got in and talked the matter over with General Grierson, he evidently hoped against any searching inquiry.

Grierson decided that "in consideration of the great amount of hardships endured, mental suffering and punishment already undergone and the present enfeebled condition of the men," they should be released "from confinement, and at

[10] Capt. P. L. Lee to Post Adjutant, Fort Griffin, Sept. 20, 1877; Nolan, "Report," as cited, 25-27.

[11] This is according to Lt. Cooper's report, *New York Tribune,* September 8, 1877, though there is some dispute on the subject.

Nolan's request, that all charges against them be dropped." Therefore he ordered them turned out of the guardhouse. But the headquarters for Texas, upon being advised of the action, showed that it was of tougher metal and sharply ordered their rearrest.[12]

Meanwhile a board of survey had been ordered to inquire into Nolan's loss, and charges had been preferred against Umbles and three other colored troopers. These gentlemen came to trial at Fort McKavett, October 1, 1877, for disobedience of orders and other transgressions, and were variously sentenced for terms ranging from four to fifteen years, though a reviewing board shortly reduced the penalties to one- and two-year terms.[13]

Thus closed one of the most dramatic and tragic incidents connected with the regular army's attempt to settle the Indian problem on the South Plains. The fact that Nolan's efforts to restore his prestige after an earlier failure resulted in his greater discredit as a leader and a disciplinarian was one of the personal tragedies in the history of Fort Concho. Yet harsh judgment is assuaged somewhat in the face of the exacting and inexorable nature of the Staked Plains.

Nolan continued in service around Concho. His trail was still a little rocky. Captain June Peak of the Texas Rangers, after an engagement with Indians on the South Plains, implied that Nolan had brought them in and furnished them arms. The incident at least illustrated the tension between the two

[12] Grierson to Assist. Adjt. Gen., Dept. of Texas, September 18, 1877, and answer thereto, Sept. 30. *Letter Book*, Fort Concho, 77, 81. For detailed movements of Nolan from Double Lakes to Concho, see his own report, 26-35; Lee's report, as cited; *Letters Sent*, Fort Concho, 511; *Letters Sent*, Dept. of Texas, 47; *Letters Received*, Fort Concho, August 4, 1877; *Special Orders*, Dept. of Texas, no. 131; *Medical History*, vol. 404, pp. 252, 254; *Charges Filed Record*, 37-39; *Telegrams Sent*, Fort Concho, December 21, 1877; *Galveston Daily News*, February 7, 1878; *New York Tribune*, as cited; *Letters Received*, Dept. of Texas, August 7 and 9, 1877.

Nolan's report and comments thereupon were printed in *Southwestern Historical Quarterly*, as cited, and the West Texas Historical Association *Yearbook*, X, 68 ff.

[13] *Cases Tried by a General Court Martial*, Office of the Adjt. Gen., Washington, D.C., vol. 546, G.C.M.O., 45, pp. 1-7, Fort McKavett, Texas, dated November 21, 1877.

services and brought from General Grierson, always quick on the trigger with words if not with bullets, an emphatic denial.[14]

Whether Nolan was a success in the sand hills or not, he enjoyed the temporary distinction of being in command at Concho for a month shortly after his harrowing experience, and it is encouraging to learn that the romantic Irish nature successfully asserted itself, even in considerable maturity, by his taking the daughter of Judge Thomas A. Dwyer as bride at St. Mary's in San Antonio, just a year after he and his suffering men were leaving the Staked Plains.

[14] *Letter Book,* Fort Concho, July 11, 1879, p. 197.

CHAPTER XV

Racial Troubles on the Conchos

Unfortunately the wisdom shown in the strategic location of Fort Concho did not carry over to the choice of garrisons. Military history too often discloses that wise conception is one thing, while outstanding execution on the field is genius of a different order. The prestige of the Army and the well-being of Texas suffered from the fact that Fort Concho and other frontier posts were garrisoned with Negro troops. It was unfortunate on the one hand because colored troops were neither apt frontiersmen nor good soldiers, and doubly unfortunate on the other because the ingrained attitudes, social customs and prejudices so strong in the South were often violent in Texas.

In view of the harsh antipathies that inevitably follow devastating war, it is likely that Negroes were designedly garrisoned in the South as further humiliation for its people. But when they were placed there in the role of military police and protectors of the peace, bitter insult was added to apparently irreparable injury. It was like rubbing salt into the wounds of fiercely proud, rebellious and individually unconquerable people. Recent history reiterates the tragic lessons that are apparently never learned, at least lessons quickly forgotten in the passions of war. Thus Negro troops came to be garrisoned among the resentful frontiersmen in the most important posts in Texas.

Under military occupation, the warlike spirit of Texas erupted into violence. Everywhere men unshucked their six-shooters and pulled down their cap and ball rifles to rectify affronts to their dignity and their rights. Violence became as common as pig tracks in the Piney Woods and many of the "best people" organized themselves into extra-legal riders known as the Ku Klux Klan, or salved their souls with personal killings and then took refuge in outlawry.

Trouble within the military service developed almost at once. Vigorous protest was made to the *San Antonio Express* in May, 1867, after a violent outbreak in the 9th Colored Cavalry under Colonel Edward Hatch. One officer was killed and another wounded before the "murderer" was shot and ten mutineers arrested. It was bootless for a rebel to protest the practice. But a Southern Unionist wrote of the rashness of a policy of inducting recently-freed Negroes into the service with insufficient officers to control them.[1]

With the founding of new posts and the reoccupation of the old ones, this policy was at once extended to the frontier. Dr. William Notson, no prejudiced Southerner but a remarkably observant and astute patriot from the North, made acid comment on the situation at Concho, repeatedly recording his grave doubts of the policy and even the use of Negroes as soldiers. He left his observations in the *Medical History* of the post.

The peculiarities of negro troops in contrast with the white garrison [he wrote], deserves probably some notice . . . As individual agents, as sentinels, they are not reliable; too liberal in their application of instructions; given to understandings usually incapable of appreciating them. Lying and thieving are the principal vices. As malingerers they are not

[1] The newspapers of the time vividly point up the widespread violence, while the army's oppressive measures sometimes checked and again accentuated it. See especially the *San Antonio Express* for the years 1867 and 1869, and for the above mentioned mutiny the issue of May 8, 1867.

so successful as the white troops confining their efforts to rheumatism, "miseries" and stiff limbs....

A little later he added:

The impracticability of making intelligent soldiers out of the mass of the negroes, is growing more evident to the Post Surgeon every day, and his opinion is concurred in by their own officers when speaking with confidence invited by the freedom and intimacy of garrison life. The discipline and police of the post is too poor to decently condemn....

Still later, July 3, 1870, as the last of the 9th Cavalry started off for Fort Davis, Dr. Notson devoutly hoped that it marked "the end" of his "service with such troops."[2]

So much for an unbiased appraisal of the troops that the Army Commands, in gross stupidity if not in pure cussedness, chose for the occupation in Texas. Little wonder that the frontier should fly into flames at the smallest spark.

The lack of settlers in the Concho country at the time of the founding of the post deferred the outbreak of troubles there, but in the San Saba region to the immediate east the explosive tensions were quickly set off, even as the post surgeon there warned against the same policy, saying:

As a rule negro troops yield to all impulses both mental and physical and 'tis almost impossible to teach them that mind is superior to matter.[3]

In that section the charming San Saba valley attracted a few settlers before the war, and with the reoccupation of Fort McKavett, April 1, 1868, and the introduction of colored troops, trouble began. The worst centered around an old Southerner named John M. Jackson, noted for his sturdy character and a distorted back that gave him the nickname of "Humpy."

"Humpy" Jackson was a native of Georgia who had come to Texas from Arkansas, settled on the San Saba, and built his log cabin near what came to be called the Five-Mile Crossing, below where the village of Menardville started a little later. During the dreary years of the Civil War, Jackson stuck by

2 *Medical History*, as cited, vol. 401, pp. 124, 147, 177.
3 *Medical History*, Fort McKavett, 1870, p. 169.

[264]

his guns on the frontier. When McKavett was reinvested, opening a ready market for the produce of the hard-living settlers and offering a little protection against the raiding Indians, Humpy seemed in a fair way to enjoy a measure of prosperity.[4]

The buildings at McKavett were badly in need of repairs and the Army set up a sawmill to cut the native timber near Humpy's home. The fort was garrisoned with Negroes, and in keeping with the use of military labor a detail was sent to run the mill. There, they were frequently observed by Humpy's family. Among the Jackson children was a daughter named Narcissus who attracted the eye of one of the Negro soldiers, a mulatto sergeant called Lanky Jim, evidently a sort of a pioneer progressive on notions of social equality.

One day Lanky Jim wrote a love letter to Narcissus. When old Humpy got the news, his Southern rage knew no bounds. He pulled his rifle off the doorsill and headed for the sawmill. He took a stand behind a pecan tree nearby and waited for his quarry to appear, though one account indicates that he simply walked up and shot the first Negro that ambled into sight.

At any rate, Humpy drew a deadly bead and then took to the tall uncut. Unfortunately he did not pick the right victim. This slight slip of justice never altered the pattern that fate was tracing, and Private Boston Henry was just as dead as if he had deserved to be. The news was carried, as only Negroes can, into McKavett. On June 9, 1869, Lieutenant John L. Bullis was detailed to apprehend a man named Jackson, who on the military records, immediately assumed the standing of "a horse thief and murderer."[5]

[4] The saga of Humpy Jackson is told in N. H. Pierce's, *The Free State of Menard*, Menard, Texas, 1946, pp. 99 ff., and 135 ff. The account of the frontier chronicler, John W. Hunter, is reproduced. It is elaborated here from these sources, from an original use of the War Records, at Washington, and hitherto unpublished recollections set down by the author.

[5] Pierce, as cited, 99, 134-136; Special Order 67, Fort McKavett, June 9, 1869, *Army Commands*.

Bullis, an able and zealous soldier, mounted and headed down the river with six men. But Humpy Jackson, who knew the recesses of the San Saba valleys and hills, had not for years been dodging Indians for nothing. He could not be found. After four days and sixty miles of riding, Bullis returned to report his fruitless quest, while a party from Concho under Lieutenant George E. Albee covered four hundred miles with the same result.[6]

Humpy dodged in and out of his home place as the chase continued for months, and he managed to raise a good corn crop on the side. He improved his time and his chances of continued evasion by digging a cellar under his house and connecting it by tunnel with the river bank. When surprised in his cabin, he ducked into the cellar and emerged out of sight along the river.

An older daughter named Henrietta, mounted on a side-saddle on a good horse, rode the country at times as a sort of picket to warn her father of approaching danger as he worked in the field. On one occasion Humpy fell sick. He took to his cellar while Henrietta, armed with her pistol—for Indian raids were still common—rode into Menardville to watch for soldiers who were continually on the prowl for Humpy. She found the village full of them. They at once placed her under surveillance and she was hard put to figure a ruse for escape. She confided her problem to John Finley, a young clerk in Tull Smith's general store, who suggested she ride leisurely from town, until near home, and then put the whip to her pony and beat the troops in if they followed her.

Finley walked with her to the hitching rack, tightened the saddle cinch, and helped her mount. She casually jogged out of the shady town and headed her horse toward home, aware that a detail of Negroes had fallen in behind her. When within running distance, she turned her horse loose and laid on the quirt, with the troopers in pell-mell pursuit. Her two little

6 Summary of information from War Records in letter of E. G. Campbell to O. C. Fisher, August 26, 1926; Pierce, as cited.

sisters, Sallie and Susie, were playing in the yard when they looked up and saw the cavalcade coming. They ran into the house in terror, screaming:

"Oh, Mother, they'll get Pap this time. Henrietta is coming at top speed and about a hundred niggers are right behind her."

Instead of stopping at the house, Henrietta raced past. When alongside the corn field she drew and shot her gun, and pulled her horse to a halt. The furious white officer in charge drew up and said:

"I suppose that is a signal, Miss!"

"It answers every purpose," she replied, and headed her dripping horse for the cabin at a walk while the officer ordered his men to tear down the rail fence and search the field. When they found no freshly worked land, they hurried to Humpy's home, searched the house, and found the hideout in the cellar. But the ailing Humpy was up and gone.[7]

After that, Humpy could rarely figure on feeling safe at home. He kept on the move while the chase continued under the ruthless resolve of Colonel Ranald S. Mackenzie, then in command at McKavett. On February 1, 1870, Humpy was passing along the Menardville road below the Peg-Leg Stage Station, riding one horse and leading another, when he bumped into a detail of Negro soldiers. He whirled his horse and took to the timber. The troops gave hot pursuit. He was about to get away until the lead horse rim-fired or circled a tree and jerked Humpy's mount under a limb. The old man was swept from the saddle and violently thrown to the ground. The soldiers surrounded him before he was able to move.

He rolled in misery and complained that his back was broken, as well it might have been, and its excessive hump, unfamiliar to his captors, was to them positive proof of his complaint. The white officer in charge—Negro troops were, by general order, commanded by white officers—told them to pick him up and take him home. Three soldiers were left as

7 Mrs. A. W. Noguess to J. E. H., September 23, 1946; Pierce, as cited, 100.

guards until an ambulance could be sent from Fort McKavett. At once the news spread far and wide among the hot-blooded sons of the frontier who would always accommodate a worthy neighbor, even to commendable homicide. Plans were drawn and the appointed minute set.

Meanwhile Humpy's wife slipped him a sixshooter beneath the suggans. The ambulance from McKavett was momentarily expected on the night of February 2nd, but the ready men of Menardville reached there first. Three well-armed Texans dropped into the place and Humpy came out from under the covers with remarkable alacrity for a man with a broken back, sixshooter spitting fire. Two of the soldiers, Corporal Albert Marshall and Private Charles Murray, were killed, while the third, at first thought to be accounted for, later escaped by making it to the river bank.

He hit a trot up the river, to Paddy Fields' place, six miles west of Menardville, where he managed to get a horse. Then he loped into McKavett and reported to Colonel Mackenzie, who at once ordered the stubborn young Bullis to take the trail. With John DeLong as scout and guide and a detail of Negro cavalry, Bullis struck down the river. He was unable to find the elusive Jackson, but placed his wife and children under arrest and burned their home to the ground.

Mackenzie, by then aroused, ordered a general roundup of the men of the whole countryside. He imprisoned Jackson's family in the guardhouse at the post and paraded the men before the escaped soldier in an attempt to identify Humpy's allies, though these worthies were out in the hills beyond the reach of the military.

Yet the army is a permanent and a persevering machine, especially in the hands of an officer like Mackenzie. Relentlessly the search went on. On February 15, 1870, Mackenzie reported that Stephen Cavaness, Peter Crane, George E. Harvey and Charles Owens had helped Jackson kill his guards. Mackenzie posted large rewards for their capture and sent implicating affidavits to Judge David Sheeks at Mason, April

[268]

12, 1870, and again put his scouting parties into the field.[8]

At the same time he arrested William Epps and B. P. Smith as possible accomplices, and kept Mrs. Jackson and Henrietta under arrest. Captain Henry Carroll and Lieutenant Bullis were sent out with a detachment of the 9th Cavalry. Carroll left the post and headed into the hills, south by west to Copperas Creek, and marched down it to camp on the North Llano.

From that point he detached Bullis with a guide and nine men to scout out the Bear Creek country in search of the fugitives. Bullis caught sight of Cavaness working in a field on Moore's Ranch on Bear Creek but failed to catch him. Bullis rejoined the command to report and they made camp. Next morning Carroll sent Bullis back to Bear Creek, where he was lying in wait with his men concealed in the brush when Cavaness returned to Moore's field, tied his horse, and walked out to see the men at work. When Bullis attempted his arrest, the fight started. The nine soldiers in ambush shot the fugitive down, and returned with his horse, saddle, bridle, spurs "and a pair of Colts Pistols," while Moore's men buried the body in the field.[9]

Mackenzie turned Mrs. Jackson and her daughter over to the district judge at Mason in response to a civil summons, April 13, 1870, while the doughty Humpy lived the elusive life of an Indian in the San Saba hills. The sympathies of the settlers were on his side, and they had their ways of helping him without making themselves liable for collusion. Of a sudden he would show up and cut a slab of bacon off the hook in a familiar smokehouse, or pick up a flour sack full of fresh biscuits mysteriously swinging from a mesquite near a friendly cabin.

[8] Pierce, as cited, 102-104; "Special Orders, no. 67," R. S. Mackenzie to Brvt. Colonel H. Clay Wood, February 3, 1870, and same, February 15, 1870, *Army Commands*, Fort McKavett; *Medical History*, Fort McKavett, p. 157; *Medical History*, Fort Concho, vol. 401, p. 157.

[9] Captain Henry Carroll Report, April 20, 1870; John L. Bullis to Henry Carroll, April 19, 1870; *Army Commands*, Fort McKavett; Pierce, as cited, 105.

His confederates drifted on to more tolerant environments, and Owens, after other stirring experiences in the Lincoln County War, died as a highly respected citizen of southern New Mexico. As for Humpy the civil law eventually had its way. He made bond in Menard, June 14, 1871, for $2000, stood trial in a court of Texans and, as Mrs. A. W. Noguess, pioneer of Menardville reports with positive finality, "of course came clear." [10]

The racial problem that stirred the San Saba country was soon felt along the Conchos. Dr. Notson's pleasure upon seeing the colored troops removed was of short duration. Other companies were sent to take their place and the volatile feelings of the frontiermen—buffalo hunters, cowboys, freighters and adventurers—flocking into the Concho country were frequently stirred by some untoward incident that transgressed their dignity, their pride and their taste.

White troops were requested by General E. O. Ord for the Mexican border in place of the colored troops because, as he pointed out, the army "cannot trust their *detachments* without officers—who are not always available." [11]

At Concho the colored laundresses were a special source of trouble, and in the summer of 1875, Dr. W. F. Buchanan, Dr. Notson's successor, asked for a detail to remove one from the vicinity of the hospital whom he had fired for "theft, disqualification to tell the truth, and general imprudence." Two weeks later Captain Nicholas Nolan filed his brief of particulars against three others because of their "utter worthlessness, Drunkness [sic], and Lewdness." Complaints were general, partly because the Negroes compounded their troubles by taking up the white folks' personal quarrels, which they were inclined to do in an excess of loyalty and through cooperation. [12]

10 *Record of Deeds*, vol. A, 19, Menard County; Pierce, as cited, 107.

11 General E. O. Ord to Assist. Adj. Gen., May 20, 1875, *Letters Sent*, Department of Texas, 886.

12 W. F. Buchanan to Post Adjut., *Letters Received*, July 13, 1875.

Of a more intimate nature was the outraged complaint of a colored private who addressed the commander of the Post at this time:

> Sir General I private William Bulger ... Respectfully have the honor to make this application so I may be justified in my undertaken sir the are a woman hear sir that I am Lawfully married to her and she is living with another man ... Sergeant Brown ... and sir I Respectfully request of this woman be Put out of the Post why sir she has been keeping up a destrubments between me and this man ever sence she had been hear she run away and come to this Post exspecting not to find me hear when she got hear.

And so in outraged dignity this properly incensed soldier signed his mark, May 10, 1875. The captain to whom it was referred endorsed the complaint with commendable wisdom. He noted that the wench had "taken up with another man (as she terms it)," but that he "could respectfully state that it is similar to numerous cases which are taking place daily in most any post ..." It was a condition that could not "be obviated except by cleaning them all out which would at the same time be the means of depriving officers of servants." Obviously, he continued, "the man is very Jealous ... which under the circumstances is correct," adding, judiciously, that "it is a very hard matter to correct the morals of these people and I can therefore recommend nothing in the case."[13]

Thus the Negroes, in post and out, at Concho stayed on until, under General B. H. Grierson's command, an all-time high was reached in general resentment. In the Fort Griffin country to the north the colored troops were called "buffalo soldiers," while around Concho they were derisively known as "Grierson brunettes."[14]

Meanwhile the village of Saint Angela, as it was first called, came to anything but innocent life across the river, and its uninhibited and wide-open diversion contributed no more to

[13] William Bulger to Company Commander, May 10, 1875, *Letters Received,* Fort Concho.

[14] See Miss Kubela's thesis, "History of Fort Concho, Texas," 65, University of Texas Archives.

peaceful racial relations than to sedate social life generally.

Its beginnings were noted in the *Medical History* of the post in February, 1870, when Dr. Notson wrote:

An effort is being made to establish a town or village on the north side of the North Concho river. The pioneer in the venture is Mr. B. DeWitt, one of the traders of the Post. Two hackel [*jacal*] or picket houses are in process of erection.[15]

Bart DeWitt, the founder of the town, had arrived from San Antonio. In September, seven months later, the name St. Angela first appears in the *Army Records,* and the observant Post Surgeon commented further on its beginnings.

The question of the sutlers . . . is interesting . . . Mr. James Trainer the first post trader, who was on duty in that capacity when the Post Surgeon arrived here in January, 1868, had purchased land adjoining the post and erected thereon a substantial stone building. Messrs. Wickes & Newton, have started another establishment with the consent of the Commanding officer, within what is supposed to be the Post limits. . . . The History of the various trading establishments of the vicinity may some day form an item in the history of this section. The village of St. Angela, across the North Concho, is almost entirely made up of traders who have been appointed or welcomed by one Post Commander, and ejected by his successors.[16]

By November, 1870, Dr. Notson was able to write that

The village across the North Concho . . . is attaining an unenviable distinction, from the numerous murders committed there. This condition of society [the surgeon continued, philosophically] seems to be almost necessarily a concomitant with the advance of American civilization, but it is certainly fostered by the residents themselves and the short-sightedness of the State authorities. From the heavy tax laid by this state (Texas) upon stores, especially where liquors are sold, (and all Texan stores sell liquors) the interest of each storekeeper is enlisted in keeping away such civil authority as takes from his sales so large a proportion of his profits, even at the risk of not having the same protection for the remainder of his stock. While the military, tied hand and foot, through the jealousy of civil powers, dares not assume any control, lest like Sheridan at Chicago it be charged with usurpation. The result

[15] *Medical History,* vol. 401, pp. 157.

[16] The same, 185.

of this condition of society is increased lawlessness. Within the last six weeks there has been seven murders in a population of less than an hundred, men, women and children all told, and during the residence of the Post Surgeon over one hundred murders have taken place within a radius of ten miles from the Adjutant's office, in a population which has never at any time exceeded two hundred and fifty.

The last murder gives some indication of having broken upon the apathy of the community. On Sunday week a man called another a louse, and refusing to retract, was for this grave offense shot dead with four balls from a revolver. On the Tuesday following the body of the murderer was found on the prairie, about a quarter of a mile from the Post with a bullet hole through his breast. Was it a "Vigilance Committee" or merely vendetta?

Dr. Notson, after this interesting commentary on the local death rate, added, without humor, that "the health of the command has been good. . . ." [17]

Obviously the Concho country placed a commendable restraint upon loose and undignified personal talk, but the penalties still seem a little generous just for calling a man a louse, especially when subsequent action seemed to prove the allegation. And as Dr. Notson suggested, "over one hundred murders" out of a population that never exceeded 250 and then totalled only about a hundred, counting all resident noses, in a brief period of two years and eight months, does seem a little excessive. [18]

Organization of Tom Green County and the local administration of civil law helped matters some. Yet Saint Angela continued to be a center of bucolic nature where a generous admixture of colored soldiers bent on recreation in her dives further inflamed the volatile feelings of healthy men responsive to pride, passion and liquor. Yet no really disturbing incident seemed to break the rather orderly procession of her homicides until the late seventies.

By then Saint Angela was not only a convenient point on the Goodnight Trail, but it was the southern center for the

[17] The same, 214.

[18] For further comment on the nature of Saint Angela, see Captain R. G. Porter, *On the Border with Mackenzie*, 53-54.

buffalo hide trade—that vast slaughter by bold and greasy meat-eaters from all over the Western World.

As such it was running in high and wide open, if anything but handsome, in its 'dobies, dugouts and picket *jacals*. As a sort of damper on its most dangerous men, the Texas Rangers scouted by once in a great while. Captain John S. Sparks came with his company from an expedition into the buffalo range in the fall of 1877 and camped nearby. On the night of arrival his rough and ready boys piled into Sarge Nasworthy's saloon and dance hall for drinks and social diversion. As they swirled through the evening with the Mexican girls, they suddenly waked up to the fact, in the dim lights, that six or seven Negroes were likewise waltzing around the place.

According to Noah Armstrong, veteran Ranger who was there, the boys pulled their guns and broke up the dance by getting "kinda rough." Next day the sore-headed soldiers reported the incident. The commander of the post called on Sparks and demanded an apology. In typically Texan rage Sparks responded to this studied insult from federal authority by saying that he and his little company could whip the whole colored garrison at Fort Concho. Grierson never called the bluff and so the matter seemed to pass. That night the Rangers camped on the Concho a few miles below the post. But the outraged Negroes slipped back to Nasworthy's while festivities were at their height, and, thinking the Rangers were again on the floor, opened fire on the milling dancers, killing an innocent hunter.[19]

The commanding officer reported the incident to Adjutant General Steele at Austin and Sparks went out of the Ranger service to make way for a hotter fire-brand, Captain G. W. Arrington.

Early in February, 1878, a festive party of cowboys and hunters cut the chevrons off a sergeant's blouse and ripped the stripes off his pants. After some preliminary fighting, so one story goes, they ran the Negroes out of Jim Morris's

[19] Noah Armstrong to J. E. H., April 25, 1945 and July 10, 1946.

saloon. The troops of Company D got their guns from the post and returned by the side door to take the whites by surprise. The shooting became general as Fred Young, a buffalo hunter, and a soldier named Brown were killed, and another soldier seriously wounded. Two white men were also wounded.[30]

On hearing of the trouble Captain Arrington came in with his men and marched across the parade ground in search of Sergeant George Goldsbury, who had apparently permitted the troops to get their guns. Colonel Grierson rushed out to challenge Arrington's appearance on the federal domain. Further trouble appeared imminent while nine Negroes were indicted by Issac Mullins' grand jury at Benficklin, and William Mace was given the death penalty. Goldsbury jumped his bond of $750 and never came to trial.[21]

Thus it went with discordant variations but no sensible revision of federal policy for many years, until in 1881, when a considerable settlement was sprawling up the slope on the north side of the Concho. The buffalo hunt had frazzled out but other vital movements were in full force. The Texas and Pacific Railroad was rushing west from Weatherford; sturdy British capital in the hands of sensitive Englishmen was hunting lands and cattle; freighters were steadily stirring the dust between Concho and San Antonio; and the dynamic nature of free men and venturesome money held the land enthralled. The trend was westerly and the tolerant town across the river from Fort Concho was the focal point for those with business, and the lodestar of fun and frolic for all.

Hence one Thomas McCarthy, "a tall, black-haired, black-eyed, manly and prepossessing person," according to the record, rode into San Angelo on diversion bent. Originally he came from Syracuse, New York.[22] After work for the Pullman Palace Car Company at Houston as assistant superintendent,

20 A detailed account of this trouble may be found in the *Galveston Daily News*, March 1, 1878, quoted from the *San Saba News*.

21 Kubela, "History of Fort Concho," as cited, 86-88.

22 *Galveston News*, February 17, 1881.

he had gone into the sheep business near Austin. Then with a brother John, and the financial backing of a cousin, Dave McCarthy, a drygoods merchant of Syracuse, he made his way to Brady Creek and established a ranch there. When Dave came down to visit him, they struck out for San Angelo to see the sights.

Horse racing and related sports made January 31, 1881, a lively day; and after taking in the races, everybody very properly took in the town, the McCarthys merrily among them. Late that night they wound up at Charlie Wilson's saloon where a Negro trooper, William Watkins, Company E of the 10th Cavalry, was entertaining those still in an appreciative mood by singing to his banjo. From here on until one o'clock next morning the accounts are, understandably, somewhat conflicting and confused.

According to John A. Loomis, who was just then making his way to the McCarthy ranch on his first trip into the Concho country, and who attended court at Benficklin, McCarthy claimed the Negro kept bothering him. He was so insistent on additional pay for his entertainment that McCarthy finally pulled his gun to move him on his way. The Negro grabbed the gun, a peculiar English revolver with a set or hair-trigger. In trying to take it from McCarthy, according to the Loomis story, Watkins simply shot himself.[23]

Yet the newspaper accounts of the time reported that the Negro was standing outside the saloon eating his lunch when McCarthy just drew his sixshooter and "shot him in the head." This may be biased too since all immediate news to the outside world was over the military telegraph line, and it is a notorious fact that government agencies are loath to disseminate information unfavorable to their cause, and the army shortly became involved. In fact, a few days later, the *Dallas Herald* apologized for its lack of details because, it claimed, "the military operator at Concho is fraid to telegraph them."[24]

23 John A. Loomis to J. E. H., January 31, 1946.
24 *Dallas Herald*, February 6, 1881; *Galveston News*, as cited.

Yet according to Ranger Jeff Milton, who got there soon after the killing, McCarthy had carelessly bowled Watkins over while innocently shooting up the town. Sancho Mazique, veteran of the colored forces, recalled that the whole shooting match was drunk and that McCarthy's party, in sheer high spirits, took over the saloon and put everybody else out. Watkins, likewise drunk, kept trying to get back in until Mc- Carthy pulled his gun and stopped him.[25]

But after all it does not really matter. Two facts are obvious and important. McCarthy was not a murderous gunman, as has been claimed, but Private Watkins was just as dead as if he had been.

It should also be noted in justice to the people generally that a substantial number of drinking men had been killed by other fighting, drinking men along the Conchos without raising the bloodpressure of the community generally. When one white man killed another white man in a local brawl, nobody seemed particularly to care. But with the Negro troops it was different. Nothing but the gentle Concho and the color line separated the high-spirited men on the north side of the river from a military mass on the south side that is too often divided from a mob only by the thin line of prestige and authority.

To make matters worse, some ten days earlier another colored soldier had been killed in Sarge Nasworthy's saloon by a gambler named P. G. Watson, when he interfered with a fight that Watson had matched with a Negro cavalryman. Watson left town on a good race horse while the temper of the Negro garrison rode high.[26]

The stage was already set for real trouble when McCarthy rushed out of Wilson's saloon in apparent bewilderment. He staggered into a sentinel on the post reservation where he was challenged and taken in charge. He was thrown into the post guardhouse but properly surrendered to Sheriff Jim Spears by Colonel B. H. Grierson about one o'clock on the afternoon of February 1, 1881.

25 Sancho Mazique to J. E. H., October 10, 1946; Loomis, as cited.
26 *Galveston News*, January 21, 1881.

Feeling ran high in the garrison, and Colonel Grierson ordered a guard about the soldiers and established check-roll calls that night. The first check of the barracks after taps showed that the arms racks had been pried into and a great many troops were absent. The "long roll was sounded" and the officer of the guard trotted off with a detachment to round up the missing soldiers from the village across the river.

He found that hell was already poppin'. The troops had taken Sheriff Spears in charge, surrounded the Nimitz Hotel, where they thought McCarthy was being held, and were demanding that McCarthy be surrendered to them. They scattered and straggled back to the post when the officer of the guard arrived.[27] Meanwhile, McCarthy was being held for his own safety in the Benficklin jail, at the Tom Green County seat, about four miles up the river.

The affairs at the post suggest a lack of rigorous discipline by Grierson and his officers. The troops got out inflammatory circulars on a hand-press at the post. As leaves had not been cancelled they scattered the handbills about San Angelo as they walked the streets in angry, muttering groups. One of these posters, dated, "Fort Concho, Feb. 3, 1881," read:

> We soldiers of the United States Army, do hereby warn for the first and last time all citizens, cowboys, etc. of San Angelo and vicinity to recognize our right of way as just and peaceable men. If we do not receive justice and fair play, which we must have, some one will suffer, if not the guilty, the innocent. It has gone far enough. Justice or death.
> U. S. Soldiers.[28]

McCarthy's preliminary hearing got under way at Benficklin. Grierson claimed that Sheriff Spears had notified him on the 4th that McCarthy's friends were gathering to release the prisoner by force, and had appealed to the post for protection, though there is nothing in the scanty civilian records to substantiate the claim. Grierson claimed, with discretion, that he could not comply "without violation of the law" and

27 *Galveston News,* February 3, 1881.
28 Reprinted in *Dallas Herald,* February 5, 1881.

without such action's being interpreted as "an attempt to overawe the civil authorities."[29]

He did send a "discreet officer" to talk with Spears, and claimed he "held a company in readiness to move promptly," apparently in case of an outbreak, while he sent another to Benficklin to arrest any soldiers who attempted to enter the county seat. Then, apparently in an attempt to appease the rebellious troops, who were still threatening to burn and pillage San Angelo, he ordered a company to fall in behind Sheriff Spears at the river crossing and help him escort the prisoner to the Benficklin jail. To a disciplinarian or a careful student of human nature, this seems not only ridiculous in an army man, but a downright foolish concession inclined to promote mutiny. What was really needed was the cancellation of all post leaves and an arrest of the rebellious leaders.

Instead the Negroes were left free to roam the village streets in muttering and threatening groups. Citizens sent their families scurrying to refuge on the surrounding ranches, while the local officials thought of the Texas Rangers. The Frontier Battalion, as that fighting organization was then known, had a company stationed at Hackberry Springs, on the extreme frontier in Mitchell County, eighty miles to the north. From there its tiny force ranged back and forth across that open world from Monument Spring, in New Mexico, to Horsehead on the Pecos, hunting vagrant Indians from the reservations and whites fugitive from justice.

This company was under the hotheaded command of Captain Bryan Marsh, a Confederate veteran with an immense contempt for the federal forces. The late war had left him short of one arm and several fingers on the remaining hand, a bitter reminder—while prowling for Indians who eluded the federal forces—to nurse his wrath against the Yankees and keep it powerfully warm.

San Angelo was the point of supply for his company, and Ranger Johnnie Miles happened to be there when the trouble

[29] B. H. Grierson to Adjt. Gen., February 8, 1881, *Army Commands,* Fort Concho.

broke out. As things really got hot, Sheriff Spears pushed a petition signed by himself, the district judge and the district attorney into Johnnie's hands, and begged him to hit a high lope for Marsh's camp.

Eighty miles is a long ride, but Johnnie spared neither himself nor horse flesh. By sundown next day Captain Marsh and twenty-one eager men were shaking out their reins on the trail to Fort Concho while Jim Werner, their Negro cook, followed in a wagon loaded with their beds and rations.[30]

Even as Johnnie left town, the shooting started and became promiscuous. Justice of the Peace Billy Russell "experienced a miraculous escape from death" when a bullet came through his window and lodged in a copy of *The Revised Statutes* that lay on his table. After all, the printed statutes of Texas had to be good for something in San Angelo.

Unfortunately just as this point McCarthy's brother rode into town and stopped at the Nimitz Hotel. He was seen by a Negro woman who on account of the resemblance spread the report: "Tom McCarthy's out of jail." That rumor hit the post with a bang, and certainly the fat was out of the pan and in the fire.

Grierson claimed a party of five men fired on the post guard that afternoon. That night "between tatoo roll call and taps"

[30] "Monthly Return," February 28, 1881, Frontier Battalion, State Archives, Austin; *Austin Statesman*, February 8, 1881; Kubela, as cited, 95.

a mob of soldiers made a rush through the barracks. They put out the lights, tore open the arms racks, and in the confusion took off for town. The newspapers claimed there were some hundred and fifty of them in all.

Captain Marsh thought they were, "both black and white, some fifty or more strong." Grierson claimed there were only "thirty to forty." Anyway, the mob marched into town, fired "several hundred shots in rapid succession," and wounded one man in front of Sterling C. Robertson's store. But they centered most of their shots on "the destruction of the Nimitz Hotel, completely riddling the building with bullets." Jeff Milton recalled that when the mob approached the Tankersley Hotel, Mrs. Frank Tankersley stepped out with a double-barreled shotgun, saying:

"Cut it out. The first nigger that shoots a hole in my hotel, I'm going to kill him." And they shot no holes!

"She was quite a lady," praised the gentlemanly Milton.[31]

At length the officers of the post appeared and the mob dispersed. Next day Marsh and his rangers rode into town. The old warrior pitched camp in Sarge Nasworthy's wagon-yard, took two quick shots of liquor and began thirsting for war. He sent J. M. Sedberry and a detail to guard the jail at Benficklin and threw others out over the town. Then with several men he headed straight for the post and Grierson's office. He sent a guard to a convenient roof to watch the approaches, and taking his youngest ranger, Jeff Milton, with him, he said:

"Get your Winchester. Throw a shell in it! Kill the first man that bothers me!" The firm and eager hand of a completely fearless young man pressed the lever down and slipped a shell into the polished chamber, appreciatively guarding this fire-eater from the Confederacy and the frontiers of Texas as he read the riot act to the commanding symbol of military power. Much of Marsh's talk was not calculated for print. But the expurgated substance of the message that

31 J. Evetts Haley, *Jeff Milton, A Good Man With a Gun*, Norman, 1948, p. 36.

crackled from the tongue of the rough old Texan to the neat man with the polished eagles on his shoulders may be reduced to this:

"I am going to kill the first man that comes across the river without a pass—nigger or anybody else. Keep these troops on this side. If they cross we'll kill every one of them."

"What do you mean?" spluttered Grierson. "You have only a handful of men."

"Yes," snapped Marsh, "but enough to kill every one of these niggers if you don't obey my orders." As Marsh turned to go, it was an obvious fact that a powerful compulsion flows from strong hearts and dominant personalities. Even with the power and prestige of the United States Army behind him, Grierson knew that in this one-armed man with the mangled hand he had certainly met his match.

Discipline was at last invoked, and that peace which is the concomitant of tolerance came again to the banks of the Conchos. But the official story of the riot of the Negro troopers was not quite over.

A few days after Marsh's arrival McCarthy's preliminary trial was completed. He was sent to the settlements for safekeeping under guard of Ranger John Hoffar, and lodged in jail at Austin pending his trial.

News of the riot quickly spread over the state. Governor O. M. Roberts approved the movements of the rangers and wired the general in command of the military district, at San Antonio, reminding him of the invasion of the civil authority by the arrest of Sheriff Spears and the riot that followed. Grierson had never even reported the outbreak. On February 8th the Commanding General of the Department relayed Governor Roberts' wires in a tart message to Grierson, wondering "if it can be possible that the statements are true, and if so, why you have not reported the matter to these headquarters." That day Grierson filed his special pleading in answer.[32]

32 Martin to C.O., Fort Concho, February 8, 1881, *Army Commands*.

He detailed the history of the trouble from his point of view. He emphasized his periodic checks of the barracks, claimed he had enlarged the guard, observed that Captain Marsh was cooperating with him, and pointed out the series of incidents that had helped infuriate the Negroes.

He did not offer this to excuse "the wrongs done by soldiers," he added, "but simply to show under what difficulties the officers are placed to control men, when their comrades are shot down without any punishment being inflicted upon the guilty parties." In spite of his bumptious brass and lack of ability in coping with a situation that a more courageous man would have prevented, herein Grierson assayed the fundamental fault in the whole business. It was one of policy. The Texas frontier was not a proper place for colored soldiers.

Grierson's official report occupied seven foolscap pages in the *Army Records* at Washington. Marsh made his report to Adjutant General John B. Jones, and it may still be read in telegraphic form in the State Library at Austin. It consists of seven words:

"Arrived here Saturday with company all quiet." [33]

On February 14, 1881, with that sense of discipline, propriety and character that has usually justified our pride in the American army in time of test, the Commanding General served orders on Grierson. Grierson was to remove the companies involved in the trouble from Fort Concho to his outposts. He was told to court-martial the mutinous individuals because "such conduct on the part of the troops whatever the provocation, cannot but react unfavorably upon the army and must be emphatically rebuked." Then in high regard for the limitations of a Constitution that should rigidly steer our conduct in dire emergency even more than in social quietude and calm, the Commanding General continued:

"Any attempt on the part of the troops to influence the civil authorities ... by threats of intimidation must be checked by the most effective measures. A failure on the part of the civil

[33] Marsh to Jones, as cited, *Adjutant General's Papers,* State Library.

authorities to do their duty will in no way justify or palliate any interference by the military. It is our duty to see that the army is right, whoever else may be wrong. Let us see that the duty is fully performed." The penalty for a renewal of the troubles, be advised, "will insure the breaking up of the whole command." [34] Thus spoke traditional military honor and character.

McCarthy made a favorable impression on all who met him, and was released from the Travis County jail on $6000 bond late in the month. He was indicted for murder at Benficklin. The case was transferred to Kimble County where it came to trial in November. The jury was out just long enough to write its verdict: "Not guilty!" [35]

Anywhere else in Texas it would undoubtedly have been the same. The moralists may contend that the Texans were all wrong. But neither defeat in the terrible war they had just fought, nor more than three-quarters of a century of peaceful development since, have convinced them that they were.

The world may disagree. But after all it is impossible to condemn an entire race for fierce pride and strong tradition. When mistaken policy runs counter thereto, the policy runs into trouble and usually fails. It is a lesson of history that has continuous application, though unfortunately for the peace of the world is too rarely applied.

The troops too evoke their share of sympathy. Those recent slaves, pushed to the frontier, where individualistic men daily flirted with danger and flaunted death, under the supposition that they were qualified soldiers, were also the unfortunate victims of mistaken policy at the hands of those who had freed them. Though they broke the tradition of the United States military by mutiny, the blame was not on them. Historically, it rests on the white men in authority who, through ineptitude or vindictiveness, set the policy and sent them here.

34 C.O. to Colonel B. H. Grierson, February 14, 1881.

35 *San Angelo Standard*, May 3, 1924; *Dallas Herald*, February 26 and November 13, 1881.

CHAPTER XVI

Transportation and Supply

In the beginning Fort Concho looked exclusively to San Antonio as the source of its supplies. Along its 220 miles, the Upper Road connecting the two points was exposed to Indian depredations, sometimes to outlaw raids, and to all those vicissitudes of terrain and uncertain weather that the times and place imposed. Freighting was a regular but hazardous business. Power consisted of mules and oxen. Mules were fine when corn or oats were available, but oxen stepped out and left them behind when the long pull depended on grass alone.

Thus Fort Concho's subsistence depended completely on mules and oxen, and the men with long whips and stentorian voices who drove them. Most of the freighting was handled on contract. Each year the *San Antonio Express* carried advertisements calling for bids for hay, wood and feed for the various frontier posts, as well as transportation of the food for the soldiers' messes.

An invitation to bid on grain for the Texas forts was published November 12, 1867, just in advance of the founding of the fort. Fort Stockton needed 15,000 bushels of oats or barley in sacks, Davis 16,000, and Chadbourne "or such Post as may be established in lieu thereof" was to get 18,000 bushels.[1] Delivery was to begin January 5, 1868.

[1] *San Antonio Express,* November 12, 1867.

Since Connelly's pioneer train had worked its way from Chihuahua City to Fort Towson in an attempt to open a short-cut for the Santa Fe-Chihuahua trade, other traders and freighters had felt their way to a practicable route. Captain Whiting had anticipated it in 1849. It had been expedited in 1852 by Major W. H. Emory's opening of a wagon road from Leon Springs, just west of Fort Stockton, directly to Presidio for the "double purpose of communicating with my parties on the lower Rio Grande," he wrote, "and of shortening the distance from San Antonio to Chihuahua." By eliminating the old round-about course to El Paso the cutoff resulted in a saving of more than 300 weary miles.[2] By the late sixties the San Antonio-Chihuahua Trail furnished a ready-made route to the new post on the Conchos.

One of the first trains loaded with government stores for Concho was "repeatedly" charged by the Indians in an attempt to stampede its grazing stock as it made its way north. A savage attack came at Rock Springs on the road twelve miles out of Fort Mason. The Mexican drivers broke open a box of carbines and ammunition destined for the post, and gave chase. After a hot pursuit of three miles they caught and charged the Indians and captured twenty head of their horses.[3]

By the middle of March, 1868, feed at Fort Concho was in short supply, and animals were reduced to half rations of forage. In early April the officers were crying for an additional 50,000 pounds of corn. Inquiry established the fact that it could be had in the settlements at the outrageous price of five dollars a bushel, and the quartermaster was ordered to negotiate for it through James Trainer, the first post trader.[4]

Even as the life of the post dropped into something resem-

2 William H. Emory, *Report on the United States and Mexican Boundary Survey*, Washington, 1857, I, 88-89. For further detail on this route see Froebel, *Seven Years Travel*, as cited, 203, 404, 410, 431; Bieber, *Exploring Southwestern Trails*, 286, 288; and that fine chronicle of freighting, August Santeleben, *A Texas Pioneer*, New York and Washington, 1910, pp. 100 ff.

3 *San Antonio Express*, December 24, 1867.

4 D. A. Irwin to Lt. C. C. Morse, April 7, 1868, *Letters Received*.

bling routine, the difficulties of supplying the horses and mules continued. Late in January, 1869, the great San Antonio merchant, freighter and contractor, Peter Gallagher, was in default on his contracts. At the most critical season for saddle stock the post was again short on grain, and the quartermaster was ordered to buy corn in the open market and notify the contractor that the difference in price was being charged to him. Gallagher replied that heavy roads since the past November had balked deliveries, and that "I will use every means that men or animals can perform to keep the post supplied." As he wrote, "three trains with corn" were on the road to Concho.[5]

In spite of the insistent demand for all sorts of supplies, the situation remained little short of critical the second winter. On February 22nd at Kickapoo Springs, some twenty miles out on the trail, about seventy Indians attacked another wagon train loaded with lumber, and killed a Mexican teamster and a span of mules. One Indian was killed, his head was cut off, and his skull sent to the Army Medical Museum by the eager and inquiring army surgeon, Dr. William Notson. A detail of pursuit troops returned in three days with "the usual negative results."[6]

Transportation continued miserably bad, and the post was still short of supplies in March, 1869. Dr. Notson was borrowing medical supplies from McKavett as he complained that he had only "a couple of bottles of Castor oil and a few doses of Rochelle salt" for the entire post. He had been trying to get supplies since the November before. In the light of the general use of these cathartics it is hard to see how the army maintained its morale.

At the same time, Dr. Notson complained, the quartermaster and commissary departments were

in their usual conditions of insufficiency. The horses have been without corn for two weeks and now the hay is exhausted. It is a great blessing

5 Peter Gallagher to J. A. Porter, Chf. Qm., January 26, 1869, *Letters Received.*
6 *Medical History*, as cited, vol. 401, p. 109.

to men and animals here, that the military stupidity ordinarily exhibited in making provision for us, can not interfere in the rotation of the seasons, and even contractors of transportation, could not prevent a fair crop of grass for grazing being at the post at the close of this month [March]. The comissary [sic] supplies can be counted on ones fingers ends, and the canned articles to two, Peaches and onions. The former the most certain and seductive form of lead poison, and the later [sic] excelling all other canned preparations in insipidity, and deprivation of those qualities, that make the fresh vegetable so desirable as an antiscorbutic.[7]

But in a free economy the pressing need usually supplies the remedy. Down at San Antonio a firm of active enterprisers known as Adams and Wickes was rising into prominence and tackling the thorny problem of supplying the frontier posts. Not only were they part owners of the land upon which Fort Concho was being built, but they had an acquisitive finger in nearly everything that was going on around San Antonio.

Major H. B. Adams, of the Confederate forces, was born in Plainfield, New Jersey, of Dutch parentage, in 1833. When still in his teens he caught a schooner and landed at Port Lavaca, on the Texas coast, fell in with John James, and came to San Antonio. He worked in a store awhile, went into Mexico, and came back to join the Confederate Army when the war broke out. He took a brief whirl in the brokerage business after the war and then meshed his ambitions and interests with Colonel Edwin DeLacy Wickes.

Wickes was born in Catskill, New York, in 1828, became a government contractor, came to San Antonio with the 4th Cavalry in 1865, and at once associated himself with Adams. Both became prominent in the affairs of San Antonio. When Wickes quit the contracting business, he concentrated on real estate and was soon able to pioneer in the fashionable trend of having a summer home in Saratoga and a winter home in San Antonio.[8] At the time of his death in 1892 he had a raft of

7 The same, 113.

8 The rise of Wickes and Adams can be followed through the Bexar County Records and the files of the *San Antonio Express*. See *Deed Records*, K, 106; vol. 106, p. 310; vol. III, 468; vol. 281, p. 494; *Probate Minutes*, vol. 2, p. 40; and *The*

city property, besides "ranches in twenty-eight counties in Texas."

These were the men who soon owned, outright, the site of Fort Concho and began contracting its supplies. The aggressive pair bought a freight outfit from Peter Gallagher, October 16, 1867, and began operating all over West Texas. The inventory of their purchase included eight wagons and seventy ox bows, eighty sets of harness, eight saddles and thirty pair of sidelines, three saddle horses for their herders, ninety mules, camp equipment, twelve guns and eight morrals, all for $5750.[9]

Thus equipped, they turned their attention from the growing pains of San Antonio to the pressing needs of the frontier. They contracted to cut and supply wood and hay for Fort Concho, and established camps for the purpose on the outlying meadows and streams. They were soon delivering the cut and corded products to the military reservation at prices approximating thirty-three dollars a ton for hay and eight, dollars a cord for wood.

For a while haying became one of the most flourishing businesses along the Conchos, and by the time the census takers of 1870 reached there from San Antonio and the parent county of Bexar, at least three big haying camps had been set up in the immediate Concho country. Christopher Shuhart was in charge of one, numbering fifty-four people, twenty-two miles west of the post. Another with twenty men under subcontractor Charles Napier, with its own blacksmith, was camped twelve miles west. Six miles out to the southwest was another made up of seven men. It was illustrative of the diverse nature of the hardy souls hunting fortune and adventure in the West and winding up on a prosaic pitchfork handle. One teamster was from Ireland, one each from Texas and Virginia, another from Ohio, one from England, and the two others were from France.

Express, 1868 through the 1880's to Wickes' death, June 17, 1892, and Adams', June 14, 1895. See also Frederick C. Chabot, *With the Makers of San Antonio*, San Antonio, 1937, p. 370.

9 *Deed Records*, Bexar County, VI, 202-203.

Yet life in a hay camp, while devoid of color, was not lacking in excitement. Frequent details of troops were sent from the post to guard the transient camps from raiding Indians. Every once in awhile some luckless teamster, concentrating on his mower and unable to keep a weather eye skinned for Indians, fell victim to their raids almost in the shadow of the fort. In September, 1872, a small party of braves disguised as soldiers rode up on a contractor named Johnson, eighteen miles from the reservation. They killed and scalped him and then rode off with impunity after shooting five or six "arrows into his back." In spite of the risk, however, the high prices so encouraged men to keep at the work that by 1873 competition had cut the cost of good hay, cured with a sprinkling of salt, to fifteen dollars a ton. Delivery was made at the post where the government put in a set of scales and a system of checking to discourage costly overestimates.[10]

Meanwhile Adams and Wickes had come in for the skimming of the cream. As others like Bart DeWitt, founder of San Angelo, took contracts for 1200 cords of wood at $3.98 a cord, they were turning their attention to bigger business such as the delivery of 1,330,000 pounds of hay at $26.93 a ton. Something of the extent of the demands for the army horses and mules can be realized from the fact that for the fiscal year beginning July 1, 1871, Fort Concho contracted an additional 400,000 pounds of hay from George Appman at $24 per ton, besides a mountain of grain from others. I. D. Burgess, of Fort Davis, agreed to supply 255,000 pounds of barley at $3.60 per bushel, while Hugo Faltin, of Comfort, and James Trainer, post sutler, contracted 870,000 and 255,000 pounds of corn at prices of $2.57 and $2.29 a bushel, respectively. At the same time a contract was awarded to Eugene McCrohan, veteran settler of the Concho country, for 1000 bushels of charcoal at thirty-eight cents a bushel.[11]

10 See various *Letters Received*, March 23 and 25, May 29 and June 15, 1871; *Medical History*, as cited, vol. 401, p. 281; *Special Order Book*, July 8, 1872; *Letter Book*, I, 14, 113; *U. S. Census, 1870*, as cited, sheets 335, 348, 349.

11 "Contracts Awarded," June 20, 1871, in *Letters Received*.

Game was abundant when the post was founded. In the spring of 1868 "vast herds of Buffalo . . . were several times seen from the tent quarters." They were never again seen within twenty miles of the post in such numbers, though the hide hunt did not get into good swing until about seven years later. Each spring the great herds moved north in their seasonal migration, though they could be found in sufficient abundance for meat at all seasons from the "many estrays that remain with the cattle in the vicinity." During the first winter, buffalo beef was common at the post, and cheap for all who wished to buy.

The post historian recorded that the "white or cotton tailed deer" was prevalent, antelope were in great herds, and "the half wild cattle of the plains are more numerous than any other mammals. They are fleet, clean limbed and often spirited. The sweep of their long thin horns will rival that of the true buffalo of Asia." Prairie dogs and coyotes were everywhere and a puma was killed right in the post. The javalinas, or peccaries, were found along the Kickapoo, two species of squirrels infested the pecan trees of the streams, and the native beaver, even four years after the post was started, were still cutting the trees alongside the reservation.

For those about the post who relished shooting, there were ducks and plover in season, and blue and bob-white quail and turkeys at all times. Trout and catfish were found in the streams, along with "a beautiful pearly" mussel, the post surgeon wrote, observing, with skepticism, that this "probably gives the name to the streams and the Post, if Concho means anything. . . ."[12] Compared with the relatively sterile and severe land that stretched westward from the Pecos to the hopeful settlement at El Paso, the Concho country was a genuine oasis for westward-moving men.

But the Pecos section, largely unwanted and unsettled, furnished in its waters and salt lakes the savor for the meat of more favored lands. For years the Mexicans of Chihuahua had

[12] *Medical History*, as cited, vol. 404, 53-55.

followed their salt trails from Paso del Norte to the Salt Flats below the Guadalupe range. After the San Antonio-Chihuahua Trail came into being, they loaded their carretas at the Salt Lake near the Pecos, in present Crane County, for hauls in either direction.

The earliest settlers on the Fort Concho frontier learned of the supply. As Charles Goodnight returned from laying out his cattle trail into New Mexico in the summer of 1866, far out on the Staked Plains he met Rich Coffey, famous first settler of the lower Concho, headed for the Salt Lake. Coffey had twelve big steers yoked to a wagon-load of watermelons that he had grown. He hoped to trade them to the Chihuahua salt-gatherers, whom he expected to find at the lake. He later told Goodnight he found none, as it was out of season. So he buried his melons in the sand and returned to his ranch at the mouth of the Concho—a unique frontier enterpriser who managed to stay without trade, and by sheer personality to lend flavor to the Concho country.[13]

Early efforts were made by the soldiers to supply their table needs for salt from the same source. In the fall of 1868 the veteran soldier, James Callihan, reported that he had sent two wagons for the purpose from the outpost at Camp Charlotte. The drivers reached the Salt Lake to find it "overflowed with water from the last rain," and they too returned, empty-handed.[14] Concho was thus forced into the open market for its supply, which, in the early seventies, was costing four cents a pound. At least half of the cost was laid to transportation.[15]

During January, 1869, "the most essential articles . . . flour, coffee and sugar [were] entirely out." The cavalry was out of corn and the medical department was out of "nearly everything including Castor oil, Iodide of Potassium, Chloroform and stimulants." The blame was laid on "difficult transportation," plus "an incomprehensible want of judgment in the

13 Haley, *Charles Goodnight*, as cited, 143.
14 Callihan to Lt. T. J. Wirt, October 24, 1868, *Letters Received*.
15 See *Letters Received*, June 3, 1872.

arrangement of contracts," Dr. Notson charged, as well as "ignorance of the natural obstacles to travel. ... The semi-annual supply of medicine for the first half of the year 1869, although shipped from New Orleans" in December, had "not since been heard from" despite a "quite caustic correspondence" between the commanding officer and the authorities at Austin and San Antonio. Three months later the Post was still out, though some disinfectants which were not wanted had been sent.[16]

The first spring brought cases of lead poisoning from canned peaches, and a danger of scurvy from a consistently heavy diet. Dr. Notson carried water cress from Kickapoo Springs twenty-four miles away, and prevailed on Brigadier General J. D. Bingham, while he was on a tour of inspection, March 7, 1869, to take it up the Main Concho and plant it in the river "at his several stopping places." Fresh vegetables were almost out of the question, and Dr. Notson thus hoped to propagate a source of salad for the future, he said, "in view of our limited supply of antiscorbutics." He planted more in the North Concho, but reported that it would be several months before a sufficient supply was available to do any good. Orders for potatoes and onions were hurried off to Fredericks-burg, and the health of the garrison was fairly well maintained.[17]

Officers and others with spare money could supplement their rations at the 'sutler's store. In the search for variety for the officer's messes, pickles were ordered in such quantity that orders followed for 600 gallons, "in excess of requirements for sales," to be issued to the troops. In 1871 while Dr. Notson was anxiously watching his transplanted water cress, another remarkable character, the Post Chaplain, Norman H. Badger, was starting a post garden on ten acres leased from the pioneer agricultural venture on the Conchos, the Bismarck Farm.

This land was broken out by German settlers who arrived about February 10, 1868, and was located seven miles from

16 *Medical History,* as cited, vol. 401, pp. 105, 117.
17 See *Letters Received,* March 31, 1869.

the post. By the time the 1870 census was taken, Jacob Marshall, a forty-year-old native of Bavaria, was the only man at the place listed with property. Yet a total of forty-two people were living there in ten separate dwellings.

The first post farm was cultivated by a detail of six soldiers living on the ground and working under Chaplain Badger. The Bismarck Farm was then thought to be the nearest spot to the post that could be irrigated. Badger claimed it was not only enormously productive but helped keep "down the extortionate prices the owners of the few other vegetables . . . were disposed to demand." But the owners of Bismarck Farm were quick to catch on to the unfair competition of government production, and in 1872 cancelled the arrangement. But the lettuce, beans, corn, squash, watermelons and cantaloupe lingered on as a fragrant memory. With commendable zeal Badger fell back on a dry-land plot—a "futile attempt to cultivate about a quarter of an acre at the Post." In spite of much labor and the daily hauling of ten barrels of water from the river, the failure threw a wet blanket, as it were, on the idea of dry-land farming for a long time.[18] An attempt to open a farm a few miles below the post in 1874 was abandoned when "a sudden rise in the river swept away nearly all the improvements and made a great expense."[19]

The prevalent lead poisoning soon gave way with better canned goods, and by the end of 1872 Dr. William F. Buchanan, who had taken over as post surgeon, was able to report an improved bill of fare. The post was "tolerably supplied with canned fruits and vegetables, butter, pickles, hams of poor quality, dried apples and peaches "for sale to officers," and—shades of Delmonico's—canned lobsters.

Fresh vegetables continued to be a problem. Scurvy, while always an immediate threat, rarely broke out, though it did

18 *Medical History*, as cited, vol. 401, p. 224 and vol. 404, 69-70; *U. S. Census*, Bexar District, 1870, sheet 334, National Archives, Washington; *Compendium of the Ninth Census*, 1870, Washington, 341; Kubela, *History of Fort Concho*, as cited, 29.

19 *Medical History*, as cited, vol. 404, p. 70.

appear in the spring of 1873. Dr. Buchanan hurriedly posted a letter to San Antonio for "Dessicated potatoes, Dessicated Mixed Vegetables, and Lime Juice of good quality." In April, seventeen barrels of Irish potatoes, a supply of sauerkraut, pickles and dried fruit reached the post in answer to his plea.[20]

Dr. Buchanan lamented that fish were not in quantity to supply several hundred men, and observed that by 1871 "hunting does not add greatly to the men's food." For three months of the year, when the buffalo range was within fifteen to twenty-five miles of the post, he wrote, "the men are allowed to go out in parties and hunt them." The same held for turkeys. Fresh meat could sometimes be had but ice was unobtainable.[21]

Like Dr. Notson he passed caustic judgment on the bread, which he found "heavy and sour and inadequate." As time wore on he considered the food utterly unfit to maintain good health, for the troops were without "codfish and saurkraut . . . two very necessary articles on the frontier." As he took stock of the health of the garrison in the month of February, 1875, he found no "molasses, canned tomatoes (almost the only article of canned stuff received fresh and fit for use) dried apples, dried peaches, Potatoes or onions." There was no flour, "on hand except a few barrels for officers use, the entire command being compelled to use hard bread. . . ."[22]

As the army activity increased in the early seventies, the freighting and supply business boomed. The trails out of San Antonio were alternately traced by deep ruts cut in the muddy sod and by wraiths of dust lazily floating into the skies. From an early start in the late sixties, Adams and Wickes kept well in the lead. By the fall of 1868 they were delivering supplies to Fort Richardson and to Fort Davis, four hundred miles from San Antonio. Their great trains moved in force and sometimes turned the tables on the Indians. One of their wagon-masters

20 W. F. Buchanan to J. R. Hammond, March 16, 1873, *Letters Received; Medical History*, as cited, vol. 404, pp. 90, 93.

21 *Medical History*, as cited, vol. 401, p. 296; vol. 404, p. 70.

22 *Medical History*, vol. 404, p. 170.

attacked a party of braves near the Riffles on the Pecos that year, put them to flight and captured about fifteen head of horses and mules.[23]

On June 26, 1869, however, an estimated 200 Indians repaid them with interest by raiding an immense train at Howard's Springs on the Lower Road. They killed a teamster, captured 150 of their mules, and forced the abandonment of the entire train.[24] Yet the freighters flourished, in a way, in spite of danger, distance and high water, and their loaded wagons were common sights around the warehouses at Fort Concho by 1871.

The same season, they were putting a million and a half pounds of corn into the corrals at Richardson. When the 6th Cavalry was removed from that post and the total amount contracted was not needed, the price fell. Then Adams and Wickes agreed to deliver on the basis of the market. This was agreeably ordered by the Quartermaster General, but Colonel Mackenzie, in command at Richardson, appealed from the order and disobeyed it. General J. J. Reynolds, in command of the Department of Texas, considered court-martialing him. But as Reynolds pondered the problem, Mackenzie was ordered "to organize an expedition against the *Indians*," which may have been punishment enough.[25]

Adams continued as a leading contractor of government business after Wickes dropped out. In a two-day period during the summer of 1876, he put on the road out of San Antonio two trains for Fort Duncan under wagon-masters Pio Santa Cruz and Jesus Hernandez, one of ten wagons under Ramon Hernandez for Fort Bliss at the western extremity of the state, another of ten under Severiano Calderon for Fort Stockton, and one of eight wagons under Maximo Cardenas for Fort Davis. During the year ending June 30, 1878, he freighted in

23 *San Antonio Express*, August 21 and September 17, 1868.

24 The same, July 6, 1869.

25 See *Letters Received*, May 31, 1871; J. J. Reynolds to Assist. Adj. Gen. Military Division of the South, July 13, 1871.

excess of 5,000,000 pounds of grain to posts along the Lower and Upper Roads between San Antonio and El Paso, all by wagon and team, and at a total carrying cost to the government of only $84,928. More than 433,000 pounds went to Concho.[26]

But all was not rosy on his far-flung horizons. As the danger of Indians decreased, the railroads arrived at the natural doorways to West Texas. In 1879 eager freighters were diverting shipments of supplies to Concho from the rails at Fort Worth, Dallas and even Waco, Round Rock and Austin. The newcomers took over the McKavett and Concho trade, and Adams reported that they were fighting hard for the Fort Stockton-Fort Davis freight.

Jack Shabatt, of the firm of Wulfing and Labatt, captured part of their trade, while in 1879 William Heuermann, with Hugo and Schmeltzer, got the contract to furnish 329,000 pounds of flour to McKavett, Concho, Stockton and other western posts. Heuermann was buying his flour in St. Louis, shipping it to Austin and, remarkably, freighting it from there into San Antonio at a great saving over railroad freight to the same point.[27]

A few years earlier, in 1876, effort had been made to improve the route to San Antonio. Army details planned a new route into McKavett and thence to Concho by way of Kerrville—the flourishing little town on the Guadalupe. Since they claimed a saving of nearly forty miles and a better line of travel, the road was at once put to use by the freighters.

But the trade from the east was swelling. A "long line of wagons" loaded with corn pushed west from Bell County in 1876, and other mule trains began pulling out of Round Rock with wagons groaning with lumber for Fort Concho and the frontier generally. James Trainer nosed out his San Antonio competitors on the hauling contract. In May, Brown County happily reported the opening of a new stage and freight road

26 *San Antonio Express,* July 23, 1876 and September 4, 1879.
27 The same, September 4, 1879.

from Concho into Dallas, and jubilantly reported that "the government will begin to have all supplies, freight, etc. hauled over the new route from Concho to Dallas immediately." The road passed through Camp Colorado, Brownwood, Comanche, Stephenville, Granbury and thence to Dallas. The stage line was set to start in June.²⁸ All of which indicated that the Concho country lay on the periphery of an active and changing world.

With the building of the Texas and Pacific Railroad west from Fort Worth, there was another radical shift in the freighting of supplies. Fort Worth had remained its terminus for nearly four years. But in the summer of 1880 the T. and P.'s newly-laid steel began to point the direct way across West Texas. On December 4, 1880, it reached Baird, passed Sweetwater in March, and reached Big Spring, April 28, 1881. Immediately, freighters swung their teams north to take advantage of the shorter haul. The army laid out a trail to Big Spring and a stage was shortly running from San Angelo to Abilene.²⁹ But those inured to the long trails out of San Antonio did not quit without a struggle.

Among these was a persistent German from the Fredericksburg country named William Wahrmund. He was actively contracting hay and corn to Concho in 1874, and he kept his freighting outfits on the road for years. He drew his teams and drivers from the frontier where the frugal German settlers, hard-pressed for money along with everybody else, were anxious to get work that paid.

One of his drivers was Albert Kott, a tall and lanky boy, who, in three years of driving ox-teams to Concho, Stockton, Big Spring, and the ends of the rails at the incipient town of Pecos, walked a total of more than nine hundred miles beside his rhythmically plodding teams. He started freighting at

²⁸ *Galveston News*, May 5 and 27, and October 22, June 24, 1876; March 17, April 26 and 27, and November 30, 1877; and June 27, 1878.

²⁹ For the westward progress of the Texas and Pacific, see S. G. Reed, *A History of the Texas Railroads*, Houston, 1941, pp. 364-365.

thirteen, whip-stock across his skinny shoulder and long raw-hide lash coiled in his hand, as a driver for Charles Henke.

Next he was cracking his whip over the sharp hip-bones of six yoke of steers for George Stehling on the long trail past Concho to Pontoon Crossing, below Horsehead, on the Pecos.

In the spring of 1881, Stehling's train left the head of the Middle Concho with lead- and trail-wagons loaded with corn. It crossed the Staked Plains without water and was met by the Irish caretaker at Pontoon Crossing with the news that a government train had so weakened the bridge that the drivers could not use it. The river was only about fifty feet across, but far too deep to ford, and flowed swiftly between steep-cut banks. Stehling and his teamsters carried their 12,000-pound loads of corn across upon their backs, pulled their empty wagons over with a single yoke, and eventually "delivered the goods" in Fort Stockton.

Then having heard that the grading crews of the Texas and Pacific Railroad were approaching the Pecos, they headed north to intercept them. When they reached the site of the town of Pecos they discovered the graders' large camp across the river. Shouted inquiry brought the answer that the nearest ford was eighteen miles downstream. Stehling's drivers packed their beds on top of the wagons and doubled their teams—twelve yoke in long tandem—and put them into the river. The leaders were soon swimming, but before the wheelers left the west bank, the lead cattle had crossed the deep water and with steady and dependable stride were leaning against their yokes as they climbed the bank on the opposite side.

The terminus of the T. and P. was still at Big Spring about 130 miles to the east. O'Donnell's grading camp, cut off by the intervening Monahans Sands, was screaming for supplies. Stehling, unaware of the nature of the terrain between, agreed to haul them across. He proceeded empty to Big Spring, and as he had to wait for his freight, he put in his time hauling buffalo bones from where others had piled them around the Spring to a loading site by the new railroad siding. At twelve dollars a ton on the frontier, the bones found ready sale in the East for commercial fertilizer. According to Albert Kott, the rick along the railroad grew until it seemed a city block long, and as high as the haulers could pitch the bones. Then the freighters hauled additional loads from Mustang Spring, on the Plains to the west, where the hide hunters had left a littered field of bleaching bones.

With the arrival of O'Donnell's supplies, Stehling's men yoked up and again pointed the horns of their leaders toward the Pecos. The going was good until they rolled off the Plains west of the site of Odessa. Gradually the sand grew deeper. Finally they dropped one set of wagons and doubled their teams, driving at night to avoid the heat. But with the coming of day they were only six miles farther toward the Pecos. They unyoked their steers, mounted their rustling horses, and drifted their work cattle to the permanent water holes in the Sands. They then repeated the performance by returning for the wagons they had left behind. For six days and nights they fought that relentless sea of drifting sand until, at last, they struck the firm alkali flats beyond and delivered the goods on the Pecos. Thus they helped keep the grading going for the railroad that was even then beginning to put them out of business.[30]

The freighters were a notable breed of western men who kept plying their whips and their profanity, to the general benefit of the West, until the motor vehicles put their weathered figures into the well-earned shade. That observant English sheepman, Robert Maudslay, in his vivid recollections of the San Angelo country, left his impressions of a characteristic figure, Jim Hewit, a freighter of the nineties.

Hewit drove a team of sixteen mules, four abreast and four strung out, with a train of five wagons and a "caboose"—a forerunner of the two-wheeled auto trailers—which held his feed and camp outfit. When he strung his personal caravan out on the road, he was a spectacular sight to behold. Everybody had to give him road. If he slightly erred in calculated aim, he never worried about the gate-posts that he hubbed nor the fences he tore down. He made a late morning start and stopped for night before his mules grew tired.

Of a morning he stretched a rope between his wagons and a tree and filled sixteen morrals with grain. At his call his well-trained mules lined up abreast along the rope. He quickly slipped the nose-bags in place and harnessed his mules while they ate. Then he swung them into position, hooked them up, mounted "his executive's seat on the first wagon . . . cracked his long whip as a signal for the start, and off he'd rumble, monarch of the road." The lonely spaces were poorer with his passing.[31]

The recipient of much of the freight at the western forts was that frontier institution called the sutler or post trader. He came almost with the first troops. His roughly constructed building was a sort of a social center where isolated troopers

30 Albert Kott to J.E.H., September 8, and October 18, 1946; John Stehling to J.E.H., October 19, 1946.

31 Winifred Kupper, *The Golden Hoof*, New York, 1945, pp. 184-185.

could spend for whiskey and tobacco the scanty pay that poker left, and accumulate a load of worthless conversation. As an adjunct to the military arm directly flourishing by government license, the sutler's tenure was dependent on approval of Washington—the Secretary of War himself. The first to occupy the post at Concho was a New Yorker named James Trainer who came to the frontier directly after the war.[32]

Competition for the place was keen and changes were frequent. The shift of commanding officers, who served more or less as agents of the Secretary of War, militated against a monopoly, and by May, 1869, there were five stores "in, or within a short distance of the Post," and the rivalry for trade was benefiting the troops.[33] But even as competition brought healthy conflict, the admixture of profits and politics with dominant authority brought favoritism and corruption.

By June, 1870, C. M. Johnson became sutler and occupied a building claimed by the government. When the post adjutant pressed its ownership, Johnson claimed the building had been abandoned by the government, and that he had repaired it by placing "most of the pickets" in its walls and by putting on a new roof. He did not agree to get out but said he would reimburse the government for its interest in the pickets out of the building itself "at any time called upon. . . ."

Meanwhile, Trainer, temporarily out of favor, bought "land adjoining the Post and erected thereon a substantial stone building." A. L. Wickes and John Newton "started another establishment with the consent of the Commanding officer" within what was supposed to be the Post limits, though nobody knew just where they were. The situation provoked the irrepressible Dr. Notson to observe:

The history of the various trading establishments of the vicinity, may some day form an item in the history of this section. The village of St. Angela, across the North Concho, is almost entirely made up of traders

---

[32] For early mention of Trainer, see *San Antonio Express*, December 24, 1867; *Medical History*, as cited, vol. 401, p. 201.

[33] *Medical History*, as cited, vol. 401, p. 124.

who have been appointed or welcomed by one Post Commander, and ejected by his successors.[34]

The confusion continued until March, 1871, when the agent of "the permanent sutler . . . arrived at the post" and made a deal with Trainer, who continued to operate. The commanding officer "ordered all other stores on the reservation closed," though the bounds of the reservations were still indefinite, and apparently always in doubt. Sometimes they extended for "a radius of ten miles from the flagstaff," as arbitrarily established by order of Major Cram, and again they were so restricted by definition of General Bingham as to leave out some of the buildings of the fort itself. It all seemed to depend on "the whim" of the commanding officers.[35]

In 1872 orders came from Washington that James H. Owings had been appointed trader, and that all others were to be removed when he took over the job. But there was chicanery in Washington, and within the next ten days news came that one J. M. Hendrick had resigned the place, and that the persistent James Trainer again held the license. Then Joseph Loeb took over, and so it rocked on with tedious variations until October 9, 1876, when he sold his store and some seventy acres adjoining the post to his partner, William S. Veck.[36] In December, Veck sold out to the colorful J. L. Millspaugh, a small, dynamic, swashbuckling New Yorker possessed more of imaginative enterprise than practical execution. He was a hearty man who appreciated good music, loved the stage, and was a zestful actor in the spirited play of life which, for him, was a continual round of adventure.

Millspaugh was mentioned as a farmer in the post records of 1874, but more nearly fitted the description of a high-powered promoter. He enjoyed his growing family but every time a child was imminent, which was often, he had pressing business elsewhere. In later years he opened a real estate

34 *Medical History,* as cited, vol. 401, p. 185.

35 The same, 209-210.

36 See *Letters Received,* March 4, 1872; December 8, 1873; *Deed Records,* Tom Green County, B, 101, 109.

division at San Angelo. But when an interested passerby stopped to ask where "Millspaugh's Addition" could be found, his wife, with the saving grace of humor, made a sweeping gesture toward his eight children playing in the yard. All sorts of business picked up when he hit his stride at Fort Concho.[37]

In 1875 he bid on the grain contracts, but with his acquisition of the trader's store he really went to town. Once when he ran out of small change he sent a Mexican to the gambling dens across the river to bring a supply. He returned with a sack of silver dollars. After abusing the Mexican, Millspaugh cut the dollars in two with a chisel and made change with them.

He jumped into the life of the region with genuine zest and struck up a friendship with General Grierson. One day he was calling on Grierson for help against Indians who had stolen his farming stock, and next day begging the commander to lend him three guns to protect his haying camp on the North Concho. The Post Council approved his application as trader, September 21, 1876, and impatient over its delayed approval Grierson wired the Adjutant General at Washington a month later to "please have the appointment made." With his license confirmed Millspaugh made his deal with Veck and actively entered into the post affairs.[38]

But "the unanimous" approval of the Post Council changed to a different tune in the course of Millspaugh's operations. In the spring of 1878 there were complaints that the trader's store was used by a gambler for fleecing drunken soldiers. Millspaugh suggested that the culprit be thrown off the military reservation, though he was shortly contending that his private land was not subject to military jurisdiction. Then he generously offered to give the government a four-acre plot from his land that was being used as the post cemetery. Mili-

37 Mrs. Dwight Hunter to J.E.H., December 12, 1945; *Letter Book*, Fort Concho, June 29, 1874.

38 See letters of April 5, July 13, 14, 16, and September 2 and 9, 1875, *Army Commands*; Grierson to Adjt. Gen., October 23, 1876.

tary Headquarters rejected his offer because of a lack of funds to fence it.[39]

With this diversionary movement thrust aside, the Post Adjutant, Robert G. Smither, emphasized the "numerous complaints" against the post trader which had been called to Millspaugh's attention "without effecting any permanent results." It was claimed that he "did not purchase his goods in the East as Stipulated," that he did not keep the needed stock in sufficient quantity or desired quality, that his prices were exorbitant, that he stayed open after the hours specified by military authority, that his store and saloon were open on Sundays, that he gave out drink checks, that he sold to "drunken enlisted men and Citizens," and that the liquors he did sell were of "a very poor quality" generally. All of which seemed to justify remedial action by the Post Council.[40]

In spite of the complaints, Millspaugh and the Post kept doing business. But in the course of the dissension the question of the private ownership of the sutler's land again intruded to worry the commanders of the post. When Millspaugh thought about losing the contract for the sutler's store, he hedged against the uncertain future by asking for clarification of his position on the seventy acres he had bought from Veck, which lay alongside the post, in the middle of the military reservation. The matter went up to the Judge Advocate General at Washington, who advised him and the Commander, October 16, 1877, that

Mr. Millspaugh . . . evidently thinks he has made a "corner" on the Government, as to that post tradership, by his being the owner of a parcel of ground within the boundaries and limits of Fort Concho. . . . The Government is not under the necessity of retaining Mr. Millspaugh in that Post-tradership, for fear that, in case of removal, he will establish a trading-post on his "own land" within the limits of the reservation . . . he is entitled to a convenient way of ingress and egress. . . . But this privilege may be limited to that exact way.

39 See *Letter Book,* Fort Concho, April 19, 1878; and letter of Asst. Adjt. General to C.O., Fort Concho, April 15, 1878, *U. S. Army Commands.*
40 *Letter Book,* Fort Concho, April 30, 1878, pp. 116-117.

While the military authorities may have no right to exclude him from his land, they can prevent anyone under military authority from going upon it, and an order to that effect would, it is presumed, make his right to do business on this land worthless.[41]

Then Millspaugh conceived the notion that in view of the exclusive tax he was paying the government for his license to operate the post store, the late owner, William S. Veck, and "all outside traders should be prohibited from going upon the reservation at the time of payment [of the troops] to collect debts from the soldiers." The military sustained him.

Meanwhile in March, 1876, a Congressional investigation uncovered the scandalous handling of post tradeships. The Secretary of War, General William W. Belknap, was involved in the selling of contracts throughout the Southwest. Traders at Forts Sill, Richardson, Griffin and Concho were involved. Trainer went on the stand to say that Belknap had referred him to General Hendrick when he applied at Concho, and that Hendrick had wanted a bonus of $6,000 for the contract. Trainer claimed that in 1870 he had paid $1500 to the General and $1000 to his agent, besides a smaller levy to Simon Wolf and an appreciative gratuity to a Texas Congressman.

A regular system of brokerage had been evolved. General E. W. Rice, of Oskaloosa, Iowa, testified that he was appointed trader at Fort Richardson and let another man run the store for one-third of the profits. At the same time he had received fat fees from the stores at Fort Wingate, New Mexico, and Fort Sill, in addition to $2000 from Jacob Loeb at Fort Concho, and $5000 from William H. Hicks, at Fort Griffin, for having interested himself with the Secretary of War on behalf of these sutlers.

General J. J. Reynolds was accused of participating in the crooked business, and it was claimed that the gift of a house to him in San Antonio was not that of grateful citizens, as originally claimed, but a part of his pay from a ring of crooked contractors. All of which sounds picayunish in view of modern

[41] Judge Advocate Gen'l to J. L. Millspaugh, October 16, 1877, *Letters Sent*, II.

government, but the exposures shook the entire country, forcing President Grant to intervene, and sending Belknap out of office in disgrace.[42]

By 1881 the question of jurisdiction, in spite of the Judge Advocate General's opinion, was still a vicious bone of contention between Millspaugh and the Concho commander. This time the trouble broke out over a number of camp followers who were living on Millspaugh's land alongside the post. Grierson directed Millspaugh, whom he called the "late post trader," to notify the troublesome women "to move away at once," and that in the future no building be rented without "his [Grierson's] sanction or consent." Grierson insisted that the post commander had "exercised jurisdiction over the land claimed by Mr. Millspaugh ever since the establishment of the Post." Millspaugh thereupon carried his complaint directly to the Secretary of War, along with his resignation as trader, which was accepted August 10, 1881, while the Attorney General of the United States sustained the commander in every particular.

As a parting shot, Millspaugh refused to pay the last assessment of the post tax, and insisted that the government should now buy the post cemetery. But even after fourteen years of active operation, no correct map of the military reservation could be had, and Fort Concho's dead continued to sleep in disputed jurisdiction as the post passed into its own inactive period.[43]

Millspaugh became a prominent figure in the growth of San Angelo. But James Trainer, the first post trader, died at fifty as a destitute alcoholic at San Antonio, July 15, 1878, and was buried by the Masons.[44] Within their respective periods they had served, not without contention and conflict, from the founding of Fort Concho to its transition to a relatively inactive post.

[42] *Galveston News,* April 7, 21, and 27, and May 3, 1876; *Free Press,* San Antonio, August 22, 1876; C. C. Rister, *The Southwestern Frontier,* 1865-1881, Cleveland, 1928, pp. 87-94.

[43] See *Letter Book,* March 11, 1879, and August 1 and September 10, 1881.

[44] *San Antonio Express,* June 16, 1878.

CHAPTER XVII

Life at the Post

THE FLAVOR of Fort Concho was quite different from that of the average frontier village. A sort of glamor seemed to mark life within a border post that the humdrum routine of military existence actually denied. Regular transportation by stage and mail lines did much to mitigate the isolation. Enlisted men and officers were removed from the stark and unremitting struggle for existence by virtue of military regimentation. They lacked the freedom of the frontiersman, but they did enjoy a measure of leisure. The stimulus of government spending spurred the economic pulse-beat of the community, and the animated social life that seems to flourish wherever the army goes enhanced the prestige of the posts in a region almost completely devoid of such diversion.

Yet the omnipotent hand of nature always kept a finger in affairs. The extremely individualistic weather was a fruitful topic of conversation and at times a matter of concern to people unused to the land. In its usual perversity it ran the gamut of temperamental change to try the patience and sear the complexions of fair-skinned women from humid lands.

The first notable dust storm in the history of the post rolled its billowy curtain in at noon, December 22, 1871, to unroof the sutler's store and awe the newcomers. Fort Stockton experienced the same storm, which next day engulfed Fort Griffin in its fury. Once in a while heavy hail flailed the pecan and mesquite trees bare of leaves. A storm on April 20, 1878, left the post a shambles. Hail stones as large "as goose eggs" badly damaged almost every building, beat out 1200 panes of glass, and left a foot of ice upon the parade ground. The storm stampeded a hundred cavalry horses and killed one. It injured five soldiers, and resulted in heavy losses of sheep and cattle.

Besides drouth and dust, floods took their toll. On the night of April 24, 1870, Colonel W. C. Merriam, sometime in command of the post, had camped with his family and a detail of soldiers at the head of the Middle Concho as he journeyed back from El Paso. A heavy hail fell that night and the river rose in a sudden torrent, sweeping his entire camp away, even to his carriage and teams. Mrs. Merriam, her child, nurse and three soldiers were drowned, and Merriam escaped only after being carried a half-mile downstream.

The next serious flood of record came on September 21, 1881, after the North Concho had been virtually dry for months. A cloudburst developed west of the post and swung up the river. The stream jumped with a fifteen-foot rise in ten minutes. Chaplain Norman Badger reported that it "swept away several drinking saloons & miserable lodging places of outside camp-followers" across the river, while the post surgeon recorded that it carried off "all houses, stores etc. on or near the river bank."

Again on September 7, 1878, a thirty-five-foot flood "overflowed the town of Benficklin," destroying the stage station and some buildings. The warning was not heeded, and the famous flood of August 25, 1882, washed the town of Benficklin away, took the lives of about fifty people, and left the most tragic memories of the bitter struggle with the elements around Fort Concho.[1]

---

[1] *Medical History*, as cited, vol. 401, pp. 166, 245-246, 261; vol. 404, pp. 156 and 329; "Post Chaplain's Return," September 30, 1874; *Galveston News*, April 21 and 23, June 29 and September 25, 1878, and August 26 and 17, 1882.

Closely akin to a healthy respect for nature is the matter of religion. Then as now the army took steps to encourage it, and apparently the first chaplain at the post was Captain Thaddeus B. McFalls, evidently a Scot and positively a Presbyterian. One Reverend Gonzales was appointed chaplain of the 9th Cavalry and held his first services the last Sunday in May, 1869, preaching "by permission" in one of the hospital wards, where the attendance was said to be "good, the behavior . . . creditable." McFalls, however, was still on hand in January, 1870, when he was granted a six months' military respite from the Lord's business.

The most notable chaplain in Concho's history was Norman Badger. This good and zealous man was born near Springfield, Massachusetts, January 5, 1812, took an M.A. at Kenyon College, in Ohio in 1834, joined the army, and late in the Civil War was ordered to Louisville. From there he was sent to Fort Concho, April 9, 1871, and served until his death, June 3, 1876, when his body was shipped back to Gambier, Ohio, for burial.

His first services were held at the post hospital. On April 30, 1871, he crossed the river and "performed at Saint Angela." The irrepressible Dr. Notson dryly recorded that it was "probably the first time that the name of the deity was ever publicly used in reverence in that place." [2]

When Chaplain Badger arrived, he found the new post a worthy field for work, observing that the moral conditions were "worse than I have noticed elsewhere, expecially in the matter of profanity." He came at a busy time. General of the Army P. H. Sheridan arrived on his inspection of the Texas frontier the same week, and shortly thereafter eight prisoners escaped from the new stone guardhouse by digging out

[2] For the life of Norman Badger see an excellent paper by Susan Miles and Roberta Thompson, "Norman Badger, Chaplain, Fort Concho," ms., Tom Green County Historical Society; copies of Badger's *Post Chaplain's Returns*, same place *Medical History*, as cited, vol. 401, pp. 123, 214; *Post Returns*, July and August, 1868, and January, 1870; *Galveston News*, June 19, 1876.

through the floor. With such a breakdown of physical restraint some resort to conscience was clearly in order.

Reverend Badger flew at the Devil with commendable fervor. Through the cultivation of a soldier's garden he made an appeal to the post's stomach, but he almost despaired of its case-hardened soul. After two and a half years he philosophically observed that maybe the morals of the troops "were as good as could be expected of men far removed from the restraints of established society." He considered the guardhouse a convenient index to local virtue, once saying that "the moral condition of the troops, judging by the comparative number of prisoners . . . is not so favorable as usual."

Yet in hospital wards or in tents, where the wind blew out his candles, he persistently preached the true faith to the few who would come and listen, and then time and time again recorded his doleful verdict with rigid honesty, "morals—as usual, unchanged." Christmas time of 1874, however, laid its benign influence upon his wayward flock. Services were held in the mess-room of Barracks I, which was "properly decorated with evergreen & mistletoe, and nearly everybody at the post attended services."

Yet with worship being bounced about between his own quarters and the hospital building, the average attendance in January was only sixteen people out of a force of 460 men. Time evidently favors those who persevere, and in February, 1876, almost five years after his arrival, Reverend Badger began the erection of God's first temple on the Conchos. "In despair of having a chapel & schoolhouse built by the government," he erected it with the volunteer labor of colored troops and "at their own expense." With its mud-plastered picket walls draped with flour sacks,[3] it must, in its indigenous but destitute simplicity, have merited a special blessing from the Christ who was born in a manger.

3 *Post Chaplain's Returns*, April and October, 1873; February, July and December, 1874; February, 1876.

The first mention of Catholic interest concerns the visit of the Reverend C. M. DuBuis, the Bishop of Texas, who arrived in July, 1871. The coming of this distinguished Frenchman had no appreciable effect on the post, Dr. Notson wrote

but for the vicinity . . . it will long be remembered and its effects felt. The number of Mexican families living near the Post cannot be easily estimated, as their burrows are frequently not discovered, until one is riding on top of them. To complete the characteristics of wickedness and villainous traits, with which the treacherous and dirty race abounds, where it is practicable to evade the fee and the Padre, even the simple ceremony of jumping a broom-stick is evaded, as a necessary prelimi- nary to maritial relationship. His Reverence put a stop to that, for the time at least, by marrying all or nearly all who had been living in such relations. And very unwilling Benedicts most of them made.

All of which was slightly suggestive of Father Muldoon's mass marriages in the early days of Texas, when men and women lived so far beyond the reach of respectability that they mated naturally until religion had time to catch them.

Bishop DuBuis indicated his "intention of building a church in the neighborhood of the mail station," near Benficklin, as he turned back into settled Texas. But religion still placed little restraint on the troops. The Bishop's visit was followed by the paymaster from San Antonio with his chest of cash, and he was immediately followed by "more than the usual number of desertions." There were twenty-three out of a total garrison that, at the end of the month, had been reduced to only 148 men.[4]

In time, of course, there were the Methodists, represented primarily by that forthright apostle of direct action when the benedictions of God left his callous neophites unmoved. With a Bible tucked in his saddle-pocket, and a sixshooter more conveniently at hand, this unique frontier circuit rider ranged the frontier on his messianic rounds, ready to kill any Indian or outlaw who got in his way, and to demonstrate the wrath of God upon the impious where forceful preachments failed.

4 *Medical History*, as cited, vol. 401, pp. 223 and 228; *Post Chaplain's Returns*, July, 1871.

Andrew Jackson Potter was born in Missouri, April 3, 1830. His father died when he was ten and he soon fared into the world for himself. In 1846 he fell in with General Sterling Price's teamsters and marched with them to New Mexico, adventured awhile on the Santa Fe Trail, explored for Arizona mines, and eventually reached San Antonio, Texas. In 1856 he attended a Methodist Camp meeting while visiting at Bastrop, and was clearly called to preach. Thus he quit the colorful pursuit of gambling, horse racing and drinking, and when the Civil War broke out, assuaged his healthy passions for religion and fighting by joining DeBray's regiment. After the war he got down to the Lord's work in earnest.

If perchance he fell into a community hostile to his message on the Prince of Peace, he pugnaciously mounted the pulpit, Bible in his left hand and sixshooter on his right hip, offering to fight to conversion any and all comers. As may be suspected the way he gathered the sinful to the Lord was little short of a miracle.

Just when his circuit took in the Concho country is a matter of conjecture. He organized the First Methodist Church at San Angelo in 1880, and moved to the town three years later. The story is told of his arrival at one of the Texas posts, apparently Concho, just after the troops had been paid. Consequently the local dives were full of sharks, toughs, and hangers-on when the Parson rode up and allowed as how he would preach. By then he was well known and a willing disciple shouted:

"Sure, parson, we'll make way for ye if we have to rent the saloon." They did rig up a saloon with kegs and barrels and all available seats, while another fervid convert, already slightly in the wind, mounted a barrel and served as the town crier:

"Oh, yes! Oh, yes! Oh, Yes! There's going to be some hell-fired racket right here on this gallery by Fightin' Parson Potter, a reformed gambler but now a reg'lar gospel shark. The jig will begin in fifteen minutes, and you ol' whiskey soaks and card sharpers come over and learn how to mend your ways, or the devil will git you quicker'n hell can scorch a feather."

They gathered and of course heard him respectfully, and then wanted to set him up at the bar. When someone reproached him for taking twenty tainted dollars from the gamblers, he retorted that the money had "served the devil long enough and now it was time it served the Lord." [5] In the days of rugged religion Parson Potter was quite a man.

The first mention of a school at Concho appears in the records of 1870. The post surgeon regretted that education, while obviously under way, had not received "the encouragement it should." Many of the officers and a few enlisted men had children "needing some scholastic training." But the fact that the teacher's salary was even less than that for regular soldiers was not calculated to encourage education.

In November, 1870, with the post crowded by eight companies of men, school was being conducted in "the well worn hospital tent." It was all that was left of the original camp just south of the permanent post site. The tent, then "standing its fourth winter against the winds of this wide prairie" was considered "an exceptional illustration of the durability of canvass," [6] rather than an index to higher education. In March, 1871, when Colonel Mackenzie marched off to Fort Richardson on his campaign, E. Hosmer, the school-teacher, went with the troops, again leaving Concho without a school—"a great loss to the Post."

The winter of 1872 found the post in the same shape, though General Hatch ordered the quartermaster to estimate the materials for a school building. Early in 1874, Chaplain Badger was giving instruction four hours a day, but "owing to the non-arrival of School-books purchased in New York" while five months before, he had lamented, "I have been able

5 See his biography, H. A. Graves, *Andrew Jackson Potter, The Noted Parson of the Texan Frontier*, Nashville, 1883; *Galveston News*, August 3, 1878; *San Angelo Standard*, May 3, 1924 and December 31, 1939; *Houston Post*, February 20, 1938.

6 *Medical History*, as cited, vol. 401, pp. 179, 195, and 211.

to benefit the colored troops only by an occasional lecture."[7]

A post library was opened in March, 1873, with a good supply of periodicals and papers. A fund of $400 was appropriated in February, of which $72 was invested in newspapers. After a year the library had 311 books on hand; by November 30, 1875, its 720 volumes, "many of them standard works," tempted those who found relief from ennui by reading, though no modern liberal literature befouled the place.

By 1880 the budget for reading was substantial, and such daily papers as the *New York Herald, Tribune, Graphic, World, Chicago Inter-Ocean, St. Louis Globe-Democrat, Cincinnati Commercial* and *Louisville Courier-Journal* were on the tables. A wide range of reading interest was served by such weeklies as the *United Service, Harper's, Leslie's Illustrated, London Graphic, Leslie's Pleasant Hours, Detroit Free Press, Scientific American, Forest and Stream, Illustrated Christian Weekly, Washington Star, Littel's Living Age,* and others. Heavier monthly magazines like *Harper's, Scribners, Eclectic,* and the *Atlantic* were there to tempt the intellectuals.

By April, 1881, the post library boasted 881 books, with a weekly attendance of about 250 men. It was the scene for two Sunday school sessions weekly conducted by Chaplain Weaver, "assisted by the ladies at the post," and by the children "comparatively well trained in singing."[8]

Such zeal aided the early educational efforts, and Norman Badger's course in adult learning gave way to a night school started by Chaplain George W. Dunbar, who arrived October 21, 1876, shortly after Badger's death. This course was opened in April with fifteen pupils, and was devoted to reading, spelling, arithmetic, geography and "some U. S. History," with no time wasted on progressive education. Books and slates were

7 *Medical History,* as cited, vol. 401, pp. 221, 297; *Post Chaplain's Returns,* January, 1874.

8 *Post Chaplain's Returns* for 1873; *Letter Book,* Fort Concho, 1880, pp. 265-266; I. O. Shelby to Geo. G. Mullins, April 20, 1881, *Army Commands; Medical History,* as cited, vol. 403, p. 11.

badly needed, but tremendous strides were obvious from the fact that while the itemized budget for 1875 totaled $8.15, the budget for 1876—for those who dote on percentages—showed a 2500 percent increase, or a total cash outlay of $200.64. There were no bonds outstanding.

Those in attendance were children of "recent recruits," but by September 30, 1878, Chaplain Dunbar had "recommended a school for officers' children, and one for the men in a small way. Lack of rooms prevents my doing more." Clearly the educational virus was at work, for on February 22, 1879, "a post school was formally established" and placed in charge of the Chaplain. After nine years the first school room twenty by forty feet was built, "by far the best finished room in the Post." The plush age in education had been ushered in on the Conchos. By the end of the year, the record indicates, three separate schools—"for white children, for colored children and for soldiers"—were in operation.[9] Obviously the jurisdiction of an authoritarian-minded Supreme Court did not reach to the Conchos. These people were interested in education and not in agitation. Nobody dreamed that it was discrimination, and in their ignorance all were proud and happy.

Shortly soldiers were doing the teaching. Private George Ruthers appealed to the Adjutant General in protest of "the legality of his assignment to a company, after having been enlisted for a school teacher." He was curtly advised that "No men are enlisted especially as school teachers. They are enlisted as soldiers . . . and should move with the companies to which they are assigned." In 1883, two years later, Ruthers officially requested that "his name be changed to George W. Gibbs, that being his real name"[10] anyway, which must have met with the approval of old-fashioned folks who think teachers should go under their own names.

9 *Post Chaplain's Returns,* April and October, 1876; September and December, 1878; *Medical History,* as cited, vol. 404, p. 5; "Post Fund Account, 1876."

10 *Letters Received,* 1881, Fort Concho, 36, 68; *Letter Book,* 1884, p. 102.

From then on education really went to town, and in 1882 it was made mandatory. The orders of the Post Adjutant read that there must be "compulsory attendance." Discipline was to be enforced by the teachers through "moderate corporal punishment . . . if necessary. The same will apply to children of servants and government employees." On the other hand "the attendance of Officers' children being optional, if they do not conduct themselves properly, they will be sent home with a note from the teacher to the parents giving reasons for the same," so the orders read.

The following year the United States Adjutant General, R. C. Drum, at Washington, officially assigned a school teacher from the army, but held that "two school teachers" were not needed at Concho.[11] This might be construed by some as the first overt act in federal support and control, but by that time education was off to a running local start.

Fortunately for the physical well-being of the post the surgeons were not changed as often as the commanders. The first birth and the first death "to an officer's family" at Concho fell to the surgeon's lot. Otis Rockwell Notson, son of the post surgeon, was born June 1, 1869, and died the same day. The "first natural death" among the settlers, the surgeon emphasized in view of the toll by widespread violence, was that of Abijah Bayless, on March 6, 1871. He was owner of one-quarter interest in the Bismarck Farm. In September the wife of General Cuvier Grover died of apoplexy at the Centralia Station on the Staked Plains while her husband was making a tour of inspection of the posts of the district. Her child died a week later at McKavett.[12]

For several years most of the deaths were violent in nature. The first killing of a soldier by a civilian took place in 1870 "across the river near St. Angela." The civilian surrendered to Colonel Hatch, who turned him loose on the basis of self-defense. With the homicidal ice broken, the deaths mounted

[11] *Letter Book*, 1882, Ft. Concho, 466; *Letters Received*, 1883, Ft. Concho, 83.
[12] *Medical History*, as cited, vol. 401, pp. 125, 138, 210.

at an alarming rate, or at what would have been an alarming rate if anyone had been concerned. Dr. Notson was helping satisfy his scientific bent by sending Indian skulls to the Army Medical Museum, while down at McKavett the way the post surgeon was performing autopsies and cutting up cadavers to satisfy his curiosity was little short of a fright.[13] He had plenty on which to carve.

Yet only twenty-two deaths were reported among the troops at Concho during the first three and a half years of its existence. Six of these were from gunshot wounds, five from diarrhea and dysentery, eight from typhoid, and the balance from other causes. The year 1870 turned out to be a trying one for the medical services at the post.

Spring wore off with little resort to the hospital, though Dr. Notson insisted that this was not due to the sanitary measures put into effect by Shafter, but because most of the troops were in the field on scouts—a fact, he emphasized, that "proved empirically against all philosophical reasoning that fewer men are sick on scouts than in garrison." With the coming of fall, the post, then designed for only four companies, was crowded with the equivalent of ten companies. It was an extremely wet year, with a rainfall of 38.18 inches. The wet weather, coupled with an improvised water system and an almost total lack of sanitation, kept the surgeon and his two assistants hard at work. The post was then nearly three years old and still had no sinks, privies or toilets of any kind except what nature provided in the ravines and on the open prairie.

The water barrels accumulated fungus and slime, and at last were disinfected by being filled with hay, which was burned until a thick coat of charcoal formed inside. The hospital overflowed with sick men, and medical supplies were short though the surgeon repeatedly requisitioned them. "All forms of fever and diarrhea have exhibited a tendency to take on a typhoid character," Dr. Notson reported in October,

13 *Medical History,* as cited, vol. 401, pp. 174 and 221; *Medical History,* Fort McKavett, 1868-1872.

"while true typhoid has been prevalent, a number of cases terminating fatally." Special sanitary orders were issued.

By the end of November the sick roll was a matter of real concern. Since the new white garrison had been moved to Concho just 172 days before, there had been 792 cases of sickness. There had been 60 cases of diarrhea and dysentery, 58 of intermittent fever, some 35 cases of typhoid; and nine patients had died. During the same period the scattered civilians had suffered six deaths. Ice was rushed from San Antonio by stage at a cost of twenty-five dollars a hundred pounds for the relief of the fever patients. The food was unsuited for the sick and the commissary was completely out of certain essentials, notably beans and tea, while the medical supplies requisitioned seven months earlier had still not been delivered. In December the men were on "beef, coffee and bread." but by the end of the year their troubles had subsided.[14]

Yet there were later epidemics, as in May, 1877, when 233 hospital cases of diarrhea accounted for "more than 50 per cent of the mean strength of the command." Over-crowding of the barracks, poor drainage, and fresh beef that was "old, tough and too lean" were all held to blame. Typhoid, always a threat, resulted in the death of thirteen-year-old Edith Grierson, daughter of the General, September 9, 1878. At last open sinks were dug and disinfected weekly with lime and carbolic acid if the weather was bad. Cases of scarlet fever were isolated about a mile from the post, and one death resulted from meningitis. There was little or no mention of tuberculosis, though the favorable climate for the treatment of pulmonary diseases was recognized at once by Dr. Notson.[15]

In January, 1871, medical supplies that had been lying in the quartermaster's warehouse at San Antonio for two and a half months, while the epidemics raged and the surgeon was

14 *Medical History*, as cited, vol. 401, pp. 80-81, 165, 190-197, 202.

15 *Medical History*, as cited, vol. 401, p. 213; vol. 404, pp. 199, 244, 248, 291, 329; *Letter Book*, Fort Concho, I, 360.

crying for such supplies, reached the post after health had been restored. In March a six months' supply came at once.

In 1871 an unidentified narcotic suspiciously like marihuana appeared. A bugler passed into a fifteen-day stupor after getting the stuff from a prostitute. On investigation the surgeon discovered a general belief "that the lower orders of Mexicans and half breeds, are in possession of some poison that will permanently affect the reason, and that the case of the Empress Carlotta is a case in illustration." [16] Months later the man was still affected, having changed from "a bright, active and rather mischievous youth" to "a dull, stolid half stupid" person, "very slow of comprehension."

At one time the entire post was alive with fleas, with "the officers quarters and the hospital . . . particularly infested." Again the men reporting to sick call were so dirty that Dr. Notson could not stand them. The surgeon prevailed upon Colonel Hatch to order them all to bathe. Strangely enough venereal diseases were barely mentioned before the middle seventies, but a plague of syphilis broke out in August, 1875, when Dr. William F. Buchanan was treating six per cent of the garrison for venereal troubles, nine-tenths of which were syphilitic. [17] It had definitely impaired the morale and the efficiency of the post, and he recommended preventive measures such as the "exclusion of known prostitutes from the garrison," and social diversions in off hours.

Like his ingenious predecessor, Dr. Buchanan found plenty of problems to engage him. He too urged completion of the hospital cistern that had languished as an unfinished hole in the ground for years. When he found his steward consistently drunk, he ordered sobriety and at last placed him under arrest. Only then did he discover that a case of brandy kept for medicinal purposes had the unremoved corks slightly slit. The bottles were filled with a vile "compound of Licorice,

[16] *Medical History,* as cited, vol. 401, pp. 198, 202, 209, 211, and 235.
[17] *Medical History,* as cited, vol. 401, pp. 120, 266; vol. 404, p. 199; *Letters Received,* Fort Concho, August 29, 1875.

alcohol, Water and Aqua Fortis." Evidently the original contents had been removed "by osmosis." The disaffection seemed general, for out of a total garrison of 326 men, thirty desertions were reported for the month.

With disease rampant in 1875, Dr. Buchanan elaborated his complaints in his monthly Medical Report. As it passed up through the military hierarchy, General Grierson, irritated by its adverse tenor, endorsed it with biting sarcasm, noting that "it appears to be a copy of former reports." Many of the matters of which Buchanan complained had already been corrected, Grierson added. Furthermore, the beef and bread the men were getting were all right, and as for the Doctor's complaint about the privies, Grierson contended he was incompetent to judge "as he is entirely deficient in the sense of smell." [18]

Dr. Buchanan was replaced by Dr. D. Hershey, who was temporarily relieved by Dr. I. H. T. King, in the summer of 1876. Hershey returned from detail work but took sick and died at Concho, September 29, 1876. King continued to serve until relieved by Dr. J. V. DeHanne a year later. Dr. DeHanne stayed until June, 1879, when he fell sick, and the health of the post largely devolved on his assistant surgeon, Dr. S. L. S. Smith. Dr. Smith had been on an extended scout to the Guadalupe Mountains with Captain S. T. Norvell in 1878, as surgeon in the field, and returned with Norvell's company to the outpost of Camp Charlotte near the head of the Middle Concho.[19] He is best remembered as a pioneer doctor of the San Angelo country, where he practiced generally after his contract with the government was annulled in 1881.[20] The last doctor at the post was Captain Charles M. Gandy.

Many of these frontier doctors, treating their army patients

[18] The same, vol. 401, pp. 289-290; vol. 404, pp. 204-205.

[19] The same, vol. 404, p. 331; vol. 407, pp. 7, 9, 38, 43, 53, 59, 71, 82; *Letter Book*, 1879, Fort Concho, 219.

[20] Other surgeons who served intermittently at Concho were Drs. H. L. Lewis, R. Gale, E. Alexander and W. F. Carter, principally during Buchanan's time. *Medical History*, as cited, vol. 403 and 404.

on contract, were genuinely outstanding characters. While serving as surgeon in Indian Territory, Dr. Smith had pursued his researches into his favorite fields of therapeutics and obstetrics, amassing a collection of paintings illustrative of the methods used among the Indians. While scouting on the frontier beyond Concho he studied the geography, the growth and the water resources, and contributed valuable information upon that region for a report that Grierson submitted to Washington.[21]

The most colorful and in many ways the most remarkable of all these early surgeons was Dr. William M. Notson. His devotion to his job under the most trying circumstances was remarkable, his ingenuity apparently inexhaustible, his courage in fighting the bureaucratic lethargy of the army unflagging, and his interest in the land about him genuine and at times profound. As already observed he induced a visiting general to plant water cress along the North Concho, he gathered specimens for the Army Medical Museum, he continually "bucked the brass" for the health of the enlisted men, he planted trees upon the barren post reservation, and by his monthly entries in the *Medical History of Fort Concho*, he left an honest and intimate record of the life of the post and the region. He was not unaware of its value, for when he made his final entry in July, 1872, he did so "with the request that who ever closes the book . . . will forward it direct to the Surgeon General's office and not leave it to mould with so many of its kind in the cellar of the San Antonio Hospital."[22] He would be pleased to know that it has, as he anticipated, served the cause of history.

It is hardly necessary to elaborate upon the crudity of their treatments. The case of the soldier who was carried out of Blanco Canyon with bowels punctured and protruding from an Indian's bullet, and still lived, is a good illustration. When

[21] *San Angelo Standard*, January 12, 1949; "Excerpts from Records of San Angelo District Medical Society," by Dr. S. L. S. Smith, ms.

[22] *Medical History*, as cited, vol. 401, pp. 211, 269, 273, 285.

a member of Major Mecklenburg's surveying party was shot in the back by accident near Concho in 1872, one "contract physician" simply plugged the hole with lint, and another applied a poultice of flax-seed, much to the post surgeon's disgust.

The most notorious "recovery" was that of a colored soldier named Ellis who came with the 10th Cavalry. He fell sick. The doctor decided he was dead and sent him to the "dead house," where his body was placed on a cooling board for burial on the morrow. Since few things are more worthy of observance than a good Negro funeral, Ellis' friends gathered in force and fortified themselves with a pot of coffee and a jug of whiskey, properly prepared to sit up with the corpse. All went well until, in the middle of the night, one watcher yelled:

"That nigger ain't dead! He's a-movin'! He's gittin' up!" Instantaneously the watchers were moving too. Three of them were wedged in the door at one time while Ellis, seeing where he was, almost killed himself again by jumping through the window sash. Thereafter he was generally known as "Dead" Ellis, and always moved among his race with a sort of an aura about him after being "dead for the first time," a familiar figure in San Angelo for years.[23]

Strange as it may seem the water problem at Fort Concho was perennial. At first, supplies were hauled in a wagon, and for years kept in barrels about the post. At a bend in the Middle Concho near the mail station, nearly three miles away, water seeped from a layer of sand about a foot above the level of the stream. A circular wall was built to hold the seepage. But as cattle and buffalo were continually dying in the river, the slightest rise overflowed the spring and polluted the water. The malaria, typhoid and bowel disorders of 1870 were thought to be the result. Yet it seemed that little could be

[23] Bill Winn, "Old Cox," *The Junior Historian,* Austin, May, 1946, p. 4; Sancho Mazique to J.E.H., October 20, 1946, Mazique thought the stampede took place when Ellis got back to the hospital.

done about it. The cistern at the hospital, though started almost with the beginning of the post, was not finished for use until nearly six years later.

Major Cram had a well dug in the late sixties, but it was put to little use. In the stubborn army way, the water-haulers were for years forced to dip the supply for the entire post, a bucket at a time, and haul it in their water-wagons, though that for washing and cooking was hauled directly from the river fords. Quartermaster N. S. Constable protested the great labor involved in 1878, because it took "the constant employment of 2 water wagons and eight mules each" just to supply the garrison. That year, in a spurt of progressive planning, the officers figured on a windmill. But instead they finally installed a steam engine pump, which the flood of 1882 inundated, forcing them back to the water-wagon.

In 1888, about the time the government was ready to abandon the post, the commander installed a Buffalo Duplex steam pump above the high-water mark, and water from two 5,000-gallon tanks on thirty-foot towers was carried through a two-inch pipe to the post. Progress had at last arrived, just when the post was dead. It merely remained for the obsequies to be read.[24]

Other modern improvements included two post clocks that marked the passing period. There was a suggestion of pioneer industry when Harris and Cartledge moved on the reservation with military approval and started a brick plant. Wood for the post became a problem, especially in the winter, since the barracks were unsealed. At one time in 1874 the quartermaster looked hopefully toward a source of coal discovered near Camp Colorado, the owner of which, writing from "Pittsburg Coal Mine, Texas," was bidding to supply the post at forty dollars a ton.

With the women, then as now, there was nothing in the

<hr>

24 *Medical History,* as cited, vol. 401, p. 124 and vol. 404, p. 117; *Endorsement Book,* 1878, Fort Concho, 423; *Letter Book,* 1878, 107; *Letter Book,* 1882, 234; "Memo. on History of Fort Concho," War Records.

way of social diversion to take the place of a wedding. First at Concho was that of Lieutenant Byron Dawson and Jennie Caldwell, April 26, 1870, who were ferried across the flooded Concho to catch the stage for their honeymoon. Dances were next in popular favor. They were merry without being frivolous affairs, calling for the best in feminine wear and evoking gallantry and good manners from the officers. Music was drawn from the string instruments about the post, though in 1882 a piano arrived by way of the freight line from Abilene on the railroad.[25]

In addition to the puny provisions of man, there was the untrammelled space of the out-of-doors. What was usually a salubrious climate always tempted those who liked to hike and ride, to sport and adventure, to fish and hunt, and simply to camp out. Notwithstanding all its petty problems, life here was not half bad for men and women of healthy, zestful spirit, and hence adaptable natures. They flourished around Fort Concho.

25 *Letters Received,* Fort Concho, May 31, 1872, and volumes for 1884, p. 126, and 1885, p. 9. N. S. Constable to Chief Quartermaster, December 10, 1873. *Army Commands; Medical History,* as cited, vol. 401, p. 166-167.

CHAPTER XVIII

The

Final

Action

T HE LAST DECADE in the history of Fort Concho definitely indicates a change of life. With the late seventies the most active period of the border forces was drawing to a close. As if in keeping with nature's rhythm, the passing dangers that meant the death of the frontier posts augured the birth and healthy growth of civilian life in numerous dynamic categories. The lusty vigor of constructive and kaleidoscopic change took over in West Texas.

Where lately the wild sweep of the Indians left but transient traces in the grass, plain trails led to bachelor-camps of cow-men pitched in dugouts along the caprock of the Plains. Soon the cavernous maws of these primitive dwellings would yawn from the faces of cut-banks along the Pecos. With the hide-hunt drawing to a close and the migratory ebb and flow of the buffalo a thing of the past, there was grass to spare for lean riders from the Rio Grande through the Concho country to the Canadian line. With the westward drive of rails along the course of the Texas and Pacific, modern transportation geared

to steel on steel was pushing the tandem teams of the freighters off the road. The man with the hoe, the hounds and the
cotton-headed kids was close behind.

Yet too, by a wise provision of nature, the withering hand
of age grips the reins tenaciously and yields the saddle but
slowly. The tougher the breed the slower it yields. The great
Comanches held on with dogged determination even though
their buffalo beef and their long-fought wars were obviously
lost. During 1877 the garrison of Concho was so reduced by
details scouting across the Plains and beyond the Pecos, and
by others working out of Fort Clark along the Mexican border,
that it was "entirely inadequate to perform the necessary
guard" and police duty, and maintain the property about the
post.[1] The Rio Grande was alive with revolutionaries, and
General Ord was rounding them up as a reciprocal courtesy
to the Mexican government, with whom, for years, the United
States had plead for relief from the Indian raids from that side.
All of which about summed up the army's activities in Texas
for that year.[2]

In January, 1878, the Comanches again struck south on
their old trail, threading through the settlements and arousing
the people of Brady, nearly eighty miles to the east of Concho,
by killing two men and making off with forty head of horses.
At the same time, they stole twenty horses on the South Concho, and in March they were prowling around Menardville.
On April 15th eleven Indians attacked the mail stage on the
road east of Fort Stockton near Escondido, killed a passenger
and made off with the horses and the mail. During the spring
several men were killed between the Pecos and Fort Davis.[3]

The final Comanche outbreak came when Black Horse led
twenty-five of his people off the reservation on a buffalo hunt.
Unable to find game they wound up by killing some colts for

1 *Medical History*, as cited, vol. 404, p. 252.
2 General Ord to General Drum, August 6, 1877; General Ord to A. J. Evans,
August 7, 1877; *Report of the Secretary of War*, 1877.
3 *Telegrams Received*, Fort Concho, 3 and 9; *Galveston News*, January 17 and
February 14, 1878; *Letter Book*, Fort Concho, 1878, pp. 109, 113 and 119.

food and stealing several horses from the Holland Ranch on the head of the North Concho. A party of cowboys and a detachment of Texas Rangers from Captain June Peak's company at once gave chase. After a preliminary skirmish with the Indians they followed the trail to a fresh water lake north of the site of Midland, where, on July 1, 1879, two Indians hidden in a buffalo wallow killed Ranger W. B. Anglin and several horses. The pursuing party pulled back, but Anglin's body was rolled in a saddle blanket and buried on the spot by Lieutenant C. R. Ward from Concho. The lake has since been named for Anglin.[4] This ended the Comanche forays into Texas. But with the Apaches farther west it was a different story.

In order to tackle the problem more effectively General Ord, in January, 1878, had established the new Military District of the Pecos, with headquarters at Concho and with Grierson in command. The district took in the country west of the 101st meridian and particularly the Trans-Pecos region of Texas. Six companies of infantry and six of cavalry were placed at Grierson's disposal. He put a party in the field in March under Captain A. L. B. Keyes for the purpose of locating all dependable water in a region that required so much of man and beast and yet had so little to offer. Later he ordered Keyes to march to Delaware Creek, opposite the point of the Guadalupe range, and inspect the area as a possible site for a permanent post.[5]

Grierson then struck out with an expedition into the Big Bend, on the way touching at the prominent spring southwest of the head of the Middle Concho, evidently discovered by Captain Andrew Geddes in 1875 when scouting for Shafter.

4 The army records gave the date of the fight as June 30; the Texas Ranger records as July 1, 1879. June Peak to John B. Jones, auly, 5, 1879, State Archives, Austin; *Report of the Secretary of War*, 1879, p. 102; C. K. Ward to Post Adjutant, July 15, 1879, Nye, *Carbine and Lance*, 238; Cox, *The Cattle Industry of Texas*, as cited, 401.

5 *Galveston News*, January 26 and April 18, 1878; *Letter Book*, 1878, Fort Concho, 109, 113, 119, 121, 161.

Geddes had reported that this "fine spring...is also an old resort for the Indians." When Grierson found it for himself, he was tremendously impressed. Its name was changed from Geddes' to Grierson's Spring—understandably since Grierson was in command of the district—and shortly chosen as the site for a considerable outpost. It lay about eighteen miles south and a little east from the Centralia Stage Station, approximately thirty-eight miles southwest from Camp Charlotte, and twenty-five from the Pecos. Thus it constituted a convenient if not vital post on the hitherto usually waterless march from the head of the Middle Concho to the Pecos.

Camp Grierson became a favored spot, soon distinguished by good stone buildings and telegraphic connections with Concho. In the summer, Grierson's command pushed far down into the Big Bend below present Marathon to establish, on August 27, 1879, another outpost called Peña Colorado.[6] From here the army began scouting the country for vagrant Apaches and made plans to "open a wagon road from Fort Davis to Fort Clark," partly to provide a more direct route to San Antonio.[7]

During the winter of 1880 other posts were contemplated. Major Anson Mills, then commanding Fort Concho, outlined Grierson's plans for "one near Guadalupe Peak, one near Presidio del Norte, and one between there...and Fort Davis."[8] Already a new post called Fort Elliott had been built in the eastern Panhandle to meet the needs proven by Mackenzie's campaigns against the Comanches. It was now felt that a reshifting of the line west of Fort Griffin to tie directly in with Concho was essential. The high command agreed.[9]

6 "Itinerary of a Scout Made by Lieut. And. Geddes," in Geddes' Report of December 9, 1875; *Telegrams Received*, 1878, p. 16; and 1880, p. 128; *Letter Book*, 1879, p. 201; and 1884, p. 93. See Shafter's maps for location, expedition of 1875, and Pressler's *Map of Texas*, 1878, National Archives.

7 *Report of the Secretary of War*, 1879, p. 103.

8 *Letter Book*, Fort Concho, 1880, p. 236.

9 The Panhandle post was first established as "Cantonement North Fork of the Red River," February 3, 1875, and then shifted to a point on Sweetwater Creek in present Wheeler County, Texas, June 5, 1875. It was abandoned in 1890. For

In 1880, General of the Army P. H. Sheridan reported congressional appropriations for new posts—one to be placed "at or near a point north of the Texas and Pacific railroad and on the cattle trail which passes through the Pan Handle of Texas . . . by way of Fort Elliott to the Arkansas River west of Fort Dodge." Another was to be located "north of Fort Davis, not far from the point where the Texas and Pacific will cross the Pecos River." Then, as Grierson had recommended, another was to be placed near Presidio, and still another "near the Guadalupe Mountains." It was clear that the restless surge of settlers was already far ahead of the army and the old posts had been left behind. Sheridan elaborated on the army's objective:

> To keep in advance of our settlers, to give protection to the surveying and construction parties of the railways, to open new paths through the mountains and across the plains, to open up the country and guard the feeble settlements and mining camps from the Indians, and to secure the Indian in his just rights against the encroachments of white men, to keep out unauthorized parties from established Indian reservations, and generally to give a place of refuge to the weak along our exposed frontier by the establishment of military posts, has been the work of our little army for years past. . . .[10]

It was something of a swan song; for before these plans materialized, an effective campaign in cooperation with Mexico put the quietus on the renegade Apaches. This action, coupled with the rush of civilian development, obviated the need of any new post and meant that the days of the old ones were definitely numbered.

Meanwhile, however, New Mexico, Mexico and West Texas were still being ravaged by the Indians, and the worst of these was Victorio. He was a Warm Spring Apache who, in the tragic uprooting of tribal homes, had been placed on the Mescalero Reservation. He loathed the place and again took

---

recommendations as to its establishment, see Mackenzie's reports as cited earlier, and "Military Sites in Texas," House Ex. Doc. 282, 43rd Cong., 1st Sess., 37-38; and M. L. Crimmins, "Fort Elliott, Texas," West Texas Historical Association *Year Book,* 1947, XXIII, 3-12.

[10] *Report of Secretary of War,* 1880, p. 56.

to the war trail, and being a marvelous leader of fighting men was joined by warriors from both tribes. His band was giving so much trouble by the spring of 1880 that General Edward Hatch, commander of the Department of Mexico, hit upon the notion of disarming the Mescaleros.

In March, General Grierson was ordered out of Concho with an expedition to their reservation, in the White Mountains of New Mexico, to aid in disarming that truculent and perennially troublesome tribe. He was joined by a detachment from Fort Davis, and the command rendezvoused with 280 men and officers near the mouth of Black River. Captain Thomas C. Lebo was detached to scout out the Guadalupes, while the main column continued up the Pecos to rejoin him on the Penasco, April 12, 1880.

From there they marched to the reservation to back up General Hatch, in charge of the ticklish operations. After considerable dilly-dallying a handful of virtually worthless arms was recovered. But there was sullen opposition on the part of a rebellious fragment of the tribe which finally erupted into a fight. Grierson, camped nearby, hurried to Hatch's support while the renegades again pulled out from the reservation and took to the tall uncut along the Tularosa. Victorio was in the mountains nearby. Grierson took up the long march back to Concho.[11] He was scarcely settled in post before Hatch nervously reported that Victorio was moving on the reservation itself.

Grierson was ordered back to support the garrison at Fort Lincoln. He prepared to move while expressing his doubt of the rumors. Before he could get away, it was positively reported that Victorio had led his forces into Mexico beyond Paso del Norte. Grierson then suggested that the District of the Pecos should be strengthened in place of his being sent to New Mexico, and the Department agreed. Thereupon Grierson placed Major N. B. McLaughlen in charge of Concho and

[11] See Grierson's detailed account in *Report of the Secretary of War,* 1880, pp. 151-158; Captain J. M. Kelley to Post Adjutant, Fort Concho, December 20, 1880.

ordered three of its companies to the far west. On July 10, 1880, he left with his staff to join them.

At Fort Davis he received a dispatch from Colonel Adolfo J. Valle, at Carrizal, Mexico, informing him that Valle was taking the field with 420 troops in pursuit of Victorio. A Mexican force of 120 cavalry was already chasing the band toward the river in the general direction of Eagle Springs, in the Eagle Mountains, roughly south and a little east of the Sierra Blanca. As Lieutenant Mills was already camped there with a detail of scouts and friendly Pueblo Indians, Grierson ordered him to deploy his force along the Rio Grande and cut sign for the fugitives. At the same time Grierson moved to increase the forces at Quitman, and in the camps at Eagle Springs, the Guadalupes, and at other vital points. On July 23rd his own party reached Mills' camp.

Meanwhile the Mexican cavalry had caught the Indians about fifty miles to the southwest, in Mexico, and defeated them in a sharp fight. Colonel Valle had then moved up with his entire force and camped across the river from Quitman. On the 28th, Grierson reached that point to confer with him. Valle reported that he had orders to pursue the Indians into the United States if necessary, but just then he was completely destitute of supplies. Grierson furnished him with corn and flour, and, expecting Victorio to cross into Texas, hurried back toward Eagle Springs in the hope of intercepting him.

On the way, he discovered advance Indian scouts in Quitman Canyon, while Captain John C. Gilmore, who had been left in charge at Eagle Springs, reported that details from his camp had been fired upon by hostiles.

"Deeming it my duty," Grierson reported to his superiors with characteristic flourish, "I camped directly in their line of march" at the only nearby water—a hole called Tinaja de Las Palmas. But in assurance of his own safety he sent orders posthaste, by "stages passing in the night," for the cavalry at the Springs and at Quitman to hurry to the spot.

Next morning a band of Indians on the move approached

the watering in force and the firing started. Captain Viele heard the shooting and hurried up with troops from Eagle Springs. Captain Nolan soon arrived with others from the west. The combined force quickly broke up the Indian assault. The warriors, leaving seven dead, fled back toward the Rio Grande. The troops lost one man and ten horses, while Lieutenant S. R. Colladay, of the 10th Cavalry, was wounded.[12]

The Apaches recrossed into Mexico where Colonel Valle seemed loath to move against them, apparently on account of his supply situation. Grierson ordered two more companies of men out from Forts Stockton and Davis, and adopted the strategy of covering the mountain passes and holding the widely scattered springs and water holes which the Apaches, in their movements north toward the Mescalero country, would have to use. Again the Indians recrossed the river, and another fight between the troops and some 150 Indians took place on August 3rd. Grierson countered their movements by sending forces to Bass' Canyon, and by covering the passes south of Van Horn's Station with his own men. Then his scouts reported that the Indians had by-passed them all and were moving north, toward the upper end of the Diablos and the point of the Guadalupes.

Grierson at once packed up and marched sixty-five miles to Rattlesnake Springs, which he reached ahead of the Indians. With detachments deployed to cover every trail and water-hole from the Diablos across the glistening Salt Plains to the Delaware's, he engaged in several skirmishes with Victorio's bands as they worked their way with all their camp equipage, their women and children, toward the rocky fastnesses of the Mescalero country in New Mexico.

Captain Lebo followed a trail to the crest of the well-named Diablos, where he fell upon and took Victorio's supply camp with twenty-five head of cattle and his other food—"a substitute for bread made of maguey and other plants, berries &c.,

[12] Grierson to Asst. Adjutant Gen., July 31, 1880, *Telegrams Received; Report of the Secretary of War*, 1880, pp. 158-160.

and a large supply of beef on pack animals." In the encounter
Lebo chased a band of fifteen Indians off the mountains.
Grierson was joined on August 8th by fifteen Texas Rangers
under Captain George W. Baylor, an old-timer always lusting
for Indian blood, hide and hair, and with renewed optimism
the chase went on.

The Mexican army was covering the west bank of the Rio
Grande. General George P. Buell's forces were to the west.
With General Grierson's hundreds of troops on the north and
east abetted by Indian scouts and Texas Rangers, and with
Hatch between the fugitives and the reservation—with all of
them holding vital water holes and guarding the passes
through otherwise virtually impassable ranges—the squeeze
was put upon Victorio and his lean warriors. At last he was
effectively bottled up.

Yet without supplies, and deprived of water, with his forces
cut to pieces by guerilla engagements, and encumbered by
his women and children, this great warrior reversed his move-

ment when he was nearly a hundred miles inside Texas. He successfully eluded the trap. He passed unscathed again into Mexico just twelve miles below the watchful garrison at Fort Quitman. Captain Nolan picked up his trail and reached the river on the 13th, just a day too late, but a day was ample time for Victorio.

When Grierson got the news, he left Sulphur Springs, in the Salt Flat country, and marched directly for his old camp, thus opening a new road west of the Diablo and the Carrizo Mountains to Eagle Springs. He at once sent Charles Berger, his interpreter and guide, with Lipan and Pueblo trailers into Mexico to locate the band, and learned to his great disgust of Colonel Valle's retreat to Paso del Norte with the Mexican forces. Berger followed the Indians into the Candelaria Mountains. They were taking the roughest route to the west, mainly afoot, as they favored their mounts and wounded, evidently on their way to Lake Guzman. General Buell's scouts later reported them there in camp, nursing their terrible wrath and licking their wounds.

Grierson proceeded up the river to Fort Bliss, boiling, in his bumptious way, over the lack of support from the Mexican side when it was needed most. He learned that the Mexican regulars had been "hastily withdrawn to Chihuahua on account of threatened revolution." Observing the perfectly natural antipathy of the Mexicans against military penetrations from this side, Grierson suspected them of outright sympathy for the Indians. He heard, however, that Governor Joaquin Terrazas was busy organizing a force of Chihuahua state troops against them. But since Victorio was then far away, and Mexico had definitely disapproved the entry of United States troops, Grierson left for his home base.

He reached Concho, October 16, 1880, and reported with great satisfaction upon his campaign. He bragged that the great "Victorio and his bold marauders were three times headed off, twice whipped; driven from their stronghold in the Sierra Diablo; and twice forced back into Mexico. . . ."

He figured their loss in the several skirmishes as "certainly thirty killed and wounded, very probably fifty," besides all their supplies and from seventy-five to a hundred horses and mules.

Grierson dropped his bombast when he came to an appraisal of that relentless land. He emphasized the indisputable fact that its "great scarcity of water," and its "rugged and precipitous ranges . . . cut into deep ravines and gullies," combined with bitter saline soil and hostile growth to produce an environment that tried the fiber of the toughest men. It has not changed. Even with all the gadgets of modernity, its exactions still force the natives to shed the irrelevancies of life and face right up to the stark realities of existence. A successful military campaign against its vagrant bands seventy years ago was an achievement for the record. Grierson could afford to be proud.

Yet he placed premature judgment on the valor of his Mexican allies. Within less than a month after his return to Concho, a courier rode into Quitman and handed Captain Nicholas Nolan a message from Joaquin Terrazas, addressed to General Buell, in command of the army forces along the border. It disclosed that in one short battle General Terrazas had put Grierson's entire campaign to shame.

Terrazas had trailed Victorio's band into the Castilla Mountains and engaged them in battle. For some reason this wily old Indian warrior, this past master of adroit maneuver, allowed his men to be caught in position. On the morning of October 15, Terrazas said,

I surrounded him . . . and by a simultaneous attack we took his position leaving Victorio and sixty warriors and eighteen women and children dead Sixty eight women and children and two captives prisoners recovered also one hundred and eighty animals of different kinds. All the arms and plunder were also left in my possession. I lost three dead and twelve wounded. There are still thirty Indians at large who did not arrive in time when I surrounded those that fell and they probably went in the direction of Bosque Bonito and Laguna de Las Palmas. Although a competent force follows them, it is not easy to know with certainty which way they go as they are scattering as soon as any of the forces who follow these despised Indians return I shall communicate to you what information they will give of their expedition . . . with great great respect &

Joaquin Terrassas,
Chief of Mexican troops[13]

Thus fell one of the greatest fighters of the Southwest as the fugitive remnants of his band were hunted down like coyotes. For awhile the two chiefs, old Nana and Ju, caught up the knife and continued to depredate with bloody vengeance, but not with the splendid abandon and generalship that marked Victorio's meteoric career. In his notable book, *The Apache Indians*, the late Dr. Frank C. Lockwood appraised him as

Next to Cochise and Mangas Coloradas, the greatest warrior in Apache history . . . Such strategy and endurance, such command over a handful of desperate warriors, such defiance of interminable mountains and arid desert, and such victory over superior numbers of white foes armed and equipped with the best that a civilized nation could provide or invent has rarely been equaled in the records of savage warfare—perhaps never surpassed.[14]

In effect, his death marked the end of an era. The fact that the final episode in this historic drama was in great part played out of the wings at Fort Concho stresses the emphasis laid early in this study. This post at the forks of the Rivers of Pearls was so strategic in place and time that it immediately became the base of military maneuver for the frontiers of Texas. For twenty years it was the principal point at which western travelers and adventurers seemed to cut the ties of settled regions behind and venture into the vast and often unknown western world beyond. From its vantage location beside the Comanche, the Butterfield, the Chihuahua, the California and the Goodnight Trails, it was the swing station for historic movements of captives and contraband, of mail

[13] Relayed by wire from Captain Nolan to Fort Bliss, October 25, 1880, *Telegrams Received*, Fort Concho, vol. 19. The name is usually spelled Terrazas, but in this dispatch as well as in Grierson's official report, the above spelling is given.
[14] Frank C. Lockwood, *The Apache Indians*, New York, 1938, pp. 226-229.

and freight, of wagon-trains of emigrants and immense herds of cattle.

Fort Concho was not only the center of significant events; it was the geographic and strategic hinge upon which history swung. From this vital pivot swung the great campaigns that swept the Comanches off the southern plains, that blocked at last the renegade Apaches along the Mexican border, and that extended a generally protective shield across the heart of Texas. All the sordid detail of its life cannot rob it of its luster in the sun. By the very magnitude of its stage and the vital movements of its time, it was destined to occupy a place in history.

Its humdrum existence dragged on until March 27, 1889, when, because of the fact that it had "ceased to be of any value as a military post, except as a comfortable shelter for troops," and was "not . . . needed for that purpose," it was ordered abandoned at the "earliest practicable date." On June 20th its flag was pulled down for the last time, and with loaded wagons and its band properly playing *The Girl I Left Behind Me*, its troops pulled out.

Wistfully the businessmen of the flourishing little city "across the river," along with sad-eyed camp followers and wondering urchins, watched them go. The sprawling plant of native stone, handsome in its durable simplicity, reverted to the private owners of the land. Fort Concho was abandoned and a new era began.

Index

Fort Groghan, 53

Fort Inge: establishment of, 36; on defense line, 103, 105; on stage line, 77

Fort Lancaster: camels at, 72; mentioned, 20, 59, 106; on defense line, 103, 105; reason for, 62

Fort Lincoln, 53, 331

Fort McKavett: after Civil War, 297; establishment, 55; freight rates to, 59; mentioned, 122, 152, 175, 180, 260, 287, 317, 318; operations from, 191, 197, 208; Shafter at, 163; supplies to, 297

Fort Martin Scott, 53

Fort Mason: establishment of 55; mentioned, 93, 122, 128, 132, 175, 287; Robert E. Lee at, 63-64

Fort Phantom Hill: cited as waste, 132, 145; establishment of, 55; mentioned, 64, 103, 111, 174, 207; on Butterfield Trail, 83

Fort Quitman, 103, 332, 336

Fort Richardson: depredations near, 174-175; establishment of, 128; Mackenzie at, 206, 314; mentioned, 144, 182, 203, 253, 306; on military road, 152; operations from, 169-172, 184, 190, 207, 215; Sherman inspects, 177; supplies for, 295, 296

Fort Sill: captives moved to, 203, 204-205; chiefs arrested at, 178, 183; Grierson at, 181-182; Indians raid out of, 169, 175, 216, 229, 247; Mackenzie at, 226, 231; operations from, 214-215, 221, 223; Sherman at, 177-178; trading scandal at, 306

Fort Smith, 39, 40, 82, 83

Fort Stanton, 167

Fort Stockton: establishment of, 10, 62; freight rates to, 59; on defense line, 103, 105; mentioned, 3, 20, 163, 253, 286, 327, 333; protected El Paso mail, 122; stage through, 76, 91; supplies for, 285, 296, 299; weather at, 308-309

Fort Sumner: Goodnight to, 194; Mackenzie to, 188, 200, 227

Fort Terrett, 55

Fort Towson, 16, 17, 286

Fort Union, 215

Fort Washita, 41, 69

Fort Wingate, 306

Fort Worth: freight from, 297; on defense line, 53; railroad from, 298; volunteers from, 102

Fort Yuma, 81

Forty-Niners *(see also* California Gold Rush): at El Paso, 29; eagerness of, 33, 42; on the road, 43-52; route for, 39

Fossett, Henry, 110, 112-118

Franklin, Tex. *(see also* El Paso, Tex.): location of, 82; products of, 89; stage at, 89-90

Fredericksburg, Tex.; Forty-Niners at, 42; freight from, 137; Marcy through, 41; mentioned, 53, 148, 248; route recommended, 35, 46; settlement at, 45, 55-57; Whiting reached, 24; workers from, 136

Freighting, 285-301

Fremont, George W., 253

French, S. G., 23, 35-37, 48

Froebel, Julius: described country, 8; El Paso mail, 76-77; scalp bounties, 10-11

Frontier Regiment, 107-109

Gadsden Purchase Treaty, 10

Gail, Tex., 246

Gainesville, Tex., 69

Gale, Dr. R., 321

Gallagher, Peter, 287, 289

Galveston, Tex., 135

Gamble, George H., 138, 139, 157

Gandy, Charles M., 321

Gasman, Hans, J., 236-237

Geddes, Andrew, 235-238, 328-329

German, Adelaide, 219

German, Julia, 219

Gibbs, George W., 316

Giddings, G. H., 78

Gifford, Tex., 29

Gillem, Alvan C., 141-143

Gillintine, N. M., 111, 114

Gilmore, John C., 332

Glanton, John, 10-12

Goldsbury, George, 275

Gomez, Chief: in Mexico, 59-60; Whiting's party escapes, 8-9, 27, 30

Goodnight, Charles *(see also* Goodnight Trail): meets Rich Coffey, 292; on